CORPORATE INTELLIGENCE AND ESPIONAGE

CORPORATE INTELLIGENCE AND ESPIONAGE

A Blueprint for Executive Decision Making

RICHARD EELLS
AND
PETER NEHEMKIS

Studies of the Modern Corporation
Graduate School of Business
Columbia University

MACMILLAN PUBLISHING COMPANY
NEW YORK

Collier Macmillan Publishers
LONDON

Macmillan Publishing Company
866 Third Avenue, New York, N.Y. 10022

Collier Macmillan Canada, Inc.

Printed in the United States of America

printing number

1 2 3 4 5 6 7 8 9 10

Library of Congress Cataloging in Publication Data

Eells, Richard Sedric Fox
 Corporate intelligence and espionage.

 (Studies of the modern corporation)
 Bibliography: p.
 Includes index.
 1. Business intelligence. I. Nehemkis, Peter
Raymond. II. Title. III. Series.
HD38.7.E34 1984   658.4'7   83–43214
ISBN 0–02–909240–X

Grateful acknowledgment is made to the following for permission to
reprint from previously published material:

Harper & Row Publishers, Inc.; William Collins Sons & Co., Ltd.
(London): Excerpt by Allen W. Dulles from *Great True Spy Stories,* ed.
Allen W. Dulles, copyright © 1968 by Allen W. Dulles.

Harvard Business Review: Excerpts from "New Attack on the
Legitimacy of Business" by P. L. Berger. Copyright © 1981 by the
President and Fellows of Harvard College; all rights reserved. Reprinted
by permission of the *Harvard Business Review* from the issue of
September–October 1981.

Walter Laqueur and *Washington Journalism Review:* Excerpt from
"Foreign News Coverage: From Bad to Worse" by Walter Laqueur.
Reprinted from *Washington Journalism Review,* June 1983.

The New York Times: Excerpts from articles by Rabbi Balfour Brickner
and Derek Shearer, both copyright © 1982 by The New York Times
Company. Reprinted by permission.

G. P. Putnam's Sons: Excerpts from *The Secret War* by Sanche de
Gramont, copyright © 1962 by Sanche de Gramont.

There must be no more intimate relations in the whole army than those maintained with spies. No other relation should be more liberally rewarded. In no other relation should greater secrecy be preserved.

Sun Tzu,
The Art of War, circa 500 B.C.

Intelligence deals with all things which should be known in advance of initiating a course of action.

Intelligence Activities, a Report to the Congress by the Commission on Organization of the Executive Branch of the Government, Part II, page 26. May 1955.

Contents

CONTENTS

✳ *Pg 149, 164, 167, 181*

PART III   Policy

Preface

WE live in what is grandiosely called the Information Age. A more accurate description would be the Age of Intelligence. Whichever phrase is used, our time is plainly an era in which a new computer technology, with amazing retrieval capability and incredible cryptosystems, has emerged.

Computer scientists are pioneering in the development of a new generation of artificial intelligence machines, which ultimately may have the capability of actually thinking like humans. Indeed, it is predicted that "by the turn of the century, ultra-intelligent machines will be working in partnership with our best minds on all the serious problems of the day, in an unbeatable combination of brute reasoning power and human intuition."* *Time* magazine, anticipating the intelligence machine still in the process of development, selected a computer as "Man of the Year" for 1982. Explaining its selection, *Time* said: "The greatest influence for good or evil is not man at all. It is a machine: the computer." Computer technology has profoundly influenced—and will continue to affect and transform—every sector of our society.

Richard Eells dealt briefly with the subject of intelligence in *The Political Crisis of the Enterprise System,* published in 1980, but this present work examines in detail the entire question of

---

* Robert Jastrow, *The Enchanted Loom* (New York: Simon and Schuster, 1981), p. 162. See also James Gleick, "Exploring the Labyrinth of the Mind," *New York Times Magazine,* August 21, 1983.

business intelligence. Our study has three principal themes: (a) a compelling need by industry and the business community generally for the adoption of an integrated system of intelligence; (b) the prevailing and widespread practice of corporate espionage whose clandestine operations frequently embody misconduct, if not outright corporate crime; and (c) observations on the functions, consequences and dangers inherent in an Age of Intelligence.

Business executives use intelligence-collection in their everyday business activities, although they may not always recognize their varied pursuits of information as "intelligence." For example: Managers survey the market to determine whether a product has consumer acceptance. Before deciding where to build a plant, a company's management undertakes a survey of a local environment to learn whether, among other things, the plant will be accepted by the local community. Before committing a company to making an overseas investment, a management studies the economic, political and social trends of the host country to ascertain what impact any adverse environmental elements might have on the investment. Political risk analyses are sought in an effort to learn what environmental factors may be favorable for the continued successful operation of a proposed manufacturing plant, or an investment in a host country's natural resources.

Indeed, multinational companies—especially multinational oil companies and multinational banking and financial firms—must, of necessity, be concerned with intelligence so that their worldwide activities can operate successfully and profitably. They need to know what the world will look like ten, twenty, or more years from now, what the size and composition of the population will be, what changes in living standards will have occurred, how such changes will affect an overseas investment; and, in the case of the international oil companies, the scope of energy requirements. Moreover, as the Third World becomes more industrialized—or more radicalized—intelligence will be needed to know whether a company can hold on to its investment, and what adjustments will have to be made in ownership philosophy to avoid expropriation or nationalization.

These and a host of other problems that beset business managers are the stuff of corporate intelligence. Good intelligence spells the difference between success and failure, profits and losses.

Although they are not strangers to intelligence-collection and espionage, most business executives are loath to discuss this subject, let alone acknowledge that *their* company engages in espionage. Some members of the government's intelligence community, like their colleagues from private industry, also have a strong aversion to having specific information attributed to them. As a consequence of this executive and official modesty, we are usually not in a position to attribute specific instances of intelligence-collection and espionage to a particular company or management, or to a government's department or official. We respect the desire of those in the business, financial and intelligence communities who have requested anonymity.

It is no doubt true that the role of government espionage is far greater than the role of espionage by the corporation. Yet there is a profound difference in the legal consequences for the agents of government and corporate espionage: government espionage in the United States is protected by national laws; industrial espionage (which we distinguish here from lawful intelligence-gathering) involves its agents in varying levels of misconduct, or the more serious perpetration of a corporate crime.

Popular writers about intelligence, who usually have government intelligence in mind, are apt to assume that government intelligence and corporate intelligence are different. In some respects they are. Corporations have not yet reached the stage where they can afford their own fleets of satellite surveillance systems. (Actually, a few companies do have satellites, but they are not, we hasten to add, corporate spies-in-the-sky.) And there are, to be sure, significant differences between the targets of government intelligence and corporate intelligence. These differences are a consequence of the purpose and function of the two institutions. Government intelligence has as its primary target obtaining the *state secrets* of another nation-state as well as economic and social data about it (usually, but not always, an adversary nation-state), as well as safeguarding its own national secrets. Corporate intelligence, on the other hand, is more narrowly focused; it has as its primary targets economic and social data about its markets and environments, and acquiring—legitimately or illegitimately—the *trade secrets* of a competitor: all needed to improve its decision-making capabilities. Yet, in reality, and in some instances, this may be a distinction without a difference. Both government and corporate intelligence and espionage are concerned with trade secrets: for example, corporate technological developments can influence an adversary's economic and, therefore, its military capabilities.

We hope that business executives may find this book useful in a practical sense. These readers may prefer to skim the early, more historical, chapters, and concentrate on chapters 4, 5, 6, 8, 9, 11, and 12.

As the research for this book came to an end it became clear that further studies should be undertaken, specifically of the implications for public policy of the private intelligence community's growth, especially in the matters of privacy, morality and ethics. For a major dilemma of our age is how to have a free flow of information and at the same time protect the rights to privacy of individuals.

Both authors, who lecture at Graduate Schools of Business/Management—Richard Eells at Columbia University and Peter Nehemkis at UCLA—are deeply indebted to their students, especially those from middle management who have returned to the classroom for an advanced degree, or those who attend Executive Management Seminars. During class discussions, they have provided us with unique and unusual insight on such subjects as plant security, pre-employment investigations, company policies toward terrorists and terrorist demands for the payment of ransom for kidnapped executives, overseas political payments, company trade secrets and industrial espionage, overseas political risk analyses, the intelligence problem of divided loyalties, and other related intelligence subjects. Indeed, it was one of Richard Eells' students, David S. Rose, who led him, via Dr. Elihu Rose, to Professor Andrew Patterson, Jr., a professor of chemistry at Yale—without doubt, in our opinion, the most informed individual in the United States on the history of the nomenclature of classified information. Professor Patterson has generously made available to us his entire manuscript on this subject.

Well over three hundred interviews were conducted by the authors. They were wide-ranging and held with corporate executives at various levels—both active and retired corporate board members, outside corporate consultants, former government intelligence officers, active government intelligence officials, and various members of the academic community. The areas covered included: energy; commercial and investment banking; heavy industry; electronics; chemicals; paper; computers; media; security consultants; legal specialists; and prison management (the transmission of information via Mafia sources).

The select bibliography which appears at the end of the book does not represent the full extent of our research, but is intended to be a point of reference for the reader, especially the senior corporate executive. The corporate enterprise system is so vast that any attempt to cover the subject more completely in a bibliographical sense would carry this book into a second volume.

The published sources from which we have derived help and inspiration are legion. Many excellent historical and descriptive works about various aspects of intelligence have appeared since World War I. Our indebtedness to some of these is recorded in the Notes and Select Bibliography. But there are no works known to us that attempt to give a rationale for, and a blueprint for the development of, an effective intelligence operation within the organized structure of the large modern corporation.

Our obligations to individuals who contributed to this study are extensive. We wish here to thank them, especially to those who found time to read all or part of the manuscript. We are grateful to each of them for their observations and comments, even though we did not always follow their advice and counsel. But whether we agreed or disagreed with those interviewed or consulted, we wish to acknowledge that their comments were stimulating and useful in the final cast of the themes of the book.

It is important to us to state that to all our students we wish the ultimate fulfillment of their work and careers.

We are pleased to acknowledge and extend special thanks to Elizabeth Parry Catenaccio for her thoughtful and skillful editing of the manuscript for this book.

To many others, who asked to remain unnamed but who, in one way or another, have given assistance and encouragement in the preparation of this study, we gratefully tender our thanks.

Finally, we hope this book will motivate and point the way to an improved curriculum in our schools of business and management.

General financial support is provided to the Program for Studies of the Modern Corporation, Graduate School of Business, Columbia University, by many business corporations and foundations, to whom we tender our thanks.

R.E.
P.N.

Part I

Rationale

1

The New Magic

Society can be conceived as a vast tapestry of many intricate patterns and images—a tapestry being woven on a great loom where the warp and woof are the intertwined threads of the events that dominate the world. Each of the world's great institutional forces struggles to impose its own design upon the tapestry. The pictures are complicated and often are superimposed, like a series of photographic transparencies laid one on the other. The weaving itself is complicated and based on formulas not generally perceived. The meaning of the tapestry can be comprehended but, over time, it has frequently been thought that the key to understanding it lies in some form of magic.

In ancient plays, the *deus ex machina,* a magical deity, would emerge unexpectedly from the stage's machinery to intervene in situations and solve human problems by Olympian fiat. The ancients used prayer, too, as a medium for establishing a relationship between man and the gods, and a formula for invoking good spirits or evil demons. Now we have a new magic: the penetration of the mind into the mysteries of the universe. It is magical only in the sense that much of modern science and technology is still incomprehensible to most people. Today's cryptography and cryptographic computer programs, for example, are little less than cabalistic magic to the average person—and are every bit as magical as our earth-orbiting killer-satellites would have seemed to the ancient Daedalian myth-makers. But cryptanalysis

3

is only one of the methods we have for dealing with intelligence. There are many others, for intelligence—or to borrow a concept from the ecologists, the intelligence "surround"—is one of the dominant features of the world in which we live. Our environment is a software jungle and is characterized, to paraphrase Hobbes, by a war of program against program. Here, the corporation like everyone else is at one and the same time producer, consumer and victim. How the corporation responds to the conditions of business in the intelligence surround will determine its future viability.

The Scope of Applied Intelligence

Since the dawn of civilization, man has sought to bring about those circumstances most conducive to his preservation. Inextricably related to the instinct for self-preservation has been an obsession with secrets and secrecy. The early locus of this secrecy was in the rituals and customs that supported efforts for self-preservation. Primitive man believed that disclosure of the secrets which were the key to his survival would expose him to the vagaries of a hostile and unforgiving environment. Conversely, access to those mysteries opened up new worlds and broader vistas previously unknown.

The Road to Eleusis[1] describes and explains one such ancient tradition of mysteries. The Eleusinian mysteries were first performed over four thousand years ago. For the two thousand years during which they thrived, they provided an awe-inspiring "born-again" experience that completely changed the life of the initiates. According to Sophocles, only those to whom the mysteries had been revealed could overcome the evil of Hades and enjoy a "true life." The "great vision" experienced by participants not only bound them together communally but also revealed answers to the individual's personal and the state's political problems.

The value of this experience for the ancient Greeks, and other people in early cultures who shared elements of that civilization, was of supreme importance. It is not surprising that initiates were sworn to absolute secrecy about all they saw or experienced during the night of the rituals. The laws of Athens even made it a crime to speak of what transpired during the Eleusinian mysteries: legislation protected secrets regarded as crucial to the welfare and security of Athenians. Society and the state had not yet become separated. In our terms, however, the Athenian city-state protected the intelligence function of a private cult.[2] Today, as public and private spheres are becoming less distinct, our society's most vital secrets are the technological products of our private labors. They require state protection to safeguard our survival.

An intelligence explosion occurred with the rise of the nation-state. Intelligence-collection became professionalized as a tool of diplomacy and was adopted by competitive organizations. Patent legislation protected the mystery-rituals of our factories, exempting inventions from industrial espionage.

Organizational intelligence, defined as strategic and tactical information (not as the mental qualities measured by IQ tests), has been a key element in the history of human institutions, especially in politics, business, religion and science. Organizational intelligence is, and always has been, basic to the survival of both public and private institutions; ironically, intelligence is also essential to the success of crime syndicates.

Since World War I, the great nation-states especially have pursued their intelligence activities with an insatiable passion and now great business corporations have also begun to rely increasingly on intelligence activities, although these functions are seldom explicitly acknowledged in corporate tables of organization. Today, numerous major multinational corporations, international investment banks and commercial investment banks, conduct in-depth intelligence operations. They do not plan and organize intelligence with the same professional zeal as the nation-state, nor should they—their needs are different and they don't fight wars. But in recent times, business firms have taken on many of the functions of the state;[3] and this has intensified their need for a more self-conscious approach to intelligence operations.

The Modernization of Secrecy

With the advance of civilization and the growth of commerce, the struggle for self-preservation became less difficult but the emphasis on secrecy became more intense. Preoccupation with mere survival gave way to a new concern for enrichment and the technology supporting economic endeavors assumed greater sophistication and required more protection. The nation-state's monopoly of intelligence functions was invaded by private institutions. Business corporations, especially, recognized the compelling link between securing intelligence—procuring it and safeguarding it—and enlarging their profits.

The emergence of private-sector secrecy has been accompanied by an increasing awareness that many other state-like qualities are also exhibited by non-governmental entities. The growing inadequacy of the nation-state system to deal effectively with global concerns has stimulated speculation that international private institutions may be called upon to conduct many of the functions once thought to be the exclusive responsibility of the nation-state.

The advance of technology and the modernization of secrecy, coupled with the rise of the corporation, raise several concerns to which modern business must respond. Woven through all the institutions of our society is an ever-present thread of intelligence. Today the corporate sector is face-to-face with the need for corporate intelligence. To achieve maximum effectiveness, business needs to have a better understanding of the relationships between information, intelligence and strategic corporate decisions. The inescapable tie between the nation-state and the multinational corporation now requires the enunciation of a new corporate ethos—a new practical philosophy for realizing corporate values—that will provide a clear perspective for the political and social role of the corporation. How American corporations respond to this need will determine whether they will merely diagnose the situation, leaving its potentials unrealized, or adopt the requisite preservative measures. For it *is* possible to devise a survival strategy.

The Warning

The warning referred to here includes several points.

The first is that business faces a significant loss in efficiency and profitability because of a *generalized* lack of integrated organizational intelligence. Within this framework certain *specific* intelligence needs stand out as being especially crucial. The first of these is *political* intelligence about the foreign states with

which the company conducts business. For example, the import-
ers of Iranian oil would have benefited greatly from an accurate
assessment of the impending collapse of the Shah's regime in
1979, and such an assessment was feasible. In 1982, the firms
that were importing Argentine beef into Europe would have prof-
ited greatly from advance intelligence of the impending crisis
between Argentina and Great Britain over the Falkland Islands.
A sound assessment of the European political climate, and the
likelihood of Common Market support for economic sanctions
against Argentina, would have made it possible to procure alternative suppliers of beef imports prior to the crisis that spring.
In each of these cases, the government had ample basis for the
accurate assessment of the crisis potential, yet failed to act on
it, because it was blinded by wishful self-delusion. Business, without that handicap, could have made sound intelligence assessments if it had had a proper intelligence function in place.

A second category of intelligence need concerns specialized
technological developments. Anticipation of new, cheaper, and
more efficient methods of manufacturing items such as superchip
computers and optoelectronic communications systems allows
a company to alter its marketing and product research efforts
so as to maximize profits, minimize losses, and avoid being out-
performed by a competitor. Here, the question is: How is such
intelligence to be acquired? The issue is dealt with in greater
detail later in this book.

Thirdly, *cultural* intelligence enables the firm to improve its
performance in both foreign and domestic markets. A business
needs to know about cultural patterns and trends in the broadest
sense because the commercial practices of a people are influenced by their cultural habits. Obviously, a market that is ge-
ographically isolated will require the acquisition of a special kind
of cultural intelligence; great mistakes that are most readily pre-
ventable are also most easily made in markets that are strange
and remote.

A fourth concern relating to intelligence is the trend toward
violence in our society in recent years. Violence has grown at
an almost exponential rate and now the threats to personal safety
that once existed only in slums have spread to every street and
home. Perhaps even more alarming is the tendency of many to
excuse violence as a justifiable reaction to the problems of poverty
or racism. Politicians and academics explain the social and eco-

nomic causes of violence, implicitly rationalizing it, blunting public efforts to combat it. The dramatic increase in violence—not only in the United States but even in Britain, where we thought it had been banished forever by traditional gentlemanly decorum—threatens the stability of government and undermines the efforts of the private sector to satisfy the needs of the public.

The Promise

Yet, there is a promise and an opportunity inherent in this turbulent situation. A properly developed intelligence function can help the corporation sharpen its competitive advantage and keep abreast—or even ahead—of rapidly changing technologies. An understanding of changing cultural patterns in attractive though insecure foreign markets will permit the corporation to enter them more readily and more profitably. Increased profitability is a function of intelligence: knowing what is new in the emerging technosciences and knowing what competitors are doing about it. The corporation able to accomplish these relatively short-term objectives will immeasurably strengthen its long-term survival capability. The firm whose superior intelligence permits it to keep up with or overtake its competition will not fall victim to the hostile forces generated by economic, social, or political adversaries. Difficult times demand innovation and greater efficiency. They will not be disastrous for the business that enjoys the benefits of an effective intelligence function.

While the corporation may be the most direct beneficiary of better intelligence, everyone else benefits too, though indirectly. The corporation is a component of the larger order and the strengthening of any one element of that system enriches the entire system. Democratic pluralism requires a complex arrangement of independent, private agencies. The decline or loss of any one of them weakens pluralism and stimulates increased demands for the state to step in and perform the services and provide the commodities that are threatened. It is not difficult to imagine the political pressures arising as a result of an announcement that a community's only garbage collection—a private one—is to be terminated. There would, quite predictably, be a call for some level of government to provide that service. If our steel industry continues to atrophy, at some point there will arise the problem of the national security interest in maintaining our domestic steel capability—in fact, the problem is already being discussed. The demand to nationalize the steel industry would be the natural public response. There are countless essential services which would become public in the event of the collapse of private enterprises. The resultant enlargement of the state and the corresponding diminution of the private sector would threaten the freedom that is the hallmark of democratic capitalism—the freedom that protects capitalism's critics as well as its proponents. Dissent is impossible where subsistence depends on the state. Thus, by strengthening the corporation, one of the most important members of the pluralist "family," we may enrich the entire democratic system and strengthen the promise of a continuation of our freedom as well.

The Emergence of Tensions between the Nation-State and the Corporation

This promise is so alluring one wonders why the corporate community has not embraced it more readily. A world characterized by cooperation between the legitimate members of the pluralistic family of associations would function with greater integrity. The acceptability of the legitimacy of an intelligence mission for all who wished would be almost automatic. Unfortunately, our world is not so angelic. There are numerous impediments to the adoption of a corporate intelligence function. Not the least of these is the generally unsavory reputation intelligence work has acquired, a matter to be examined later in this book. Another impediment is the distrust that exists between government and business, those two most important elements of pluralist democracy.

While more will be said later about the tensions between the corporation and the state, it is important to recognize early in this examination of corporate intelligence that considerable animosity exists between them. In the United States this has been true throughout our history. The fact that industrial leaders are invited from time to time to enter government as heads of departments or senior advisers does not dissolve the basic tensions that still exist (and probably should) between government and business. One of the most obvious explanations of this antagonism

9

is the rise of the corporation to such status that it can quite properly be considered as a rival to the authority of the state. The newly acquired power of the corporation, especially the multinational corporation, enables it regularly to evade and sometimes defy the rules and regulations of the nation-state.

The issue of illegal foreign payments by corporations—the media call it bribery, ignoring the element of extortion, which frequently is more significant—demonstrates the difficulty of enforcing corporate compliance with the Foreign Corrupt Practices Act of 1977. In the opinion of many foreign trade experts, this legislation represents an effort by our government to impose our domestic business ethic upon the world economy—an extraterritorial effort that is greatly resented overseas. Here is a case where the business intelligence of Congress may have been inadequate. Nevertheless, Congress passed the law. A 1982 report by the International Telephone & Telegraph Corporation concluded that, in spite of the stated desire of ITT leadership to comply, it would be virtually impossible to guarantee even a minimum observance of the law. According to the report, ITT representatives who deal with foreign nationals continue to pay up to nearly 20 percent "commissions" to meet so-called "local requirements" in arranging foreign deals for ITT.[4] In view of the fact that many other corporations are undoubtedly even less inclined to comply with the legislation, it is reasonable to surmise that, in at least this instance, multinational corporations regularly evade the rules and regulations of their home nation-state.

As the nation-state loses its domestic consensus supporting its efforts to curb overseas corporate expansion, tension is produced. Our prerequisite to a national consensus is a sound economy, which is largely dependent upon the availability of jobs for those who want to work. But when the multinational corporation, for a variety of reasons, locates its plants overseas, it "exports" some jobs and creates others outside this country. The trend toward the globalization of business makes it difficult for our government to prevent this practice.

In the broad historical sense it is certainly plausible to argue that the corporation is widening the basis of its power.[5] Corporate power is founded on control of jobs, access to money for investment, control over the raw materials used in production, and numerous related factors. Taken together, these factors mean that the modern corporation has become an international entity that cannot be limited by the ordinary sanctions available to the governments of the individual nation-states. Moreover, as the basis for corporate power continues to grow, the authority of the nation-state continues to decline. The government loses revenue sources when a corporation locates its facilities abroad, yet if the corporation remained in its homeland, in some cases, the government would have to acquiesce in the depletion of its own natural resources and the degradation of its environment. The government is forced to spend enormous sums to provide for the welfare of its disadvantaged citizens and it must also maintain an enormously expensive defense establishment. While the state continues to expand its military might almost to the point of national bankruptcy, military force has become less and less effective as an instrument of national policy. Parallel to this is the growing tendency of people to regard all politicians and all governments with apathy and mistrust. Electoral participation in the United States regularly falls below 50 percent of those eligible to vote and some political scientists soberly propose the remedy of placing the category of "none of the above" on the ballot.

But the nation-state is not, as yet, completely enfeebled. It can, for example, impose a variety of punitive measures against businesses and many of these regulations are not so easily circumvented as the Foreign Corrupt Practices Act. In fact, the growing anti-business climate inside many Western capitalist states makes restrictive legislation politically popular. In addition, as a regular course of action, governments adopt policies with adverse impacts on the business environment. There are ultimate limits to this, but even a minor change in policy can have a dramatic impact, for example, on the price of a foreign automobile imported into the United States.

Finally, today's nation-states employ weapons against corporations that traditionally were thought to be appropriate only in the confrontation of state versus state. Most prominent here is espionage. With the development of the modern corporation's own independent sources of power, it should not be surprising that it finds itself a prime target of professional espionage. After all, the technological developments of business can be just as important as the secrets tucked away in the foreign ministry building in the capital city. (In 1980 it was disclosed that East European industries conducted regular espionage against West-

11

ern corporations, demonstrating that the state versus the corporation spy scenario is common not only in the world of James Bond but also in the world of Carl Zeiss.)[6] At times, governments utilize their espionage services to conduct operations against the corporations of their own nation.[7] Under certain circumstances and subject to administrative procedures, the National Security Agency—the largest, most influential and most secretive organization within the intelligence community—is permitted, after securing the approval of the Foreign Intelligence Surveillance Court,[8] to examine electronically-intercepted communications to, from, and about individual U.S. companies. The states that practice counter-corporate espionage are simply embracing one of their more effective weapons in their struggle for survival, enrichment, and the pursuit of advantage against their adversaries. In the search for advantage, no one is immune from surveillance.

Changing Concepts of Loyalty

Changes in the twentieth-century conditions of the nation-states mean that they can no longer offer their citizens many of the advantages people have come to expect from government. It is not surprising, therefore, that concepts of loyalty, allegiance, and citizenship are undergoing transformation. The most obvious result of this development is that the multinational corporation is now able to offer individuals many of the opportunities that were once regarded as flowing only from the state. Commitment to a powerful corporation may mean much more to an individual than his identification with his native land. This is especially true in modernized industrial states—those in which the corporation is best developed—where traditional ideas of nationalism and patriotism have declined in respectability. Popular notions that extreme nationalism has often caused warfare have produced—in this nuclear age—a belief among many people that patriotism is both obsolete and hazardous to human life.

The rise of nationalism in the industrial states produced the patriotism that was the source of civic loyalty. Everywhere, the cultural basis of loyalty has been eroded. The decline of nationalism has weakened loyalty to the state. Loyalty was formerly strengthened by the emotional identification of a people with their native land. However, in this age of constant exposure to other cultures, people everywhere experience values in vehement opposition to each other. Foreign places hold out exotic attractions. And because of the domestic economic failings of the nation-states, many people have become convinced that their prosperity cannot be assured by their governments. They have begun to realize that their well-being may derive more from a domestic, or even a foreign, corporation than from their own government. Studies of the Japanese worker indicate that his identification with his corporation rivals his loyalty to his country.

This brief survey of the predicament of loyalty in the modern world reveals the ambivalence of our allegiances. Where, then, does the prime loyalty of the San Diego Chicano, the Chicago Black Muslim, the Beverly Hills Jew, the Miami Latino, or the Manhattan Marxist, lie? Uncertainty, at least for some citizens, has always existed, but present trends have increased split affinities and nation-state alienation. It is interesting to note that several centuries ago it was common for ambassadors of one state to receive upon retirement a gratuity or even a life pension from another state, usually one in which they had ostensibly served as the representative of their own country. The point, of course, is that they were being rewarded because while they represented one nation, they served another. Their loyalty was, to say the least, divided.

Division or commercialization of loyalty is more prevalent today because of the diverse ideological, religious and economic interests that pull people in diverse directions. It is certainly understandable for people to have divided loyalties. A person with ethnic origins in another country, a church prelate, an executive who has had a long and successful career with a powerful corporation—all might feel deeper loyalties elsewhere than to the state of their citizenship. Ours is a world of nations made up of citizens with dissociated bonds. The existence of these new model "elective" affinities encourages people to believe, as did a prominent General Motors executive who later became Secretary of Defense, that what is good for General Motors is good for the United States, and, of course, vice versa. But with the weakening of the nation-state and the dissolution of its primacy as a collective repository of component loyalties, people's emotional identifications devolve upon their immediate institutions. This is not a conscious process but rather an instinctive response to the demands of one's immediate interests and needs.

Corporate executives and religious activists who devoutly promote the illegal sale or transfer of sensitive defense equipment to another nation, or employees who—out of misplaced idealism—purloin trade secrets of their employers and hand them over to the agents of a foreign power, are seldom forced to come to grips with the question of where their primary loyalty lies. Undoubtedly, the business executive simply does what an economic or business opportunity requires, insisting all the while that the items in question are really of no military significance— that if he does not sell to the Soviets, for example, someone else will—or that the deed is in the larger interests of the nation. The "sincere" employee not infrequently confuses his dislike of capitalism with a distorted allegiance to the Soviet Union. It is seldom thought of as a matter of stark disloyalty but often as one of simply pursuing the ordinary objectives of business or individual rights in the ordinary way. This is all too easy to understand. Even our Presidents make the same sophistic rationalizations, as when Reagan distinguished guilefully between Europe's sale of pipeline equipment to the Soviets and his own pre-election grain sale proposal. That the loyalty of Soviet citizens can be eroded in a similar fashion was illustrated in an excellent study by Max Ralis of the attitudes of workers in the USSR. According to Ralis, industrial workers and plant managers regularly develop perceptions of self-interest that are completely at variance with official views.[9] Soviet double-agents and defectors are nearly as plentiful as are those from our side.

Technology Transfers

The development of advanced technologies also contributes to the dissociation of loyalties. Modern technology is so complicated, and its possible uses are so difficult to anticipate, that questions of which aspects are, and which are not, connected with the nation's security interests become matters of arcane technical judgment. A subtle technical rationalization may easily obscure the fact that a transfer of loyalty from one's country to one's company has occurred. The development of dual-use technology, often as a result of a nation's explicit preparedness policy, makes things even more complicated as it enables foreign governments surreptitiously to derive military advantages from exports that can be specified legitimately as civilian commodities. The sellers, of course, need not look beyond the stipulated domestic designation of what they have sold. An American firm, to take a difficult example, sells the USSR a powerful computer ostensibly designed to facilitate the centralized management and scheduling of guest registrations for the nationwide hotel system. The fact that the USSR needs, and cannot buy from us, essentially the same computer to control its missile guidance system may be only coincidence, but no knowledgeable person thinks so. The diversion of the computer, the firm claims, is either something for which it is not responsible or a mere fabrication designed by the competition to discredit them. The difficulty of verifying the actual application of dual-use materials purchased by closed societies means that we can never be certain when the purchase order of a totalitarian regime tells the truth.

In 1982 a report to the United States Senate revealed the extent of the problem of technology transfers. According to Senate investigators, much sensitive information is now being sent by American firms to the Soviet Union and its allies. Although there is legislation designed to prevent this, the Compliance Division of the Office of Export Administration in the Commerce Department lacks enforcement ability. The Senate report states that this inability is due in large part to the Division's shortcomings as an investigative and intelligence unit, and to the fact that too few Division personnel have the specialized training required for evaluating sophisticated technologies. Senate investigators concluded that "significant amounts" of dual-use technology that contribute to Soviet military strength are being shipped to the Soviet bloc despite formal restrictions. One witness who appeared before the Senate maintained during his examination that the Soviet Union was mounting a "deliberate, massive and longstanding effort to acquire Western technologies for direct incorporation into their military and defense-related industry."[10]

Technology transfers are, of course, exchanges of science-based processes and products for money. In some cases the exchange is legal, in some cases illegal. Technology transfers may supplement the more traditional methods of acquiring secrets by means of espionage and, in many ways, they are even more effective. Because of the growth of Soviet-U.S. trade, the exchange of some of the West's most sophisticated technoscientific innovations has usually taken place in the course of implementing the policy of "detente." Difficulties in assessing the real value of some exotic technologies, coupled with the strained or divided loyalties of many corporate leaders, make technology transfers especially difficult to regulate. More effective intelligence—by both public and private entities—could do much to limit the scope of damage resulting from many of these exchanges. The U.S. government is currently making an effort to develop better intelligence with regard to this issue, and the Federal Bureau of Investigation, in particular, has been studying technology transfers.

Disclosure in 1982 of efforts by Japan's leading computer manufacturer to make illegal purchases of advanced confidential IBM computer information indicates the seriousness of the problem of illegal technology transfers. In this case Hitachi, Ltd. authorized payment of $622,000 for the purchase of proprietary information belonging to IBM. This was part of Hitachi's government-backed effort to become the world's leading exporter of computers and telecommunications products. IBM's own intelligence operations first revealed that the Japanese-financed plot was under way. IBM then requested the FBI to set up a "sting" operation to arrest the seventeen Japanese businessmen and their American assistant in the act of procuring the secret information. This incident shows that in some cases there is little difference between technology transfer and corporate espionage.[11]

This quandary is not solely the result of dual-purpose equipment but also the consequence of the present stage of the scientific revolution. Scientific innovations reach to ever more fundamental processes and, accordingly, possess ever more general applications. Genetic engineering can be used to produce both pesticides and homicides.

The Problem of Classifications

As a result of our growing technoscientific sophistication, the simple systems of information classification used in the past are no longer adequate. Dual-use technologies and protomilitary sciences especially demand a more subtle classification system to take into account the multiple uses of innovations. In chapter 3 we shall see that the U.S. Army as long ago as World War II developed a special area designated as "technical intelligence" in an effort to examine more fully the implications of scientific advances by friend and foe alike. The rapidly accelerating pace

16

of present-day scientific advancements requires that still more be done by all agencies that deal with classified material.

The corporation is affected by these developments just as directly as are national governments. The fact that businesses have for years been stealing trade secrets from each other in their struggles for competitive advantages should make the corporation especially aware of this need.

One problem is to devise new ways to identify and designate the intelligence value and security importance of secret devices and processes. These new classifications must also accommodate rapid change, for what is secret today may be discovered or duplicated by someone else tomorrow. Accordingly, there must be enough flexibility so that, at the proper time, classifications can be downgraded to facilitate the wider civic dissemination of information that is already possessed by other nations. The same thing is true of business intelligence. If information that is no longer strategic to a nation or a firm is unnecessarily kept secret, it restricts consumer applications and inhibits the type of research needed to encourage a rapid pace of technical and scientific change.

The Problem of Private Government

Awareness of the valuable scientific information at the disposal of corporations, and the extensive use by them of intelligence systems, lead to the recognition of a fundamental fact about our society, namely, that our private firms are able to exert an enormous amount of power over the lives of our people. Government is not alone in making decisions that affect how our citizens will live. In fact, actions taken by large corporations may, in many cases, affect larger groups of people more directly and severely than do those of the government. The "pink slip," notifying a worker that he has been laid off, is a powerful sanction—more powerful than many in the state's arsenal. The individual's livelihood is at stake.

This merely reinforces in a new way the fact that the corporation is actually a government—a private government. The term private government is not one that enjoys common usage, except among political scientists and a relatively small number of students of corporate America. Others often react negatively when they encounter it, feeling that in some sense it must mean that private groups are trying to usurp the legitimate power of public government. In spite of these somewhat sinister connotations, the term is gaining in currency and it is important to understand what it implies.

It should be made clear at the outset that a society full of private governments does not of itself constitute a threat to the freedoms of the pluralistic democracy we all cherish. On the contrary, only where private governments are totally outlawed is freedom in jeopardy. Private governments facilitate the self-sufficiency and the enrichment of our people as well as the strengthening of our social system. Business is not our only private government. There are numerous others, including churches, labor unions, professional associations, and most basic of all, the family. There is a negative side as well: in many places the Mafia constitutes an essentially noxious but powerful kind of private government.

In examining business as a private government, the late Beardsley Ruml, who was something of a specialist in the governmental aspects of business, once proposed a concise definition of this phenomenon:

> A business is a government because within the law it is authorized and organized to make rules for the conduct of its affairs. It is a private government because the rules it makes within the law are not reviewable by any public body.[12]

Of course, conditions have changed since 1945 when Ruml made this statement and many of the internal rules of private business are now studied and "reviewed" by public government. The courts protect our public and private rights against encroachment, and agencies like the Securities and Exchange Commission and the Department of Justice also review aspects of private government which are thought to be inimicable to the public interest, or when it is deemed that a private government has made insufficient disclosure of its activities. However, Ruml's most important point was the distinction between private authority and public authority. This, rather than private ownership or independence from public accountability, is what makes business a private government. Yet the individual, scarcely aware of the existence of private authorities that exercise political functions, still reserves the term government to mean the exercise of public authority, in a general sense.

18

Businesses, unions, churches, and professional associations are all legitimate operations; earlier we mentioned other kinds of private governments that operate outside the law. The families of La Cosa Nostra (the Mafia) are the best-known organizations that fall into this category. There are numerous offshoots of La Cosa Nostra and there are the so-called Jewish Mafia and Black Mafia, as well as others.

Some measure of the significance of illegal private government can be seen in the amount of money that reputedly circulates in the "underground" economy that flourishes in the United States. According to a recent estimate nearly 15 percent of the overall GNP of the United States is associated with illegal activity.[13] Illegal private governments such as the Mafia are deeply involved in a variety of economic endeavors that support their organization and increase their profits. Others may have only a modest investment in activities with an economic aspect measurable in terms of the GNP, so their significance must be evaluated by different standards. Revolutionary organizations, for example, constitute a separate class of illegal private governments.

Private government is a supplement as well as an alternative to public authority. It regulates departments of life with which public officials may not concern themselves, such as matters of morality or private belief. Hence many circumstances may arise in which private governments become the adversaries of public government, as in the case of draftees who resist military service on religious grounds. The role of private government, especially its intelligence function, will be considered in more detail in other parts of this book.

The Problem of Terrorism

Among illegal private governments, terrorist groups—ranging from street gangs and motorcycle bands to revolutionary bomb throwers, kneecap gunners and assassins—are on the rise. Like members of other illegal private governments, terrorists operate outside the law and utilize violence to accomplish their objectives. However, the revolutionary objectives of terrorists are different from those of the Cosa Nostra organizations in one special way: violence is often enough the primary vocation of revolutionaries rather than merely one of several alternative means for

19

achieving other goals. The members of a crime syndicate are more likely to use intimidation or some threatening form of persuasion. Terrorists have little use for persuasion, except to solicit ransoms or demand release of their confreres. Violence is their end product in the same way that law is the end product of legislators. Hence they differ from mobsters in that the members of an organized criminal group depend for their livelihoods upon the enduring health and prosperity of the public order on which they prey. They violate certain of its rules but they never work for its complete destruction. In fact, during World War II, underworld leaders often used their connections to aid the Allied cause. A business may, on occasion, reach a *modus vivendi* with a Mafia gang or even right-wing terrorists; many have done so here as well as in Latin America. It has recently been revealed that the Mafia was instrumental in locating Brigadier General James L. Dozier, who had been kidnapped in Italy by members of the Red Brigades and who was subsequently rescued by American and Italian intelligence personnel. But this amounts to extending the analysis of private intelligence operations into an entirely new sphere of private government, one that is beyond the scope of the present discussion.

One dimension of the terrorist problem was revealed by a Department of State bulletin of 1980 which reported that from January 1968 to October 1980 there were more than 7,300 international terrorist incidents. During this period of just over a decade, 173 American citizens were killed and 970 were wounded as a result of terrorist attacks. The cost of terrorism must be calculated in hundreds of millions of dollars, in the enormous fear and suffering of the individuals who have been affected by or who must live in dread of terrorist attacks; and in the costly disruption of commercial as well as governmental and diplomatic activities.[14] There is also the other side of the coin, however: some firms engage in counterrevolutionary participation with right-wing terrorists, as in the overthrow of the Allende regime in Chile.

An additional problem created by terrorism is the weakening of the loyalty of the citizens of target nations, or of the employees of target institutions, for the erosion of institutional loyalties is the prime aim of the terrorist. Terrorism subscribes to an alternative morality and it promotes the acceptance of its creed by those outside the organization, as it did so effectively with Patty Hearst. Consequently, those who demonstrate continued loyalty to an institution that comes under terrorist assault risk serious physical injury or even death for themselves or members of their family. The objective of a terrorist is to deprive the enemy organization, usually a state or a corporation, of the loyalty (or at least the visible loyalty) of its citizens or employees. In doing this, terrorists threaten to undermine the foundations of the support necessary for the proper functioning of the institutions of government and business. To sum up: the growth of terrorism means the decline of the ability of the state to protect its citizens, the weakening of security, and the acceleration of the dissolution of conventional loyalties. Border installations designed to protect against invasion by foreign armies are useless against terrorist onslaughts.

The Power of Organizational Intelligence: Modern Man's Answer to the Eleusinian Mysteries

Secret rites perpetuated the power of religious leaders of ancient times. Twentieth-century people, when they think about the objects of secrecy in antiquity, regard them as quaint and irrational. Many of the secrets of the ancients were, after all, related to drugs and based on magic. The modern Westerner would doubtless consider the efforts of Athens to preserve the secrecy of the Eleusinian mysteries as rather foolish. But in a way he resembles ancient man. He shares the urge toward secrecy and uses secrecy to protect his exclusive possession of certain elements of his knowledge, hoping thereby to safeguard his personal power. In a sense, the complexity of the new technologies—the new magic—creates an aura of incomprehensibility that gives power to technocrats as effectively as the secret rites of the ancients.

Intelligence networks can penetrate and interpret the mysteries of the new magic. These networks have great potential, for they can be used to demystify or steal or transfer technology. To the modern businessman, in the most immediate sense, knowledge is both power and profit. Even marketing is to a large extent a function of knowledge: knowledge of what the competition will be selling, knowledge of how to produce better and more durable goods, knowledge of what people are buying; and above all, knowledge about how to see that all this knowledge is properly utilized. The Ford Motor Company's Edsel illustrates for all time the misapplication of industrial knowledge.

Today we have a new and brilliant marketing tool, the compu-

21

terized consumer credit reporting service called credit data. TRW, for example, in April, 1983, stated through its Information Services Division that it "maintains credit information on more than 90 million consumers." (The company also publishes a booklet, *TRW and Credit Reporting*, commenting on "Laws, Legislation and Consumers" and stating that "all consumer credit information is treated in a confidential and ethical manner.") In the U.S. we have many such computerized consumer credit services, and taken together these private services are a vast intelligence network.

The chief executive officer has a crucial role in the proper use of industrial intelligence. In fact, it may be argued that the chief contribution of the CEO is simply the ability to see the truth and—unlike Cassandra—to be believed. Yet the CEO must also act practically. He may be a dreamer, a visionary, or, privately, even a religious mystic; but failure to deal with the truth in a practical manner is unforgivable. Consider the reverse: a CEO who seems practical and pragmatic, but has no capacity to divine the truth. Such a person may have invulnerable job security but stolidly and inexorably he leads his firm toward disaster.

The role of cultural values in management is seldom considered. In all the vast literature on Japanese industrial superiority there has been little discussion at all of the religious sources of truth that remain vital in Japanese culture and inform the judgments of Japanese CEOs. To see the truth requires objectivity and insight but to benefit from it requires the moral strength to follow the dictates of the truth. That quality must be based in the first place on the access to complete, often exclusive, intelligence.

Without sufficient intelligence the formulation of effective and profitable policy is impossible. Policy formation processes in an organization—public or private—are only as good as the intelligence on which they are based. Hence, it is imperative for the corporation to develop effective systems of intelligence-gathering and analysis so that relevant judgments can be formulated from the mountains of information, most of it useless, now available as a result of new communications technology. Later we will deal with this problem in greater detail.

The new challenge to the corporation is to develop an intelligence-gathering function of considerable scope and magnitude.

But this requires a new fail-safe executive staff function to see that the intelligence function is actually used to improve business operations, and for the benefit of society in general. The only restrictive stipulation is that it must not in any way threaten the liberties or privacy of individuals in our society.

War, it is said, is an extension of politics by other means. It is appropriate to ask, then, of what politics is an extension. Politics, many would say—businessmen as well as commissars—is an extension of economics or of the power of industry. Certainly, in many respects, war, politics, and economics are all alike. All three involve continual struggle. Conflict is inevitable in the market place, among politicians, and between nations. The validity of the strategies applicable to all three of these battlefields is commensurate with the accuracy of the intelligence underlying them. And while in this country the main contestants in at least one of these settings are private governments, their needs are not qualitatively different from those of public governments. If it is taken for granted that government, in the public sense, requires intelligence, why should the requirements of private government be different?

Intelligence is clearly a necessity for all sectors of society. A business that abdicated its responsibilities in this regard would be one that decided, in effect, to dissolve its own power and simply pray that the government would keep it alive through subsidies. Such a decision is neither realistic nor possible for, as the late Adolf A. Berle, Jr., observed:

> Power has laws of its own. One of them is that when one group having power declines or abdicates it, some other directing group immediately picks it up. . . . The choice of corporate management is not whether so great a power shall cease to exist; they can merely determine whether they will serve as the nuclei of its organization or pass it over to someone else, probably the modern state.[15]

Business is constantly involved in a struggle to maintain its autonomy. It cannot abandon that struggle without irreparable harm to pluralistic democracy, for the corporation is one of the most powerful components of pluralism. There is a continual struggle between the public and private aspects of life in our society; business in all its forms represents one of the most influential of our private interests.

Although an intelligence system is a necessity in this setting, it is a dangerous necessity. This book provides a defense of the use of intelligence by business. Since it employs primarily a conceptual approach, it also considers the dilemma of intelligence systems and all they involve: they are necessary to defend freedom but they also endanger it. This requires us to consider dispassionately the actual benefits and disadvantages of the large-scale system that is presented here. It would be the darkest of ironies if a system of corporate intelligence, once created, evolved into a technological and bureaucratic leviathan that destroyed the free society it was designed to aid. A careful analysis that takes into account philosophical as well as operational concerns may help us avoid this tragedy.

Conclusion

Among the bastions of pluralist democracy, business stands out with a special prominence. It is also charged with a special responsibility: it has an obligation to us all to maintain its vitality and its leadership. This involves a paradox: business today, in the shape of the great corporation, is naturally acquiring many of the attributes of a governing institution. Although this appears to violate the basic principle of maintaining a healthy adversarial relationship between business and government, such is not the case. On the contrary, the acknowledgment and even enhancement of the political attributes of corporate power is required today to safeguard the survival of the corporation. This requirement is nowhere better illustrated than in the need to institute formally organized intelligence functions in the corporation. That need is the subject of the analysis that follows.

2

The Evolution of Intelligence

A Brief History of Intelligence

INTELLIGENCE dates back to the beginning of mankind. Earliest man sought answers to questions relating to his own survival and well-being. Members of the most primitive civilizations not only had a need to know what their enemies were doing and how those threats could be countered, but also were concerned with matters relating to their survival and daily comfort, such as the best sources of food and shelter.

Early Intelligence Efforts

The earliest "intelligence officers" turned to seers, oracles, and prophets. *I Ching,* or, as it is otherwise known, *The Book of Changes,* a collection of mystical teachings from China which first appeared around 1200 B.C., served for centuries as an inspirational and instructional guide for generals and spies. While giving no simple, direct answers, *The Book of Changes* was widely believed to provide, if consulted with appropriate rituals, important clues which an intelligent decision-maker could decipher.[1] Similarly, the ancient Greeks consulted oracles.

Yet one of the earliest written accounts of an intelligence operation shows a departure from relying on spiritual surveillance reports. A Biblical account in Numbers 13 records God's instructions to Moses to send men to Canaan to act as spies, which Moses did. The men were to note what riches the land offered and what enemy forces the Israelites were likely to encounter when they journeyed to Canaan. Still earlier in Biblical history, when Noah sent out a dove to see if the flood waters had receded it might be said that he was conducting the first known form of aerial reconnaissance.

The dozen men sent out by Moses and Noah's dove were on simple reconnaissance missions. Their tasks were to do no more than report what they observed. An effort to add some sophistication to this intelligence approach was made by Xerxes who, in 480 B.C., captured three Greek spies sent to learn about his troops. Rather than execute the three, Xerxes gave them the opportunity to view his impressive array of forces and then allowed them to return to the Greek army. Xerxes' plan was to deter his enemies from attacking by revealing the magnitude of his power. This psychological gamble, unfortunately, did not work and the attack, when it came, was better organized and prepared for the large force it encountered. Xerxes came closer to modern intelligence practices when he sent a spy to observe the Greek soldiers and attempted an analysis of the behavior reported. This is the first recorded instance of analysts being employed to explain foreign behavior.[2]

Chinese Intelligence Pioneers

The Chinese were the first to show real sophistication in the use of intelligence, as is shown by the writings of Sun Tzu, a contemporary of Confucius and author of *Principles of War*.[3] Sun Tzu, whose work dates back to 500 B.C., provides us with the first recorded effort to examine the intelligence-gathering process systematically and intellectually while developing principles and systems of espionage. Sun Tzu gives us a good overall picture of the intelligence systems of his era, and offers detailed lessons on the functions and techniques of those systems. He shows that for the leaders of the different Chinese kingdoms at that time intelligence was already a refined policy instrument which was seen as an indispensable part of military endeavors. Deception had become a hallmark of intelligence, as spies were dispatched in the uniforms of enemy soldiers to aid their infiltration of an adversary's camps. Another deceptive practice Sun

Tzu reports was to allow exposed agents to continue their missions while providing them with false information. Sun Tzu argues that a better course would be to arrest detected spies and attempt to win their allegiance. Sun Tzu writes that the spy should always enjoy a privileged position and have continual direct access to his leaders. No honor, he insists, is too great for these heroic figures. This elevated conception of the espionage agent stands in sharp contrast to the prevailing Western view of spies as contemptible individuals whose existence should, if possible, be denied. Sun Tzu also identifies several categories of spies and gives detailed instructions on how each should be employed. An interesting point is that Sun Tzu, stressing how valuable spies could be in defending a nation against war, advocates maintenance of a permanent espionage service in friendly as well as enemy states.

Another use of intelligence developed by the Chinese was in the maintenance of domestic control. If it was important to know what a foreign adversary was planning, it was even more vital to know the intentions and activities of potential domestic opponents. In the tenth century A.D. the Chinese emperor's Privy Councillor, Wang Anshih, established an elaborate family spy system to deal with the excessive banditry and lawlessness that afflicted the country at the time. Under his system, families were organized into units of ten, fifty, and five hundred, as well as by relatives and guests visiting their homes. Citizens were to report to the authorities on good deeds—and also on evil ones—and in return received protection against bandits or other exploiters. Wang's family spy system was accepted as a model for future regimes, including Mao Tse-Tung's communist order.[4]

The Development of Intelligence in the West

Europe was far behind China in developing sophisticated intelligence methods, perhaps because of the influence of ancient Rome. The Romans long suffered from a self-imposed handicap because espionage was rejected by the Roman leadership. Julius Caesar opposed the establishment of any secret service and Tiberius continued that opposition even though the existence of such an instrument might have prevented Caesar's assassination.[5]

Failure to understand the culture and customs of the East led to numerous mistakes by European leaders of the Middle Ages.

They knew little of the Byzantine Empire, the Eastern Slavs, and the Moslem peoples. Efforts to make contact with these civilizations were denounced as heresy and, being unable to see beyond their cultural biases, the West Europeans consistently discounted the threat posed by Turkey.

European ignorance of the East was not, however, total. European merchants had opened numerous markets in that region and had developed a thorough understanding of its people. European political leaders, unfortunately, did not avail themselves of the knowledge which was already at their disposal. By the fifteenth century, the Italians recognized the folly of isolating political intelligence operatives from commercial operatives and established embassies and missions in foreign states. Utilizing all possible contacts, including those established by merchants, Italian embassies generated the highest quality of strategic intelligence. This Italian innovation soon became an accepted practice for all European states.[6]

The consolidation of the nation-states brought the greatest advances and expansion in the uses of espionage. Espionage had a major impact on the outcome of the Hundred Years' War between France and England. In that conflict, the English—unable to defeat the French forces, inspired by Joan of Arc, on the battlefield—chose a subterfuge. They employed a covert agent among the French clergy to organize a plot which led, eventually, to the death of Joan. This event illustrates the link between information and action. With the exposure of weaknesses in an adversary's position, it becomes possible to exploit faults to one's own advantage. By combining information-gathering with an action-capability, the intelligence organization becomes doubly valuable. From the time of the Hundred Years' War and the Turkish wars, it became obvious that intelligence was not only essential to a more efficient military operation but also, perhaps, the key to victory.

An important contributor to the development of national espionage in Great Britain was Henry VII who, during the time he was hunted by Richard III, had to learn the skills of effective espionage in order to survive. Henry VII devoted a great deal of his time to perfecting what was essentially an instrument for his personal protection rather than an agency to serve the nation. However, the techniques he introduced were of great value to the later national services and his experiences also demonstrate how very fine the line often is between public and private intelligence.

Sir Francis Walsingham built on the foundation begun by Henry VII when he created for Queen Elizabeth I the first modern political espionage system in the formal, recognized service of a state. Almost every technique of espionage was practiced during his service to the Queen as Secretary of State and chief of the nation's secret service. Walsingham's organization combined domestic and international responsibilities; for example, he dispatched students from Cambridge to penetrate the French court.

The English poet and dramatist Christopher Marlowe was involved in this plot, although his precise role has never been absolutely determined. The circumstances of his death remain suspicious four centuries later. Another literary figure who supplemented his income by employment in the secret service was Marlowe's friend Matthew Roydon, and even Ben Jonson, his biographers have thought, was a secret agent of the English government. (It is also alleged that other great and famous men such as John Donne, Sir Philip Sidney, Sir John Dee, Daniel Defoe, Francis Bacon, Samuel Pepys, and more recently, even T. S. Eliot and W. Somerset Maugham, were from time to time intelligence agents. How different would be the popular American attitude toward espionage if the history books taught that our foremost example of a foreign agent was none other than Ben Franklin!)

Walsingham is credited with breaking up the French-backed conspiracy to elevate Mary Queen of Scots to the English throne and with procuring the naval intelligence that enabled England to defeat the Spanish Armada.[7]

The art of secret communications improved dramatically under Walsingham because of his employment of Thomas Phelippes, a cryptographer capable of devising codes that no enemy agent could decipher. Phelippes was, of course, equally skilled at breaking codes and thus improved Walsingham's ability to monitor enemy communications effectively.

Under systematic state tutelage, the art of intelligence advanced rapidly. Intelligence technology was the first beneficiary with improvements in map-making as well as cryptography. State tutelage also led to a specialization of intelligence functions. With the increasing complexity of assignments, secret services found it desirable to separate political intelligence, internal security, and military intelligence. The work of Frederick II of Prussia, widely regarded as the founder of modern military intelligence, firmly established the concept of military intelligence as a distinct, specialized endeavor. The continued development of embassies, whose espionage missions were first recognized by the Italians, established the dominance of diplomats in the area of political intelligence.

Another pioneer in the development of espionage was Joseph Fouché, organizer of Napoleon's political secret police and counterespionage machinery. By this time, the importance of intelligence was widely recognized throughout Europe and most nations were seeking to improve their intelligence capabilities. Sweden and Holland became the premier examples of small states which enjoyed considerable prominence because of their outstanding intelligence systems. The Swedes successfully played on religious connections in the recruitment of foreign nationals in the service of Swedish espionage. Such religious recruitment was a precursor of Soviet ideological recruitment in the name of Marxism-Leninism in the twentieth century.

Twentieth-Century Intelligence

While the art of espionage had reached relative maturity by the first World War, its acceptance was not universal. The primary recalcitrant among the major powers was the United States. The American response to the development of espionage systems by the other great powers was passage of the Espionage Statute of 1917, an effort to engage in passive resistance to espionage assaults against the nation. The exploits of Mata Hari, the German spy who obtained information by seducing French officials, were seen as suitable for novels but not appropriate for policy imitation. Even German espionage efforts under the direction of Admiral Canaris in preparation for another war were an insufficient stimulus. It was not until World War II was upon us that the United States joined the other nations in developing an organization for national intelligence. The U.S. still suffered from the legacy of Secretary of War Stimson's debilitating dictum that "gentlemen do not read other gentlemen's mail" and his subsequent dismantling of the United States' cryptographic unit.

This distressing picture was fresh in the minds of those men who agreed to set up the Office of Strategic Services to manage the only preexisting intelligence offices, those at the departmental level which were concerned primarily with the limited informational needs of their specific departments. Under William Donovan's direction, the OSS became the first comprehensive American intelligence organization. Although it was initially limited in space, staff and funding, it made such a great contribution that with the end of the war there was a general recognition of the need to perpetuate many of its functions.[8] The 1947 National Security Act produced the organizational successor to the OSS, the Central Intelligence Agency.

The advances in technology since World War II have had a considerable impact on the methods used by intelligence services. Computers, reconnaissance satellites, and other space-age innovations have in many instances allowed machines to replace agents on the ground. Exotic devices for assassination of political enemies have also been perfected by numerous services. Technology has enabled the intelligence operative to find new uses for his product. The ability to conduct surveillance of so much of the earth's surface means that our natural resources themselves can now be the target of the spy's attentions.

The instrument of intelligence, which was finally accepted by the governments of most nation-states in the early twentieth century, is now a useful tool of business. Today, intelligence—operating with varying degrees of sophistication—provides commercial customers with information ranging from credit checks to analyses of natural resources available for major investment projects. Technological advances of the mid twentieth century have created a situation in which the functions and abilities of intelligence increasingly intersect with the needs of the corporation. The natural growth of both entities has enabled the two to work together effectively. In contemporary global society, both the corporation and private intelligence agencies make fundamental contributions to the society of which they are a part.

History of the Nomenclature of Intelligence

No history of intelligence, however brief it is intended to be, is complete without an examination of the nomenclature of classified information.[9] The words used to designate an item's value or sensitivity are in themselves an indication of official thinking on intelligence policy and a study of them helps to chart the evolution of that policy. They should denote specific types of information to which access is restricted, as well as the reasons for and the extent of those restrictions, and there should be clear guidelines regarding who is empowered to affix them to information in the possession of the government. The evolution of governmental policy is instructive for an examination of corporate intelligence policy because, as we will see, it reflects common problems, uncertainties, and inconsistencies. In fact, early reactions to the institution of governmental restrictions on access to information were based on the assumption that officials were simply trying to hide their ignorance and incompetence. Indeed, the cry that restrictions to access to government information are excessive is heard even at this writing. In an era of public skepticism regarding corporate leadership, one may observe similar critical evaluations of efforts by business to adopt security procedures resembling those of governments. Popular suspicions embrace both government and business and the security measures of each are subject to equally adverse reactions. However, since government has an advantage over business in terms of the longevity of its security programs, its experiences offer valuable lessons to corporate leaders attempting to respond to similar adversities.

When governmental classification systems first appeared, they were characterized by a failure to discriminate between different classes of information and by lack of precision on the part of classifying authorities. Officials generally assumed the authority to classify their correspondence as they saw fit. They were guided by current customs rather than set rules. The result of this unsystematic arrangement was that familiar words were used without an agreed understanding as to their legally prescribed meaning. Consequently, often little was being done to insure special handling of documents which required much more than normal treatment. The system thus suffered from a lack of precision that seriously impaired its effectiveness.

The use of the term "confidential" illustrates the early failure of security systems. The word had multiple meanings. The lack of a precise, generally accepted meaning, and the frequency of the term's appearance, led to confusion and it came to mean little more than a courtesy that extended to both governmental and commercial matters. A confidential classification did not bring any assurance of special handling or even limited access.

Necessity of Restrictions

Nevertheless, the desirability of restrictions on information has been widely accepted—ever since Biblical times when God was said to have warned Adam not to eat from the Tree of Knowledge—as a matter of necessity in the struggle for survival. Both business and government respond to the pressures of competition and challenge by attempting to guard secrets, including technology, that give them a competitive advantage. Over the centuries, many different things have been classified as secret. Rituals thought to give special powers to their performers were guarded with the same determination exhibited by a modern nation protecting military information, or an automobile manufacturer trying to keep private its plans for the introduction of a new car model on the market. Survival is at issue in all of these cases. Secrecy is not a luxury but a necessity.

The struggle for survival inspired U.S. legislation in 1776 to forbid correspondence with enemy soldiers. British forces operated under similar restrictions. More recently, wartime censorship of newspapers has been introduced to prevent publication of information that might reveal troop movements and thus give an advantage to the enemy. In the years that followed World War I and World War II, more and more legislation was passed empowering the U.S. government to withhold information from the public in order to deny enemies access to data that could be used against the nation. Even in the absence of legislation, American presidents have restricted access to information by invoking the president's power as commander-in-chief of the armed forces.

In all of this, what emerged was a rather haphazard system. Wartime conditions were sufficient to prevent critics from making a concerted effort to oppose censorship, but during times of peace it was more difficult to justify some of the restrictions and, as a result, there was a relaxation of security. This had to change. The advent of modern technology changed the ease with which a nation could shift from war to peace and raised serious questions regarding the ability of a potential adversary to make extensive preparations for war long before a state of war came into being. Technology, which radically altered the operating methods of espionage agents, has also had a dramatic impact on peacetime security policy. The indifference to technological advances

33

which was once characteristic of most nations has become a dangerous flaw to be avoided at all costs. Vigilance about a nation's own technology as well as its neighbor's has become the hallmark of the security policies of nations at peace.

Technology and the Rise of Military Intelligence

In his pioneer study, "Confidential: The Beginning of Defense Information Marking,"[10] Professor Andrew Patterson, Jr., observes that the U.S. Civil War was a turning point in the development of security systems. Prior to the 1860s, the protection of the secrets of military technology was not crucial to the outcome of a battle because communications and the ability to exploit new military innovations were limited. According to Patterson, numerous breakthroughs occurred at this time which increased the need for security. New uses for electricity, remote controls for explosives, searchlights, steam power, nitroglycerine and guncotton were all developed by the period of the Civil War. New weapons and new combat techniques promoted an awareness of the need to protect defense information at all times. Defense requirements could no longer be summarized in terms of a few thousand muskets and primitive artillery pieces. Technology was creating weapons of increased accuracy and sophistication which were products of a nation's scientific research and industrial strength. A technological advance falling into the hands of a potential enemy meant the neutralization of an advantage that one's own nation might otherwise have enjoyed.

Formal recognition of the new importance of military intelligence came with the appearance of military attachés in U.S. embassies. The use of military personnel for espionage parallels the earlier employment of merchants for a similar purpose. Since the time of the Civil War, the military attaché has become an integral part of the diplomatic staff in friendly states as well as potential enemy states. Today, the mission of the military attaché varies enormously in terms of the responsibilities assumed, and, in some cases, the dangers faced, by officers serving in that position. Frequently the attaché does little more than care for the needs of U.S. servicemen traveling within the country, but in many other instances he is actively involved in the collection of military data about the host nation. The military attaché also

34

serves as a symbol of his country and, more and more, is the target of terrorist forces wishing to strike against the United States. The assassination of a lieutenant colonel serving in the American embassy in Paris in 1982 demonstrates one possible consequence of this role. Throughout Eastern Europe, U.S. attachés provide a convenient barometer through which the Soviet Union and its allies can register disapproval of American political and military action. The increase in physical assaults against U.S. embassy personnel over the past five years has coincided with political differences between America and the Communist states.

Technology has also made the drive toward recognition of the concept of state secrets more urgent. Before the advent of relatively sophisticated weapons technologies, it was generally maintained that a new formula or system was ultimately the property of the inventor. Restrictions might be imposed during times of war, but with the end of hostilities the new device—or the science which produced it—became the exclusive property of the person who developed it. For example, Matthew Fontaine Maury, who had introduced the use of mines during the Civil War, gave instruction after the war on how to use mines. The classes were offered in return for payment to Maury while he was in England and he continued the business of selling his invention in France, Russia, Sweden, Holland and other nations. At the time, the mine was regarded as a remarkable, perhaps even revolutionary, development in military technology. Even though this innovation was developed under governmental tutelage, it remained the "property" of the inventor who was free to sell it as he saw fit and profitable. Because a full awareness of the significance of this new technology had not yet been formed, no serious effort was made to restrict access to it. It was the British who first recognized the need for some effort to restrict access to the mine and who assigned restrictive defense information markings to it. This was the first peacetime use of such markings and represented a significant step in the direction of a fully developed concept of state secrets during both war and peace. The British action, however, caused a public outcry on the part of several editors of journals and writers who were interested in studying these new weapons. Americans joined the chorus of critics complaining that those who knew the most about such developments were going to be denied access to them. In Patterson's account he remarks that most people saw these restrictions as novel, unnecessary, and unlikely to be retained for long.[11]

Acceptance of the concept of state secrets relative to technical material during peacetime carried with it a new concern for agencies to regulate access to classified information. British specialists recommended creation of a standing committee to deal with questions relating to the utilization and development of new weapons technologies. Establishment of special committees, of course, heightened public speculation about the nature of the weapons and the reasons for the secrecy surrounding them. Many commentators expressed fear that excessive secrecy would not only limit readership and scholarship in newly developed technological areas but would also inhibit research, as scholars would fear that success would simply lead to classification. In such an emotional atmosphere, it was difficult to establish the point that much information could have an impact on national security even though the country was not at war.

It was not until the 1870s, when foreign governments exhibited an interest in British experiments on how to sink the double-bottom ships possessed only by Britain, that much popular support was generated in favor of restrictions on information. Letters to *The Times* of London pointed out that observers from various foreign states, most of which had been at war with England at some time in the past, had been allowed to look on as mines and torpedoes were detonated from different distances and angles in an effort to determine how to sink the iron ship the British had constructed. Journalists and scholars who had previously denounced governmental measures limiting access to information began to demand rigid restrictions that would deny foreign governments and others access to sensitive information. In response Queen Victoria issued a proclamation in 1878 forbidding the export from the United Kingdom of any devices such as torpedoes or related materials. This action, however, was probably no more than symbolic by the time the proclamation was issued, because so many other nations had already acquired and exploited the necessary technology. The effects of the proclamation were further limited by its failure to consider restricting the publication of the information required for construction of such devices. An inability to purchase a torpedo could be overcome by simply procuring the instructions on how to build one's own torpedo.

The Official Secrets Act

The Admiralty itself initiated efforts to protect its weapons technology in 1887 by awarding separate contracts to different companies for individual components of the new Brenan torpedo. Officials reasoned that if no single firm produced an entire product, then it would be impossible for one individual to betray the government to a foreign power by selling a classified weapon. This step was taken during a time of considerable public concern about the transmission of secrets to hostile powers. In 1888 there were numerous scandals in England regarding officials who, for various reasons, shared information with foreign military officials. All of Europe, it seemed, was embroiled in a spy scare involving English, French and German espionage agents.

The British government's response to this concern was the Official Secrets Act of 1889. This Act ended the long controversies about what could and could not be properly shared outside the British government by making criminal the communication of any defense information to foreign representatives. Imprisonment from two years to lifetime could result from conviction under the terms of the Act. Even the sketching of an English fortress or factory was forbidden. Later questions regarding the legality of transmitting information not to foreign governments but to British newspapers were resolved by additional legislation. Other countries passed similar laws, some of which went still further, such as the French law which prohibited foreign carrier pigeons from being brought into the country. Generally, the British Official Secrets Act has been regarded as the model legislation establishing a systematic security program.

For some time, however, there was disagreement about the precise purpose and function of the Act. In fact, the bill was first introduced in 1888 but was withdrawn because of complaints regarding the necessity for such legislation. Some critics even suggested that England had no secrets worth keeping and therefore needed no protective legislation. During the first two decades of its existence, the Official Secrets Act was used infrequently. One reason for this may have been that the law punished only the person revealing the classified information and not the recipient. It may also be significant that most of the prosecutions under the Act did not involve the disclosure of defense information but rather related matters, such as the offering of defense contracts. Efforts to amend the Act so that the prospect for convictions would be improved were generally unsuccessful and the law continued to be regarded as a deterrent more to British citizens than to foreign spies. With time, the public concern over foreign espionage declined and there was little support for a significant strengthening of the law. In the absence of a major threat to England, the belief was advanced in the press that espionage was nothing so sinister but merely another legitimate profession. Some public figures even argued that it was useful to have foreign agents active in one's country because a careful monitoring of their activities enabled the nation's security services to learn much regarding the intent of foreign nations toward England.

The paranoia of 1888 regarding foreign spies in general was replaced in the early twentieth century by a new paranoia regarding the activities of German agents. There was soon a widely held belief that German spies had penetrated every level of British society. The emergence of this German threat prompted passage of the Official Secrets Act of 1911. The Act was much more stringent than the earlier legislation and, unlike the 1889 Act, it was not based upon the assumption that a person might have an innocent interest in military fortifications or installations. The state was no longer obligated to prove criminal intent in asking for prosecutions under the Official Secrets Act. Mere possession of certain defense information was, by itself, regarded as a violation of the provisions of the Act. Furthermore, the new law allowed authorities to designate any area of military significance as off-limits and to punish a person simply for intruding into the facility. The penalties imposed under the 1911 Act were also more severe than those specified in the 1889 Act.

The breadth of the 1911 Official Secrets Act was so great that it affected much of the legitimate work of journalists. Numerous topics were soon designated as being of a sensitive defense-related nature and "D" notices were issued, warning that journalists should not attempt to write about them without consulting with the proper authorities. Service and engineering publications were covered under this system along with the general newspapers. The rationale of the "D" notice system was that much information served to warn the Germans that England was making preparations for war and that such a warning would give them an obvious advantage over Great Britain. With the coming of war, full press censorship was instituted and remained in force until the end of hostilities. The threat of another war in the 1930s brought a reinstatement of the "D" notice system and it remains in force today. The wide range of possible topics covered by the system has continued to worry critics fearful of a loss of fundamental domestic freedoms in the effort to protect against foreign threats such as espionage and sabotage.

The Classification of Ideas

Efforts to devise the best warship types and designs, naval tactics, and armament raised questions that could be answered only by the careful utilization of ideas advanced by individuals in the employment of the government. The sorts of problems which became apparent to governmental decision-makers have become equally obvious in recent decades to the leadership of businesses doing highly technical work. For both business and government today, the problem arises of how to control or at least limit the activities of individuals who leave their service. The employment of outside consultants to assist with research and development makes the task of the security specialist even more difficult.

This question was highlighted by an incident near the end of the nineteenth century in which the U.S. Navy Department advertised for designs of an armored cruiser and an armored battleship. British authorities viewed this as an open attempt to bribe someone in the employment of the British government, which had done much development of such naval weapons. Although there were individuals in private employment capable of doing much of the work desired by the United States, British officials felt that the overwhelming majority of them were working for the British government.

By this time, governments had come to regard ideas—as well as instruments—as exclusively the property of the state. Clearly, secrecy about the devices built for the military services meant little if the builders themselves could immediately sell the ideas that brought the weapons into existence. The problem was more than theoretical since there were dozens of nations, such as the United States, desperate for modern military technology. It was concerns of this nature that helped build support for passage of the Official Secrets Act in Britain and for a more rigid enforcement of patent laws where possible. While this problem was by no means uniquely British, it did seem to affect Britain more than many other nations because of the significant advances Britain was making in industrial and scientific matters.

The Growth of Military Intelligence

Patterson shows how concern for gathering military intelligence grew side by side with the concern for protecting sensitive information during the latter years of the nineteenth century. It was in 1873 that the British Army finally created a formal intelligence branch to replace the "Topographical and Statistical Department of the War Office" which had been responsible for the limited intelligence activity of the army since the Crimean War. The new military intelligence branch was responsible for far more than the mere collection of maps and plans and made a serious effort to acquire information about foreign armies. British military intelligence was to be responsible for restricted documents—including their marking and storage—and was also to provide information on developments in the far-flung British colonies. In view of the important global role of the British Navy, it is not surprising that the most remarkable development of intelligence was in the Navy. British difficulties in Egypt during this period stimulated the development of a serious program for strengthening the British Navy. The need for a Naval Staff to plan major operations was recognized and many felt that planning was more heavily dependent on the quality of knowledge used by planners than by their ingenuity. A Russian threat to Afghanistan in 1885 provided the final impetus to proposals that major resources be devoted to a Naval Intelligence department.

Although there was agreement on the need for such an agency, bureaucratic infighting and jealousy delayed final deployment of the plan for an intelligence department. The safeguarding of defense information and collection of information to support military operations were still not seen as important enough concerns to override questions about the ranks and salaries of the officers who would staff the new Naval Intelligence department. Military and civilian bureaucrats suffered from a general short-sightedness about intelligence needs. Civilian administrators were concerned that too much money might go into the program, while military officials were often more interested in the maintenance of glorious but obsolete naval traditions that did not seem compatible with the possible activities of an intelligence branch. (These objections are similar to frequent complaints by contemporary business leaders who feel unnecessarily constrained by the intelligence demands frequently faced by the corporation. Like the venerable British admirals, they often resist pressures for their organizations to adopt new functions that appear to have little in common with the widely accepted definitions of their mission.) Naval leaders argued that, after all, their service was very different from the Army and must, therefore, operate differently in terms of internal operations and planning approaches. However, the alarming growth of the German Navy and of German espionage, coupled with an awareness of the global responsibilities of the British Navy in meeting the German threat, were eventually sufficient to bring about the creation of a major intelligence apparatus within the Navy.

Like the British military, the U.S. Army was late in establishing a military intelligence branch. The need for one became apparent during the Civil War when Southern spies could learn about Union military plans by simply reading Northern newspapers which were not subject to any censorship. By contrast, the Confederate forces placed great importance on intelligence activities and were able to exploit Northern weaknesses by superior intelligence in spite of having weaker military forces. A formal military intelligence branch was set up in 1885 but it suffered from the numerous administrative changes in the U.S. Army and developed no accepted standards of operation until World War I. Because of uncertainty about routing classified information to the next higher command level, documents often fell into the hands of officials who were unfamiliar with required handling procedures. Numerous leaks of classified information resulted as untrained individuals found themselves in possession of sensitive material. Until American forces arrived in Europe in World War I, the Army had developed no defense information marking system or procedures for classification of information according to its intelligence value.[12]

The U.S. Navy was equally hesitant in establishing an intelligence branch. The Secretary of the Navy ordered the creation of such a branch in 1882 but it was forced to operate with borrowed personnel and no funding at all until it finally demonstrated that it was useful. In the following years, naval intelligence worked through a system of naval attachés assigned to U.S. embassies. Their reports were forwarded to Washington for evaluation and dissemination to agencies capable of utilizing their material. Naval intelligence set very high standards during this time although it was not involved in the handling of sensitive defense information. It was not until the Spanish-American War that the Office of Naval Intelligence began the use of covert methods and agents and adopted the attitude that not all the necessary information could be acquired by simple reciprocal trading of facts about nonsensitive matters.[13] The increasing sophistication of military hardware by the early twentieth century was also creating a concern for the protection of some American information. Thus, the earlier policy, which was based on the principle that governments could casually exchange "secrets," was abandoned in favor of a policy reflecting a concern for protecting the nation's unique technologies.

Military Intelligence During World War I

World War I had a dramatic impact on the nature of military intelligence and led to a realization of the enhanced importance of this function in modern conflicts. All involved expected the war to be short and decisive. As it dragged on year after year, analysts began to realize that military strength was only a small part of a nation's capacity to fight a protracted conflict. Suddenly, the national economic potential of an adversary became significant: everything from transportation and communications systems to industrial plants and population characteristics became valuable "intelligence." Enemy newspapers were carefully read for data on national political and economic activity. By the end of the war, this new understanding of conflict had spawned a new weapon—psychological warfare.

A little-known incident of the postwar era gives a sense of how intelligence was viewed. When Harry Stimson was Secretary of War, he inadvertently learned through one of his military advisers that the War Department had a cryptanalysis section by which it intercepted messages from other countries to their ambassadors in Washington, D.C. Stimson was outraged, and ordered the practice stopped, saying it was ungentlemanly to read the secret messages of nations with which we maintained diplomatic relations. This order fortunately did not prevail too long. Eventually, the United States developed one of the most advanced cryptanalysis capabilities in the world. This curious example of morality interfering with national survival is discussed in *The American Black Chamber*—once a rare book—by Major Herbert O. Yardley.[14]

As psychological warfare and cryptanalysis developed during World War I, the United States military was forced to reconsider its still immature system of classification of information. The term "confidential" had been in use for years but no widely accepted meaning of the word had yet been generated. When the American Expeditionary Force arrived in Europe, it established a three-level system for classifying defense information. Three categories of sensitive information were identified and special arrangements for the handling of each were required in order to prevent the compromise of restricted material. At the lowest level was "For Official Circulation Only," a designation reserved for orders, pamphlets, instructions, maps, diagrams, and intelligence publications not intended for the public because their disclosure might harm the Allied cause. The next category was "Confidential" and included matter restricted to a minimum number of people with the A.E.F. The highest level was "Secret"—a term to which was applied an absolute meaning: there were to be no degrees of secrecy, only absolute secrecy. Secret matter was to be used or viewed only by the officer receiving it. That officer enjoyed no discretion in sharing it with others. The receiving officer or his clerk was responsible for the safe storage of all secret documents as well as any confidential papers in his possession. Both categories of documents were to be kept in a locked container except during times of use. Unless specific exceptions were stated, material bearing these restrictions was not to be taken to the front-line trenches, reproduced in any manner, or allowed to circulate at lower headquarters. A short time later this order was modified slightly in terms of specific definitions and nomenclature ("For Official Use Only" replaced "For Official Circulation") and provisions were made for penalties to be imposed in the event of violations. Patterson observes that many of the modifications actually reduced the already limited precision of the definitions and made their application more difficult.[15]

Intelligence During World War II

In the years between World Wars I and II, few advances were made in intelligence work. Attitudes such as those expressed by President Coolidge made it difficult to give realistic consideration to intelligence requirements. Nevertheless, World War I did create an interest in maintaining a communications intelligence capability and for at least a brief time the Departments of War and State cooperated in a joint venture to advance this purpose. When that undertaking came to an end, the Army and the Navy continued their programs in cryptography and, as a result, were able to break the so-called Purple Code which the Japanese used to transmit classified diplomatic and military messages to Japanese representatives serving abroad before the attack on Pearl Harbor.[16] Because of this capability, American officials were able to read secret Japanese communications almost immediately. In fact, the communications indicating final preparations for the attack on Pearl Harbor had been intercepted and a report was on the way to the responsible U.S. officials as the first wave of the Japanese assault forces arrived. Another contribution of the Army and the Navy during the period between the wars was less dramatic but nonetheless important. The Army and Navy used this time to resolve differences between their defense markings and to establish uniform handling procedures for defense information. As a result, it was finally possible to transfer sensitive data from one service to the other without serious discontinuities in its handling.

It was World War II that generated pressures for the establishment of a fully coordinated national system of intelligence. The outbreak of war in Europe prompted new activity by Military Intelligence and by 1941 "country digests"—summaries of political, military, and economic conditions with projections in each field—were being composed about every country in the world.

The next major conceptual leap occurred in the wake of Pearl Harbor. In an atmosphere thick with recrimination and hints of espionage, Congressional investigations were held to fix the responsibility. Gradually it became evident that documents which had crossed the desks of many officials, if pieced together, clearly indicated the likelihood of such an attack. In other words, the investigators concluded, it was not ill will, ineptitude, or treasonous sentiments, but the lack of a coordinated gathering and evaluation of information on Japanese military, social, economic and political developments that had allowed this major U.S. military disaster. This version of the events of December 1941 set the stage for the creation of a centralized facility on intelligence to replace the various department operations. The events and activities prior to that "day of infamy" in 1941 have never been fully revealed, but it was the general understanding that there had been an intelligence failure that led to a push for centralization.[17]

The centralized intelligence facility which emerged was the Office of Strategic Services. Organized and run by Colonel William J. Donovan, the OSS utilized covert operations and espionage as well as scholarly research in an effort to produce the information necessary to accomplish the defeat of the Germans and their allies. Most of the work of the OSS was not dramatic escapades involving agents dropped behind enemy lines but rather systematic research of the sort conducted in libraries and laboratories. Yet the OSS did establish paramilitary units behind enemy lines and conduct psychological warfare against the enemy. OSS operatives maintained contact with agents in German-occupied France and elsewhere as a means of keeping track of German military units. With the approach of D-Day, reports radioed out of hostile territory enabled Allied commanders to anticipate German military movements and save thousands of lives. The message, from the military's point of view, was that intelligence was an extremely good investment. It allowed forces to accomplish their missions more effectively and at a much lower cost.

It is a contention of this study that the military's lesson about intelligence is applicable to other endeavors, including those of the business community. Policy—whether corporate or military—is only as good as the knowledge upon which it is founded.

The Founding of the CIA

At the end of the war, some American officials felt that the OSS had done its job and that there was no further need for it. In September 1945, the temporary organization was dissolved and its secret intelligence and counterintelligence branches were placed under military control. Rivalry between the OSS and military intelligence had persisted throughout the war and that same spirit delayed creation of a successor agency after the war. In his farewell to the men and women of the OSS, Colonel Donovan spoke of the end of an unusual experiment, implying that no similar organization would replace it in the future. Nevertheless, the temper of the times was such that in 1947 the National Security Act created the Central Intelligence Agency. The turbulence of the early postwar years—Soviet troop movements throughout Eastern Europe, Soviet-backed guerrilla war in Greece, and the constant threat of a new war over the Berlin issue—had clearly indicated a need for another institution capable of satisfying the informational needs of the United States government. According to the National Security Act of 1947, this new agency was "to correlate and evaluate intelligence relating to the national security, and provide for the appropriate dissemination of such intelligence within the Government . . ." A further requirement was that the CIA "perform such other duties" relative to national security at the direction of the President. Under this mandate, the CIA assumed vast information-collection functions, research and analysis activity, and created sub-offices for various kinds of covert activities.

The CIA, during its early years, was greatly benefited by having a cadre of people who had worked for the OSS, the FBI, and the military, but countless organizational matters remained to be resolved. Behind the organizational questions were still larger questions about what the CIA could and should properly do in advancing United States interests around the world.

The Korean War created new circumstances in which the CIA was forced to resolve many of the questions about its role. During this conflict the CIA found itself called upon to satisfy demands of the military, of civilian policy-makers who needed information, and of policy-makers who wanted the agency to undertake a variety of covert operations. It was during this period that the Air Force, wanting to know more about the latest Soviet fighter plane, requested the CIA to furnish not only one of the new planes, but also a Soviet fighter pilot! In order to keep pace with as many of these demands as possible, the intelligence community moved toward coordination and centralization. As Director of Central Intelligence, Lieutenant General Walter Bedell Smith used all of his prestige and influence to end the countless jurisdictional arguments among intelligence services. Smith set up new, detailed procedures for interagency cooperation and developed support agencies to provide the personnel, training, communications, and security needed for effective intelligence operations. The many specific intelligence functions—research, estimates, and operations—were reorganized and assigned to separate commands.

In the Eisenhower Administration, the CIA was under the leadership of Allen Dulles, the brother of the Secretary of State, a pleasant coincidence which did much to help problems of coordination among the different intelligence services. This was a time of expanding political action on the part of the intelligence community and an administration that felt many national objectives were better met by effective covert political action than by direct political or military confrontation. Once again, intelligence was viewed as an economical way to accomplish important policy objectives. Even more important during the Eisenhower-Dulles years was the establishment of mechanisms to review the varied work of intelligence organizations.

After the Bay of Pigs disaster in 1961 a newly critical attitude to the CIA emerged. New oversight agencies were established, and in August 1961 the Defense Intelligence Agency was set up to assist in coordinating military intelligence and meeting the intelligence needs of the military. The United States Intelligence Board was also a product of this era of re-evaluation. The Vietnam War produced still more criticisms of the U.S. government's intelligence apparatus. Faced with the overwhelming demands for operational intelligence in Vietnam, and at the same time with demands to limit expenditures, the CIA was apparently unable to keep pace with developments occurring elsewhere in the world. For example, the CIA was unable to devote the resources required to anticipate rapidly breaking political situations in Eastern Europe and Indonesia during these years.

The trend throughout this period was one of ever-increasing centralization of intelligence functions in order to avoid the difficulties associated with the rather haphazard and unsystematic intelligence system of earlier years. However, the advantages wrought by centralization were offset and, in the view of some critics, completely overshadowed by the problems. Most of the centralization was a product of the National Security Act of 1947, which was intended to enable policy-makers to obtain a more concise picture of an intelligence situation. The new American intelligence community had developed very differently from that of Great Britain, which has at least five separate intelligence organizations. France has four individual organizations while West Germany functions with three. Only the Americans have placed such a wide array of responsibilities in the hands of one individual. The U.S. Director of Central Intelligence is responsible for paramilitary operations, technological collection, military order of battle estimates, as well as political and economic analysis. It has been argued that this great concentration of responsibility in one individual makes the CIA's decisions more likely to be influenced by the prevailing climate; and that it was this weakness that resulted in the gross underestimation of the Soviet Union's military effort in the mid-1970s when policy-makers were wedded to the perception of the USSR as a nation making approximately the same defense efforts as the United States.[18]

3

Intelligence Today

Haʌɪɴɢ surveyed the general historical development and problems of intelligence systems up to this point—concentrating primarily on the American experience—we must consider how the system functions today. Two concerns give us a comprehensive view of current operations: first, the contemporary nomenclature of classified information, and second, the handling of technical intelligence and what it reveals about an increasingly important matter—technology transfers.

Contemporary Nomenclature of Classified Information

All intelligence organizations—public as well as private—are involved in the handling of sensitive information. In order to distinguish between various levels of sensitivity, intelligence specialists have retained a variety of terms which are descriptive of the nature and value of information contained in classified documents. A classification system is necessary for two fundamental reasons. The first is that information varies in degree of value to adversaries—whether these are business competitors or hostile foreign governments. Since the utility of information varies, it is to be expected that the efforts made by an adversary to obtain it will also vary. A higher classification should guarantee greater safeguards for protection of the information. The second has to do with the use of information: a system which does not accommodate the needs of potential users is destructive of the larger objectives of the organization. The information possessed by an organization is of no value if organization members are denied access to it. However, the wider the dissemination of information, the greater the danger that the information will fall into the hands of adversaries. An effective system balances the need for security with availability requirements by insisting that users have both the proper security classification and a "need to know" with regard to protected information.

Governmental Nomenclature

The United States government relies upon three levels of classification of defense information: top secret, secret, and confidential. The standards used for application of these classifications are clearly stated and are fairly straightforward. Top secret is the term applied to information which, if disclosed without authorization, would cause exceptionally grave damage to national security. Top secret information generally relates to national defense plans or cryptological and communications intelligence systems. Scientific or technological developments in the area of national security are also generally included within this classification. If the unauthorized disclosure of information could be expected to cause only "serious damage" to national security—rather than "exceptionally grave danger"—then a secret classification will be given. Finally, where only "identifiable damage to national security" would occur in the event of unauthorized disclosure of information, a confidential classification is employed. Data indicating the strength of military forces are classified as confidential.

In addition to these three standard security typologies, two special categories must be noted. First, one designated as "for official use only" is reserved for nondefense, unclassified information which requires protection in the "public interest." Material of this nature is exempt from disclosure under the Freedom of Information Act. Second, it is widely maintained that there are more sensitive designations above top secret, designations which depend on the nature of the information and the use being made of it. It may reasonably be assumed that at this level information about the classifications themselves becomes classified, since security training manuals insist that there are only three categories of classified information, and to reveal the nomenclature of this special classification would reveal something of the nature of the information being restricted. According to hearsay, such "classified" classifications frequently shift as the nature of the information and the needs for which that information is reserved also change. New situations generate new classifications which may or may not become permanent designations. Questions of access are also used as a method of classification. Certain information is generated for only a very few individuals, frequently no more than five or six officials in key positions. Hence, to enjoy a very high security rating does not entitle one to read all information classified at or below that level inasmuch as data may be reserved for the eyes of a select few.

Identification and Storage of Classified Information

Special classifications are used to insure special handling of sensitive material. The first step in this process is labeling and identification. Physical markings and notations are commonly used to warn holders of the nature of the documents in their possession and indicate the degree of protection required for them. Documents are given overall classifications while major components of certain documents—items which might be used separately—are often given separate classifications. Files, folders, or groups of documents are marked according to the highest classification of any one document included in the collection. Drafts or studies used in production of a finished document which will be classified are also classified according to the highest classification of any item of information contained in any of the material.

Elaborate procedures such as these tend to produce a proliferation of highly classified materials. In an effort to control this tendency, U.S. governmental security procedures require that a review date be set for reconsideration of security classification. No U.S. document may retain a classification without a review for more than twenty years. Nevertheless, numerous critics within and without the governmental system complain of overclassification which, they feel, does much to limit legitimate access to materials useful in continuing specialized research as well as in informing the public about the activities of their government.

Special security containers and storage areas have been developed by the U.S. government in an effort to insure the protection of sensitive materials. Generally, these storage facilities are guarded or kept under either direct or indirect surveillance, with by far the greatest protection assured for top secret documents. Much less protection is provided for mere confidential documents. Document registers, receipting requirements, periodic inventories, and destruction certificates are utilized as protective measures for awide variety of classified materials. In the event that classified information is compromised, governmental regulations require that the security violation be reported as soon as it is discovered and an outline prepared of steps to be taken in order to minimize or neutralize the loss. There are also specific and very often severe punishments meted out to individuals who are responsible for the occurrence of security violations. Fines, loss of employment, and even imprisonment can be the result of one's failure to maintain proper security.

There is one final method for the protection of governmental secrets that should be mentioned. Quite often, in order to prevent the compromise of classified information, the data are simply destroyed. Where the material is no longer of immediate use to the United States government but might nevertheless cause detriment to the nation if it were in the possession of a foreign agent, destruction is regarded as the most appropriate measure for safeguarding its contents. Security regulations specify that classified material be destroyed by burning, melting, chemical decomposition, pulping, pulverizing, shredding, or mutilation sufficient to preclude its further use. The wide range of methods of destruction reflects the diversified nature of the material that may be subject to the protection of classification. Because of advances in technology, far more than mere documents have sensitive content and use.

The government takes so seriously a decision to destroy top secret or secret materials that extensive records are required as documentation of the completion of that act. Witnesses are required and records must be maintained for periods of up to two years. Those witnessing the destruction of such material are personally required to sift through ashes or other resultant wastes so they may attest to the thoroughness of the destructive process.

Even certain waste materials—notes, carbon paper, typewriter ribbons—are classified and must be given complete security protection until such time as they are destroyed.

Technical Intelligence

The development of intelligence, as noted above, has progressed with advances in technology. The instruments as well as the concerns of intelligence have changed dramatically with scientific progress in a wide variety of areas. Technology—whether publicly or privately generated—is a necessary preoccupation of intelligence organizations. The public, of course, has a legitimate interest in what is done with private technology. In recent years, our attention has been increasingly drawn to questions about the use of private technology. For the nation-state, the phrase "technology transfer" has come to imply the possible "loss" of its technology to other states, frequently those with hostile intentions. The U.S. government has frequently dealt with the issue of technology transfers by imposing limits on what may be sold to foreign states in general or to specific nations, especially the Soviet Union and other Communist states. A wide assortment of critics of the corporation have commented upon the apparent willingness of high technology producers to sell their most advanced and sensitive instruments to hostile states. In the early 1970s, a number of American firms specializing in advanced police surveillance and detection devices indicated their willingness to set up displays at a Soviet trade exhibition and to offer their products for use to Soviet agencies responsible for suppression of dissent in the USSR. Vladimir Bukovsky, a dissident ally of Alexander Solzhenitsyn, who was expelled from the USSR shortly after Solzhenitsyn, observed ironically that, as he was being flown from his homeland, he examined the handcuffs on his wrists and noticed the inscription "Made in USA" stenciled on the side of the lock.

In the view of the French historian Alain Besançon, Western businessmen are actually threatening the survival of the West by enabling the USSR to meet its needs for technology, finance, and food.[1] The entire debate has had enormous philosophical implications for private interests in that it has drawn attention to the extent to which private science is viewed as public property. Nevertheless, few will deny the public's very real stake in the uses made of private innovations of possible military and scientific interest.

In an effort to understand the significance of technical intelligence and to control the uses made of it, the United States government has developed a broad category of military intelligence to deal specifically with technical intelligence. In the military's view, technical developments—even those which are foreign— have a practical application for military purposes. For the military, technical intelligence includes a study of the principles of design and operation, nomenclature, physical characteristics, performance, operational capabilities, and limitations of foreign material. Thus, the military's concern is a rather restricted one. The U.S. government generally recognizes a much broader value in technical intelligence produced by foreign states. The technical intelligence units of the military have a mandate to further national security through the collection and processing of scientific and technical information and data, and the dissemination of the resultant technical intelligence to be used by the government.

For the nation-state, history offers numerous examples of the value of a careful study of foreign technical intelligence. One of the most dramatic examples occurred when England's Edward III launched his invasion of Normandy against the numerically superior French forces under the leadership of King Philip. While they were badly outnumbered, the English troops were armed with the longbow, whose power, range, accuracy, and penetration were far beyond all other weapons of the period. French knights advanced on horseback only to fall when their horses, wounded and terrified by the English marksmen, threw their riders in panic, trampling them as they ran away. In this battle, the English lost only fifty men while the French army was destroyed as an effective military force. If the French had paid careful attention to English technology and studied the longbow at all, they would have realized that their cavalry could not be effective in combat against this weapon.

A more recent example of the breakdown in technical intelligence was in 1950 when the Chinese Communists were preparing for an invasion of Chiang Kai-shek's stronghold of Taiwan. Since the last step of the invasion would require his troops to swim for a short distance, Mao Tse-tung ordered an intensive program of swimming instruction in the fresh water canals of northern Fukien and southern Chekiang provinces. Most of the highly skilled troops selected for the invasion were non-swimmers, so the program was an urgent requirement. Unfortunately for the Chinese Communist leadership, which was unfamiliar with the regions in which the training was being conducted, these fresh water canals were infested by the Asiatic blood fluke, the carrier of schistosomiasis. The blood fluke is a parasite which burrows through the skin of the host, invades the bloodstream, and infects the liver and intestines. The infected person suffers headaches, internal pains, fever, and diarrhea—the combination of these ailments making him totally unfit for combat. As a result of the swimming program, almost fifty thousand of the very best troops of the Red Chinese army were incapacitated and, given the poor medical support the army had, little could be done to help them. The invasion date had to be set back six months, and by that time the United States had committed itself to the support of the Nationalists and was patrolling the Formosa Straits. If the Chinese had had the benefit of an adequate technical intelligence organization to study medical hazards of the region, the outcome undoubtedly would have been different.

The United States Army early recognized the importance of technical intelligence, but it was not until World War II that the organizational structures serving technical intelligence assumed what is roughly their present form. With the assistance of the more advanced British specialists, the U.S. Army established a comprehensive training program for personnel to serve in technical intelligence units. A Foreign Materiel Branch was established at the Aberdeen Proving Ground to study all of the items forwarded from front-line combat units or other acquisition agencies. During the war, large amounts of foreign equipment were shipped back to the United States for tests and evaluation. The examination process helped military commanders understand the capabilities of enemy forces and also provided many opportunities for incorporating foreign technology into American weaponry.

Today, technical information and intelligence are collected by teams stationed throughout the world in military and civilian service. Collected information is sent back through intelligence channels until it finally is processed by the Directorate of Scientific and Technical Intelligence of the Defense Intelligence

Agency. This office was established in 1963 to develop and maintain the Department of Defense technical intelligence production program. As an element of the larger U.S. government intelligence community, the Directorate is able to guarantee that information of great potential value is made available for use by all agencies involved in the evaluation of foreign technical intelligence. While decentralization can be disadvantageous, as discussed previously, the just-mentioned Directorate helped to avoid the problem seen in the very first days of the classification and restriction of sensitive information, namely, that data would be hidden from legitimate users and jeopardize the prospects for scientific research and advancement.

Major Intelligence Failures

Vast flows of money and talent have not, however, saved government intelligence activity from major embarrassments. Indeed, the history of intelligence activity has been punctuated by a series of miscalculations that have been costly in terms of both economics and prestige. Such misreading of information has been mentioned earlier with reference to the British and the Falkland Islands, the turmoil in Iran that led to the long captivity of Americans in Teheran, the Bay of Pigs fiasco and the inaccurate estimates of the situation in Vietnam.

The sources of these glaring failures are not hard to find. As intelligence has evolved from a military-related concept to a much more inclusive activity, it has become ensnared in the problems of politics that dominate our governmental system. A former CIA analyst on Iran sees the agency as a typical bureaucracy, in which the primary interest is in not being wrong rather than in being right. An individual takes no chances that might jeopardize his career. Our informant was given an adverse fitness report after a superior told him that his reports critical of the Shah were inconsistent with the prevailing beliefs of those who formulated American policy on Iran. Confirming reports that the CIA did not even attempt to make direct contact with student activists and dissenters in Iran, he concluded that policy determined reporting rather than the other way around. Private sources at one of the nation's largest private international banks indicate that, on the other hand, Israeli intelligence foresaw problems more than a year before the crisis and began shifting oil purchases away from Iran and toward Nigeria and Mexico. It is in response to this tendency to let politics set the guidelines that Robert F. Ellsworth, in his study cited above, recommends that the National Security Act of 1947 be loosened in such a way as to promote independent, competitive centers for collection of intelligence and analysis of that data. He also advocates a legal separation of the duties of the CIA director and a sharing of his responsibilities.[2]

Private Intelligence

Just as advances in technology have increased governmental intelligence capabilities and responsibilities, they have created numerous opportunities for development of private intelligence operations. In this concluding section, it might be useful to examine the nature of the many private intelligence organizations and to consider possible implications of the private use of sensitive information. One of the most rudimentary private intelligence operations began around the time of the Civil War: the Pinkerton Detective Agency, a large organization which worked for the government as well as for private clients. Throughout the next century there were many imitators but little qualitative change in the work they did. In the twentieth century, with the growth of credit purchasing, still more agencies were created to serve private needs by conducting credit investigations. Yet most of these operations were relatively modest and unpretentious endeavors not generally regarded as threatening the public.

The advent of the computer, however, marked a radical departure from the operating styles of credit verifiers and Pinkerton detectives. This new technology, with its almost unlimited data storage capacity, gave private companies much the same intelligence capabilities as the government. As more restrictions were placed on governmental agencies by politicians responding to public skepticism, private agencies began to enjoy some decided advantages over governmental ones. Unlimited data banks, generous and successful corporate funding arrangements, skilled marketing of informational resources, and superior pay for gifted personnel are but a few of the weapons that have supported the rise of private intelligence organizations in recent years. Giant information companies of the 1970s and 1980s have been able to process far more data than ever imagined possible earlier. With the use of new technologies such as aerial photography, infrared photography, and special radar, these companies can literally scan the earth's entire resources in a matter of hours. Because of modern instantaneous retrieval systems, they can process, index and search the equivalent of hundreds of newly published books every day, with thousands being possible in the near future.

The potential for abuse in such a system is considerable. First, in a market where information is a valuable commodity, quite often the easiest way to get it is to steal it. Telephone lines are commonly used for transmission of computer-based information so it is possible to tap into a computer through the telephone. The absence of effective security systems makes this process relatively simple in many large institutions. Second, since much of the information being generated today relates to the activities of individuals, those individuals often find themselves at the mercy of operations which, in effect, blackmail them. Information is a convenient weapon to be used against people and, with so much information being kept seemingly for all time, human memory is no longer a limiting factor. Finally, as more and more data in private hands are being put to private use, the question of loyalty emerges with increasing frequency. To whom is the possessor of these enormous storehouses of knowledge loyal? Will this weapon be utilized in service to the public or against it? If the perception develops that it is being used against the public, there is a danger that more and more challenges will be mounted against the very nature of private interests. Such a confrontation would threaten the distinctions that exist today between the public and private sectors and, in so doing, undermine the pluralistic nature of Western society.

Nevertheless, maintenance of those distinctions does not mean that there may not be cooperation between the public and private organizations. Such cooperation is widely regarded as a hallmark of pluralistic society: many private organizations assist the government in conducting its legitimate business. Even organizations involved in intelligence-related activities can work together to accomplish common objectives.

One of the most interesting examples of this was during the Italian campaign of World War II when the American services sought to enlist the aid of the Mafia in defeating the forces of Fascist Italy. The Mafia was viewed as a private intelligence source. The approaches taken by the two allies in dealing with the Mafia illustrate the different consequences that may result from efforts to enlist the aid of private organizations which sometimes engage in illegal activities.

The Mafia secret society, of course, was regarded as a rival of the Italian Fascist party, so Mussolini had set out to destroy this dreaded criminal organization. Thousands of suspected members were arrested and imprisoned and Mussolini announced in 1927 that the war against the Mafia had been successfully concluded. In fact, the Fascist victory was at best only temporary; the more important and astute members of the Mafia had simply bought political protection by joining the Fascist party while continuing their Mafia affiliations. American policy, recognizing this fact, was predicated upon an effort to organize the Mafia as a covert anti-Fascist force. The Sicilian-born "Lucky" Luciano, serving a thirty-five-year prison sentence in the United States, was freed in order to help direct this campaign, and approximately fifteen percent of the American troops selected for the Italian campaign were of Sicilian origin, which emphasized the strength of the U.S. commitment to Sicilian and Mafia interests. Many Italian crowds cheered the announcements of Mafia appointments to head local post-war governments with the chant "Long live the Allies! Long live the Mafia!" The identification of the two was almost complete and most Sicilian towns soon had Mafia mayors.

The British policy was more restrained. The British actually preferred to utilize independent anti-Fascist bandits in preparing for their invasion rather than to enlist the Mafia. After British forces landed in Sicily, Scotland Yard was requested to send in investigators who would round up and arrest the most notorious Mafia leaders on the island. However, while the American policies may have fostered the revival of the Mafia in Sicily, they were more successful than the British policies which moved with what some observers and participants saw as painful slowness. Some native leaders were actually driven into the Mafia for support because the British leadership was so hesitant to advance the necessary aid.[3]

In spite of this less than satisfactory conclusion, Allied experiences with the Mafia during World War II serve as an extremely valuable lesson in how a public service should—and should not—work with a private organization. Accomplishment of the primary objective—the defeat of the Fascists—was the most obvious result. It was the secondary result—a revival of the Mafia and an identification of that illegal organization with the victorious powers in Italy—that highlights some of the dangers of a union of the illegal and legal agencies in achieving a legitimate goal. One must never lose sight of the question of who is using whom.

The Business Application

It is the authors' position that the military and governmental lessons about intelligence have a direct application to the business community—as well as to other institutions of the private sector. The great intelligence battles of the future will not be waged only by nation-states. They will be fought among the great multinational business corporations, the great law firms and international banks and investment houses—even the major international public relations and advertising firms.

From earliest times, governments and individuals in possession of secret information have employed the principle of a "need to know"—or a similar concept—with respect to releasing highly classified information.[4]

Today, both the nation-state and the business corporation have their secrets. They share a similar, but not identical, nomenclature for classified information. It is most likely that in the future such presently conventional classifications as Secret, Top Secret, Top Secret Ultra, and the like, will give way to classifications such as Computer Access Levels, reflecting the language of the computer. Indeed, this trend has already begun.

But specific information about a corporation's intelligence practices is even harder to obtain than information about the federal government's. To give but one example, a group of five major investment banking houses in the United States were selected to explore the simple question: What is your system, and what nomenclature do you use, for classifying sensitive information?

One firm responded, after hours of discussions, that they could not tell because that information itself was confidential.

A second firm responded that they really didn't have a system, but used "confidential" for private information concerning clients, and that such information was strictly limited to a very few persons within the top management of the firms.

A third firm responded, again after a long interview, by declining to say whether or not they had a "system," and whether or not their sensitive information was computerized, but assured one of the authors* there were absolutely no "leaks," especially with their international clients. They added that they wished to tape-record any future conversations on the subject.

A fourth firm responded that the most secret information, regarding mergers, for example, was simply never written down until the firm was ready to go public with the information. The reason was obvious: a possible run-in with the SEC on the charge of using insider information before the anticipated merger was consummated.

The fifth firm responded that they had no system; they did classify some information "confidential," but the words "secret" or "top secret" were not used. On the other hand they did have, as did all other major investment banking houses, a risk arbitrage department, that collected information from *all possible* sources.

Of the five firms, no one wished to be quoted directly, and all requested their firms not be identified.

Major commercial banks were more forthcoming, as were major multinational corporations. The very large multinational corporations, with years of successful operational experience, were the most cooperative. In this category, the overall reaction was most favorable for a study of corporate intelligence. Indeed, a high official and director of a major multinational oil company advocated, and said he had been advocating for years, that his company develop an organizational structure for what would be in effect their own state department, their own intelligence department and their own cryptanalysis unit. Actually, practically all large multinational corporations have these functions in one form or another but they are not formally and systematically organized and, therefore, not nearly as effective as they could be (as discussed in the following chapters).

A significant difference between a nation-state, such as the United States, and a corporation concerns the habit of reducing everything to writing. In Washington, the memorandum reigns supreme. This is not always true in the private sector; for exam-

* Richard Eells.

61

ple, in the investment banking community, as just noted, the most sensitive of all information is *not* recorded.

The problem of how multinational corporations and international banks in the future will handle the matter of the classification of their sensitive information is an enormously interesting subject. Because of the great data banks and powerful computers, business has already begun to devise new methods of acquiring and protecting sensitive information through computer access. But as Joseph Weizenbaum, a professor of computer science at the Massachusetts Institute of Technology, has stated, "There is no such thing as absolute safety. You cannot guarantee the security of a computer system if it is not physically or electronically isolated."[5] Thus, one of the serious problems of the present, as well as the future, is the illegal penetration of computer codes.

4

Corporations and the Intelligence Function

The Polycorporate Firm

THE growth and interdependence of world commerce and industry call for new institutions. One response to this demand is to envisage the multinational corporation as a polycorporate firm with multiple nerve centers that functions across national boundaries. The polycorporate company may take the form of a group of autonomous corporate firms acting in unison from numerous home bases—"home" being the locus of the originating or creating or domiciliary sovereignty. Eventually, we may come to describe these new business institutions in ecological terms, and analyze their problems in the language of natural zones or ecosystems of the global ecosphere, applying the mathematics of "niche theory" to understand their market shares and product mixes. Oceanography, in particular, is creating opportunities for the extractive and other industries that make new demands on our powers of conceptualization, necessitating a marriage between economic and ecological theory. In the areas of agribusiness, aquaculture and space-dimensioned corporate efforts, the polycorporate firm may need to give way to new units of political authority. Corporations organized for the development of the seabed under an ocean regime may be neither national nor inter-

63

national. Indeed, the ocean regime of the future may bring into being a new kind of political body not presently known to the traditional international system.

In recent times, the corporation has evolved into something more than a device for doing business. The modern corporation represents a new system of cooperative social organization that brings together the skills, the labor and the investment of large numbers of people. Nor can its social role be measured in terms of its size and wealth alone. The old combative individualism, idealized in classical economic theory, recedes before the advance of this more irenic cooperative enterprise.

The vulturine caricature of the corporation has been encouraged by the general unwillingness of those in corporate leadership to adopt a broader concept of the place of the corporation in society and to equip themselves with the instruments that would allow them to function effectively in a broader political environment. The costs of this reluctance have steadily mounted as society itself has begun to view the modern corporation as more than an economic instrument, but also as a sociological and political institution.

The decline of public confidence in the leadership of business, according to Paul McCracken, must be attributed, in part, to the popular adoption of a more demanding view of contemporary business activities.[1] The public is more critical because its expectations are now much higher.

The polycorporate institution is in reality one of the twentieth century's leading innovative forces. It has been an effective agent of social and political change as well as of social justice. Its impact on contemporary society has been revolutionary.

That the corporation has not received political "credit" for its contributions must be attributed largely to the inability of its managers to express themselves in a way that could obtain a fair hearing in a frequently hostile political setting.

Although the private corporation was established primarily to fulfill economic purposes, the motivations of its foundation were also social—to increase the "wealth of nations" and to generate sustained economic development for the nation-state. The corporation, Michael Novak writes:

> . . . depends upon and generates new political forms. . . . It has brought about an immense social revolution. It has moved the

center of economic activity from the land to industry and commerce. . . . The idea of economic development has now captured
the imagination of the human race. This new possibility of development has awakened the world from its economic slumbers.[2]

In a more immediate sense, the impact of the corporation upon
society has released enormous free time as a consequence of the
introduction of labor-saving technologies and industrial practices. These innovations have reduced the workweek and the
workday and engendered a higher level of consumption through
increased commercial productivity. The incredible personal mobility provided by mass-produced automobiles was, in and of
itself, one of the twentieth century's social revolutions.

These and other technological innovations have drastically altered our culture as well as our politics. These consequences of
corporate inventiveness have profoundly affected the rising social and economic demands which confront nation-states, particularly those that compose the Third World. In some instances,
the innovations of the corporation have actually enhanced the
ability of the nation-state to survive. In others, they have generated social unrest and have created a challenge to the nation-
state as a viable device for fulfilling the revolution of rising
expectations.

Much of the bitter criticism directed against the multinational
corporation has come about because of its manifold successes
and its growing political as well as economic power. The multinational corporation is denounced not because it has failed to attain
its stated objectives, but rather because it has succeeded in realizing them. The latter-day multinational corporation is perceived
as a threat to the continued power of the nation-state. To the
consternation of its critics, the multinational corporation is in
many respects a more viable instrument than the nation-state
for attaining stated social and economic objectives. The special
ability of the multinational corporation to rise above an ethno-
centric orientation has enabled it to avoid many of the pitfalls
that have had disastrous impact on nation-states—pitfalls that
have made it impossible for nation-states to respond to the social
problems of their populations.

Polycorporate institutions have multiple personalities. They
are, on the one hand, an integral part of the world's industrial
operations; and, on the other, they constitute essential ingredients

of the economic development of the nations in which they are individually incorporated.

The emergence of polycorporate organizations requires a new philosophy of business. The role of the polycorporate firm within a single nation—and its place in the structure and dynamics of that nation—is an issue that exists not only in the United States but also in every technologically developed and developing nation. The great polycorporations of America—IBM, Xerox, Exxon, ITT, for example—are objects of deep suspicion among the Third World nations, as is the entire private enterprise system. Yet polycorporate institutions are capable of helpful collaboration with states and public international organizations. They undertake cooperative tasks as great as the industrialization of Africa, Asia and Latin America. They provide cultural interchange on a worldwide scale through their presence in thousands of localities. Polycorporate companies play a major role in lifting world living standards to higher levels. Through their intelligence services, the polycorporate corporations scan the universe for investment opportunities to maximize the results obtained from their research facilities, technical and managerial skills, technologies, capital and business experience. As catalysts and achievers, polycorporate organizations are indispensable for the world's economic development.

For the present, however, polycorporate managements must plan most of their tasks for a world that is still dominated by sovereign states wielding coercive powers and punitive sanctions—a world that may be profoundly antagonistic to the polycorporate organization and the private enterprise philosophy it embodies.

Alternative approaches, if only to facilitate short-range corporate planning (to say nothing of twenty- or thirty-year perspectives) are essential. Some observers suggest that only five nation-state powers will be of consequence in the future: the United States, the Soviet Union, the European Economic Community members, China and Japan. Others say that the age of superstates is nearing its end and that we are entering an era of polynational pluralism in which different kinds of organizations can be expected to proliferate in the world arena, some nationalist, some local, others functional. The much-discussed and controversial Trilateral Commission is a harbinger of a new polynationalism.

Meanwhile, the course of the polycorporate firm has to be

charted amid the polarities of the world arena and the economic overlordship of sovereignties, both large and small, in which it conducts its business and has its investments. Beyond the constricting political boundaries of the nation-states lies that vast realm of the open frontiers—the oceans and outer space—where the problems of establishing a realm of public order are yet to be faced.

The task demands certain capabilities of the polycorporate firm: skill in the decision-making process; knowledge of the strategies of nation-states and other institutional participants in the world arena; and management's ability to define business goals. In the absence of a polycorporate intelligence function these capabilities cannot be achieved.

The polycorporate firm at best is not the servant of a single market or nation-state. Its constituencies include all the interests that must be balanced to achieve profitable operations. The essential characteristics of organization needed to attain business goals in a tension-filled world are only gradually being understood by the management of polycorporate firms. One specific characteristic is especially significant: the use of intelligence—not only for survival but for attaining growth and for meeting social responsibilities.

Several long-term considerations have a bearing on any decision to establish an intelligence function. The factors are not immediately economic in nature and, therefore, cannot be as directly weighed in the balance as conventional accounting items. Yet, as they affect the general climate of activity—and, by extension, the political climate inside various national sites—they are relevant and need to be evaluated.

Decision Strategies

Decision-making, whether by nations, groups, individuals, or corporations, can be regarded in part as a continuous operation involving the perception of streams of input, the processing of alternative options, and the formulation of a course of action based on these data. In very complex organizations, however, a transformation occurs because of the inertial institutional force of prior decisions and traditions. Decision-making becomes a more ponderous and elaborate operation.

The world arena (in reality, it is not a regime of law) is a place where all participants must at times fall back on four types of strategies: coercion, diplomacy, barter and persuasion. Each of these strategies depends on accurate and integrated intelligence.

Direct *coercion* can seldom be used by a corporation except by its own security forces—and then, as a general practice, only for the protection of its own property and personnel. With poly-corporate firms operating in host, or capital-receiving, countries, it is hazardous to attempt to enforce corporate policy with military or other support from the country of origin. No regime will soon forgive or forget an attempt by a foreign corporation to unseat it.

A full spectrum of possibilities has to be considered. At one end, an organization or corporation of any nation can operate entirely on its own with no support whatsoever from either home or host government. At the other end of the spectrum lies the unlimited intervention by sovereign governments which identify their own national interests with those of the firm—approaching, for example, the relationship between Amtorg (the New York City Soviet purchasing organization) and the Soviet Union. Perhaps the closest non-communist parallels are found in the relationships between Japanese firms and their government. The ITT/CIA episode in Allende's Chile is not a typical example. Neither extreme is realistic. In practice, all American corporations overseas can count on some support from their government, depending upon the degree of national interest involved.

The strategy of corporate *diplomacy* is an essential tool of both corporate and national policy, not only to attain economic advantage but, more importantly, to achieve status in the world arena. Status as a matter of law, or prestige or rank, or preferred position in a given situation, is an outcome that depends as much on negotiating skill as it does on economic assets. For example, a corporation which, in theory, is not among the major "actors" on the world scene, may, nevertheless, be represented in national capitals and other power centers. Corporate representatives may be received with more consideration (if less pomp and circumstance) than ambassadors, and the weight of their words may be far more persuasive if for no other reason than the fact that their corporations have command over valuable resources.

In the past, *economic power* was often regarded as the sole ingredient required of the multinational corporation in order for it to play a role in the world arena. But the economic instruments of corporate policy are only a part of the story. Economics, in national strategy, involves an effective allocation and use of scarce resources, just as it does in corporate strategy. But the assets of nation and corporation include all resources that can be sold in, or withheld from, the market. Insofar as these resources include land (the title to which is controlled by sovereign states), minerals, money and other negotiable instruments—the value of which is subject to legal regulation—an economic strategy must be in harmony with national policy. As the polycorporate firm operates in a world arena that lacks a unified system of world law, it is dependent on and responsive to the laws of many different—and sometimes hostile—regimes. As a result, an economic strategy in the world arena must be different from one that is applicable exclusively within the home nation. For the polycorporate firm, as for the modern corporation generally, an economic strategy must always be in alignment with the public interest. For any extended period of time, the economic goals of the corporation cannot be at odds with the goals of national communities (whether at home or abroad) and still offer any hope of safety for the polycorporation.

The use of *persuasion* has a special character for the polycorporate firm. Communication and information systems are of paramount importance in this intelligence approach to corporate strategy. However, the present concern is mainly with input. In national governments this is called intelligence, and at the corporate level we speak of a "comparable intelligence."

Narrowly considered, intelligence is that knowledge which our higher governmental and military leaders must possess in order to safeguard the welfare of the nation. Viewed more broadly, intelligence is the knowledge that any person or group must have to safeguard his or its own welfare.

The conventional wisdom of economists and political scientists is inadequate for conceptualizing the systemic nature of today's polycorporate firm and its need for an effective intelligence organ. This new kind of transnational organization struggles for place and meaning in a world arena that constitutes neither an "international economy" nor an "international regime." It must, therefore, be newly outfitted for survival. One of the most challenging tasks of contemporary business management is to intro-

duce a modern intelligence function into emergent polycorporate
firms and foster the attitudes and organizational forms capable
of meeting the onrush of world change.

Political Stability

Today's business abhors anarchy. Our largest corporations cannot operate in a chaotic environment. The need for secure supplies of basic resources and dependable markets shapes corporate
planning and strategy. The global web of economic relationships
is so tightly interwoven that any substantial and unanticipated
disruptions—wars, natural disasters, or even unanticipated
changes in climate—can throw highly evolved intercorporate
economics into disarray and reduce the economies of developing
nations to even greater chaos.

Global political stability is a dominant corporate interest. To
be sure, the polycorporate enterprise by its very presence in the
host country contributes to political, economic and social stability. With rare exceptions, the overseas managements of polycorporate firms eschew involvement in local politics. Their
neutrality provides an anchor of stability in the turbulent political waters of local regimes. As instruments for the transfer of
technology and the application of the West's management practices, the polycorporate firms help to sustain normality. Nonetheless, this stabilizing influence of the polycorporate firms should
not be exaggerated.

Whether or not the polycorporate enterprise can function effectively in the absence of political and economic stability may be
the ultimate test of the polycorporate firm's ability to survive.
The search for stability may be the pursuit of a will-o'-the wisp.
Capital- and technology-receiving countries in the underdevel-
oped world are racked by political, economic and social unrest.
A chronic incapacity on the part of the few democratically-
elected leaders, and the more numerous self-appointed despotic
and totalitarian figures, to achieve their oft-proclaimed social
goals of a better life for the population; economic stagnation as
a consequence of ruinous commodity prices; and tribal, ethnic
and religious fratricide—these diseases create instability
throughout much of the Third World. In the relatively more sophisticated Third World countries, there is present a recurrent

management nightmare that the regime currently in power will expropriate or nationalize foreign-owned assets with or without payment of compensation or will unilaterally change the rules of the game by cancelling a raw material development contract, or promulgating a decree prohibiting remittance of dividends or the transfer of profits.

Intelligence is the key that enables corporate management to determine whether it can adapt its operations to an unstable environment, or whether marketing and investment plans must be postponed or abandoned.

Summary

Changing world conditions necessitate new institutions. The polycorporate corporation is a response to the altered global environment. As one of this century's leading innovative social forces, polycorporate institutions have become an indispensable organizational instrument in a world of rapid social change. Through their intelligence services, they provide insights into investment and marketing opportunities, and have become catalysts and instruments for the transfer of technology as well as modern management practices—elements that contribute to host country stability.

Part II

Execution

5

Elements of Intelligence Strategy: Diplomacy and Survival

INTELLIGENCE," as the Hoover Commission Report of June 1955 observed, "deals with all the things which should be known in advance of initiating a course of action." This concept of intelligence, though devised in a governmental context, is a central aspect of any successful organization. As this notion is illustrated below, we shall see that the large corporation can indeed profit from a more direct recognition of the role of intelligence in its corporate decision-making.

Intelligence, as the term is used here, is the product of the collection, evaluation, analysis, integration, and interpretation of all available information that may affect the survival and success of the company. Well-interpreted information, provided by a properly designed intelligence function, can be immediately significant in the planning of corporate policy in all of its fields of operations. Stated in both operational and organizational terms, the main purpose of intelligence is to help the chief executive officer fulfil his wide-ranging responsibilities.

A business corporation—or any other large organization—depends on effective means of knowing what is going on both within and without its walls as a prerequisite of wise and effective policy. Workable methods of receiving messages from outside the organization, integration of these messages with already accumulated knowledge, and use of the combined intelligence as a factor in formulating the policy of the organization as a whole (as well as then sending out the necessary messages to appropriate receivers) are all the standard requirements of survival and growth.

Adequate "information input" and "intelligence output" are critical elements in the government and management of corporations, though they are not generally recognized as such. It is particularly important to emphasize this point because the large multinational corporations have become politically significant entities in the international arena. Their sheer size and organizational proficiency place them in a conspicuous public position, and their actions influence the options and attitudes of political or politically-oriented bodies: governments, media organizations, political parties. Today's multinational corporation operates in a realm where the collection and interpretation—as well as communication—of information vital to the corporation is of the first magnitude of difficulty and importance, not only for the corporation but for society at large. For these reasons, the managements of multinational corporations must formalize and strengthen their intelligence functions.

Given the multinational corporation's involvement in world politics, it must, in addition to developing its intelligence activities, establish a staff of people who are competent to represent it, both in lobbying and in the way that a diplomat represents his nation to other nations. Large corporations should (and many do) maintain a Washington office, and such an office should strive to increase its capacity for both lobbying and diplomatic representation. The Washington office is not only a vital part of a strong and capable intelligence activity of the company, but the advance outpost for the initial intelligence collection.

The argument here is that a strong intelligence function will enhance the ability of a company to survive and grow and prosper economically. Viewed in a larger context, effective intelligence is a response to the challenge of formulating astute and effective corporate strategies in a world beset with complex opposing forces; it is itself of strategic consequence in the contest between statism and an open society.

Just as political payments of various kinds have been used since the dawn of commerce to secure various services essential to economic success, so has intelligence activity been part of commercial life throughout history. Trade brought about the earliest contact between the world's major civilizations, and successful merchants and traders sought to learn all they could of the financial resources, specialized knowledge and skills, and political and social contacts of potential trading partners.

The great financial empires of medieval Europe—the Italian city-states, the great Germanic merchant princedoms—were built on extensive knowledge of market factors as well as the political fortunes of rulers. Looking through the earliest files of old merchant banks, one finds information on trade operations throughout the world: reports on gold shipments; descriptions of railroads and waterworks; lists of shippers and duty schedules in foreign ports; ship capacities; memos on crop cultivation; proposed regulations; and accounts of ship movements and correspondence for every conceivable commodity.

In the nineteenth century, the Du Ponts established themselves in the forefront of the U.S. chemical industry (and the world market) through their own use of intelligence. The firm regularly sent its scientists to the top laboratories in Europe, where researchers would explain recent findings and important breakthroughs. Dupont thus had access to valuable data long before published accounts were available. These trips also played a recruiting function for the firm as it began to expand.

In our own century, the early history of Aramco under James Terry Duce provides an excellent example of a high executive officer being a master intelligence officer in his own right. Until Citicorp's careful intelligence work on the royal Saudi family, which detailed the relationship of each family member to the government, Duce's knowledge of Arabian oil market conditions was unrivaled anywhere in the world. As far back as 1972, Aramco spent five million dollars annually on "government and public relations," a program that included monitoring daily Saudi and other Arab press and radio broadcasts, closely following political, economic and cultural developments in the Arab world, and carrying out the exhaustive anthropological, cultural, economic and linguistic studies of the Arabian peninsula for which Aramco is well known.

In recent times, intelligence work has taken on new dimensions. Transnational activity has grown with the recognition that many regional and worldwide needs could not be met effectively through the conventional system of sovereign states. The numbers of economic and political factors to be taken into account have grown exponentially as advanced communications and transportation have transformed global policy coordination.

Some Corporate Applications of the Intelligence Concept

Many authorities claim that modern corporate intelligence organizations mirror the structure and design of governmental organizations in some essential ways. The outside observer is unlikely, however, to spot the intelligence function of large firms on an organizational chart, since the lingering public associations described earlier make it ill-advised to mention intelligence functions. If a large multinational corporation planned to create a specific intelligence operation, it might be suggested that the new activity be referred to as "policy information" rather than "intelligence."

Problems of nomenclature aside, the basic organizational principles for intelligence are essentially the same in both government and business. Sherman Kent, an authority on national intelligence organizations, writes as follows:

> Intelligence can be thought of—indeed it often is—as an organization engaged in the manufacture of a product (knowledge) out of raw materials (all manner of data) and labor (highly skilled, but not practical in the business sense of the word). The product, to be worthy of the label, must be up to standard.[1]

It is natural that the language of intelligence organizations should be weighted with words from business. Whether in government or corporate structures, intelligence organizations must package a product that meets consumer demand. Some consumers want this output in semi-finished form, as field notes, for example, with accompanying comments. Others want it finished, in bulk and in encyclopedic form. The most demanding want succinct statements, often in the form of executive summaries.

Three Kinds of Knowledge

These various kinds of customers (whether branches of government or offices within a corporation) utilize the three basic kinds of knowledge an intelligence organization generates: 1) basic descriptive knowledge; 2) current reportorial knowledge; and 3) speculative-evaluative knowledge.

The first category includes necessary background information, analyses, and in-depth and spot studies. Much of this material comes from published sources such as encyclopedias, scholarly monographs, the serial press, and other public media. Often it is collated, stored in files or computers, and made available for decision-making when required.

The second category—current reportorial knowledge—follows the basic descriptive work, which is apt to spoil with time. Priority topics are selected for continuous surveillance. In government intelligence these might include biographies of national leaders, political and social developments, scientific and technological developments, new geographical information, and religious and cultural data on many classes of people.

The third kind of knowledge—that with speculative-evaluative content—deals with the capabilities, intentions, and options of allies and potential adversaries. This aspect of intelligence work is most closely tied to strategic thinking in corporations and governments.

The three kinds of knowledge correspond to knowledge of the past, present and future of the people, places, plans and things in the corporation's business environment.

Basic Strategies

Strategic thinking is the highest level of corporate managerial responsibility, just as it is the highest form of governmental responsibility. It is inherent in the dynamic of the large corporation that it must plan its activities far ahead. Constantly projecting its activities five or more years into the future, corporate leadership makes decisions on products, processes and projects that may be as much as twenty or more years distant. All firms are subject to the economic penalties of failure, and the healthy survival of the corporation is the basic concern of its managers in framing plans and in reaching decisions based on them. In practice, healthy survival is considered synonymous with growth, and long-term growth requires skillful strategic planning.

As detailed in chapter 4, there are *four strategies* available to any actor operating in an environment subject to few rules or laws of conduct: coercion, negotiation, use of economic resources, and persuasion. In other words, actors in our present international context can either fight with each other (coercion), argue about whether they have some common interests (negotiation), limit the value exchanges they have with each other (use of economic resources), or try to talk it through (persuasion). States have the monopoly on armed forces; for non-state entities, therefore, noncoercive means are of prime importance.

The application of these basic concepts will vary in each instance of corporate intelligence activity. Cultural, political, and economic differences are major factors affecting the kind of information the company needs. And the countries and areas where large multinational corporations operate cover the face of the earth.

Strategic Mix

If cultural variations can affect a firm's strategic options, so can the organizational setting. Relations with governments—both here and abroad—will require the firm to mix its strategic options in certain ways. Work within political, financial, religious and industrial organizations will require other kinds of approaches.

Thus, the shape of the corporate intelligence function will be defined by the interaction of the corporate strategic imagination, and the characteristics (more or less knowable) of the objectives of corporate activity. Like the pattern in an oriental carpet, the structure of an intelligence function emerges as the role it plays in various corporate ventures is defined. And just as the fingers of a rugmaker grow adept with time, so the intelligence function develops its capacity to meet the firm's challenges and opportunities.

Sources of Corporate Intelligence

Banking

The relation between banking and intelligence is a two-way street: good banking relationships can extend the firm's intelligence "reach" significantly. At the same time, a good intelligence operation can aid in the development of new banking relationships. Mutual assistance of this sort between intelligence and other corporate activity is a basic operational rule.

Major international banks do a great deal of investigation and research on the social, political, and economic conditions in countries where they hold investments. Preparation of reports costs these banks money, and the finished products are tangible corporate assets. This knowledge, while not "classified" or secret, is not accessible to the public. Sometimes the reports include findings on poor investment decisions by the bank's corporate loan officers, a factor that makes bank officials doubly reluctant to make reports available.

Relationships at the highest level between a bank and a corporation can, however, create a climate of confidence in which bank intelligence can be made available to corporate executives.

From the other direction, top corporate management can receive information on bank activities from the company's intelligence sources that can be extremely important in considering overseas operations. Information on a bank's lending patterns to Third World governments is a good example. Private banks from the United States and Western Europe carry an increasing amount of government debt from Third World countries, which means that banks have some capacity to evaluate the accounting methods and general fiscal accountability of government agencies and state-owned industries. Thus, it is useful to know which banks are underwriting governments in various parts of the world and to what extent they are doing so.

Knowledge of banking relations of Third World governments can be an important element in planning large-scale ventures in a particular country. Firms investing in a developing country will often establish substantial indebtedness to banks that carry that country's public debts as well. This provides the firm with a shield against government expropriations, since the government is unlikely to tamper with a good customer of its own bank.

And, obviously, high-level relationships between United States banks and United States business corporations could affect ties with important foreign financial institutions. Such relationships, in turn, could have valuable intelligence possibilities.

Public Interest Groups

"Consumer advocates" such as the Ralph Nader organization and other groups which claim to speak in the "public interest" have had some impact on energy issues and consumer rights, particularly in regard to nuclear power and efforts to regulate oil companies. Any political assessment for the next decade or two must take account of the pressures these groups can generate.

There may, however, be a more comprehensive approach to this new political phenomenon that American business corporations can utilize. Nader's initial success was made possible, it should be recalled, by the automobile industry's injudicious squandering of good will it had established in the first part of the century. Planned obsolescence based on trivial stylistic modifications and a virtual moratorium on basic automotive technology innovation through the 1960s and early 1970s left that industry vulnerable to the kind of campaign that catapulted Nader into political fame.

Nader's continued success hinges on his ability to detect areas of public discontent and to promote them as causes in Washington. Viewed as a private business enterprise, Nader's "product" is reports and findings "manufactured" from the views of dissident bureaucrats, professionals, and technical people. His "profit picture" is positive only when he successfully taps an area of public concern or discontent.

Thus, the work of "public interest" groups can be seen as a market survey of public attitudes on social and political issues. A corporation that stays abreast of developments in that area through an intelligence scanning system can anticipate potential controversies in which it might become embroiled. This "lead time" can be extremely useful in planning corporate strategy.

There is a specific operational use of this information that may become important to a number of corporations. Social activists of various stripes are increasingly using stockholders' meetings as a forum for demanding corporate decisions on social issues. As activity of this sort increases, so does information on this phenomenon. Continuous scanning of the activities of "corporate dissenters" or "corporate reformers" can be provided by a corporate intelligence function.

Philanthropy

Corporate philanthropy is frequently associated with aid to college scholarship programs, hospital development programs and the like. In the international context, corporate philanthropy can serve as an important vehicle for the firm's informational operations. Research in developing countries has always suffered from a lack of funds, though native scholars are often well prepared to evaluate significant change in the national climate. By involving itself in support for research and conferences, the firm can advance national educational opportunities in foreign countries, improve the corporate image, and provide itself with information sources that may prove more reliable than those employed by its own government's intelligence services.

In addition to fulfilling an informational need, corporate philanthropy can (with the aid of solid intelligence work) provide a useful instrument in economic negotiations with foreign governments. Gifts in support of educational institutions or charitable organizations could be an important part of developing stable relationships with foreign governments. The donations, made through a company foundation, or its contributions program, could obviate the need to make political payments to foreign officials, which U.S. corporations may not do, under the terms of the Foreign Corrupt Practices Act. On the other hand, they would have a positive spillover effect in cultural, economic and even political areas from which the corporate donor can benefit.

An intelligence function within the firm should also regularly scan news of changes in foreign laws regarding political payments, current controversies involving such payments, and changes in U.S. law regarding payments abroad.

Summary of Specific Strategies

The purpose of this discussion of strategies is to demonstrate some of the varied circumstances in which the intelligence function can be of assistance.

In each setting, the chief executive officer can enhance his options on major corporate decisions by maximizing the information available to him. Flexibility of response and maximum lead time in decision-making are increasingly important elements in long-term corporate planning, given the uncertainty and the instability of global politics. It follows that the top corporate management of any large firm can only fulfill its functions properly if it is provided with maximum support in the form of reliable information.

The most successful firms of the future will be those capable of seeing their own activities in a global perspective. However, policy decisions in this broader context require more than economic information. The farther the executive staff looks beyond immediate operational matters, the more important it becomes to put economic information into a relationship with other major variables.

Economic activity happens in a social and political environment, no matter where in the world it takes place. That environment is in turn shaped by cultural and psychological forces with long traditions firmly rooted in custom and belief.

The goal of an intelligence function is to allow the senior management of a major corporation to merge the economic information it receives with political, social, and psychological information in ways that enhance its strategic planning capabilities.

If well designed, such an intelligence function also enhances a firm's capacity for conceptualizing and designing alternative strategies.

The Lobbying/Diplomacy Connection

Lobbying and corporate diplomacy are two key areas in the utilization of an intelligence function within a company. The information the firm receives, as well as the ability of its senior executives to use those contacts effectively in the firm's behalf, will depend in large part on how well principal corporate representatives have been oriented beforehand.

In the following section, the evolution of lobbying and corporate diplomacy is briefly reviewed. Lobbying is now a highly sophisticated art, in which many large and small organizations influence the legislative process and gain vital operational information from the use of a wide range of pressures and channels. The true value of an intelligence function only becomes evident when the advanced state of lobbying is fully understood.

The same holds true for corporate diplomacy. In many respects, corporate relations with foreign governments are an international equivalent of lobbying on Capitol Hill, and the full impact of the intelligence function only becomes clear when this diplomatic work is understood in its fullest dimensions.

The Lobbyist Label

The mass media have tried to categorize lobbying as an unsavory activity. Most people associated with lobbying, as a result, avoid the term studiously. Visions of shady characters are evoked in the public mind, a result of many exposes on television and in the press. One study of the Washington operations of major firms indicates that 76 percent of the heads of Washington offices were not registered as lobbyists in the early 1970s, an indication of the stigma attached to the label.[2] Executives typically responded to the survey question in this manner:

> No, I do not lobby. No, I'm not registered. My primary function is marketing and I only brief Congressmen when they ask for information.

More recently, Clark Clifford, former Secretary of Defense, a partner in an influential Washington law firm, and probably the dean of the capital's lobbyists, explained his refusal to register by saying his firm provides his clients with legal services "topped off by an intimate knowledge of how the government works."[3] Lobbying, in other words, is an inappropriate term, in Clifford's view, for the precise and informed relationship he can provide for a client.

The late Ralph Cordiner, as chairman and chief executive officer of General Electric, had another and more realistic view. He insisted on being registered on the grounds that it might keep him out of trouble, since he testified before Congress on matters relating to GE and the business community. Other chief executive officers have followed this stance. In our own view, lobbyists' registration as such will help overcome the media effort to derogate a vital and sophisticated form of representation of corporate interests, protected by the First Amendment, which the media fallaciously regard as something which "belongs" to them. Walter Laqueur, the distinguished editor of the *Washington Quarterly* and chairman of the Research Council, Center for Strategic and International Studies at Georgetown University, where he is also a university professor, has said:

> Our media have frequently reported in loving detail—and not without justice—government intelligence failures. Yet, their own more numerous intelligence failures are seldom, if ever mentioned: no post-mortems are arranged; no conclusions are drawn and no lessons learned.[4]

It is of interest that many companies try to upgrade their Washington offices in terms of symbolic nomenclature. For example, the chief lobbyist of Occidental Petroleum Co. has held the title "President of Occidental International."

The Founding Fathers' Perspective

Congress has from the beginning been subject to pressure from private interest groups, a state of affairs that the framers of the Constitution clearly anticipated in 1787. Their concepts of government and society included provision for a role for private interests, and their working model of a governmental system—as embodied in the Constitution—was partly a product of these ideas.

The drafters of our Constitution recognized the existence of what they called "divisive factions," and they were concerned about the potential influence of these factions in the conduct of government. They were so acutely aware of the importance of interest groups that James Madison stated that "the regulation of these various and diverse interests forms the principal task of modern legislation, and involves the spirit of party and faction in the necessary and ordinary operation of government."[5] Thus we see that the Founding Fathers conceived Congress's role as being principally to mediate between conflicting private interests in society, an idea which is still remarkably current.

Today, many observers call group representation the "Third House" of Congress to symbolize its true significance in the legislative process. Though the Constitution makes no direct reference to the right of association or the right of interest groups to gain access to Congress, there are certain constitutional clauses that the courts have interpreted as protective, to some extent, of both these rights.

The pertinent clauses are the "due process" clause of the Fifth Amendment ("nor shall any person . . . be deprived of life, liberty, or property, without due process of law"); the First Amendment ("Congress shall make no law . . . abridging the freedom of speech . . . and to petition the Government for a redress of grievances"); and the Tenth Amendment ("The powers not delegated to the United States by the Constitution, nor prohibited by it to the States, are reserved to the States respectively, or to the people").

Coordinated Lobbying Activity

Corporations can work most effectively in lobbying if they understand the many pressures on Congress and coordinate their lobbying activities to maximize their impact. This understanding comes from the sociopolitical information that intelligence work provides.

Let us consider one example of this. Mexico has petroleum reserves that could serve as an excellent source for American refinery corporations in the near future. A stable and mutually cooperative relationship between an American refinery corporation and Pemex, however, depends in large measure on United States-Mexican relations, where a legacy of mistrust and hostility must be overcome.

A historical centerpiece of this mistrust is illegal immigration to the United States by Mexican nationals. The Mexican government perceives this export of people as an important "safety valve" for its own problems of underdevelopment, and is unhappy about the prospects of Congressional action to tighten immigration control along the border.

The House Select Committee on Population, among other things, researches and writes reports on Mexican illegal immigration. These reports are important elements in shaping potential legislation on this issue.

An effective intelligence organization can spot situations such as this. A firm with such an organization might aid in shaping legislation domestically, and such a step could be helpful in building a closer working relationship with Pemex.

As every experienced Washington lobbyist knows, the time to affect the legislative process is before the bill is even written. As one representative of a major firm described it:

> The trick is to get the bill before it gets into the hopper. Once it gets in there the job is really tough. But if you can get it before, it's much easier and you can be much more effective.[6]

Corporate Diplomacy

The multinational corporation today has become one of the main institutions of Western society and a major factor in the

87

societies and economies of the rest of the globe. Indeed, short of the nation-state itself, the large business corporation is the most important and powerful force on the earth today.

Thus corporate diplomacy emerges. Today, large corporations often deal with nations in the same way that nations deal with each other. Thus, the head of a multinational oil company will deal directly with the president of an OPEC nation, and the head of an American automobile company seeking to invest in a Western European nation will be received by the prime minister of that country.

The success of corporate negotiations is already measured as much at the political level as at the economic level. A real need that follows from this development is for the corporation to develop a staff of people who are competent to represent the corporation in the same way that a diplomat represents his nation to other nations. Just as the Foreign Service of the State Department trains its people, so should the corporation prepare its people to deal with the complex environments within which they must exist.

The late distinguished Columbia Law School professor A. A. Berle, Jr., who served as an Assistant Secretary of State and Ambassador to Brazil, observes in his *The 20th Century Capitalist Revolution:*

> relations carried on by private corporations directly with foreign governments, when handled by enlightened men, with broad human sympathies, and with respect for the countries in which their companies operate, and for the people with which they deal, are at least as satisfactory as the economic relations worked out by government-to-government negotiations.

Corporate diplomats, in Berle's view, give a good account of their activities. Moreover, to offset the lack of experience in foreign diplomacy among their own headquarters personnel, corporations have been drawing on the skills of retired Foreign Service officers of the Department of State, as the United States Steel Company did when it added to its staff Mr. Walter Donnelly, a distinguished Foreign Service officer, with long experience in Latin America, and in effect made him the company's roving ambassador for South America. Another example is former Ambassador George Messersmith, who became Electric Bond and Share Company's resident "ambassador" in Mexico. We have previously alluded to Aramco within the oil industry. Standard Oil Company (New Jersey), now Exxon, has enormous competence in Middle East relations. And, General Motors Corporation provides special training in foreign affairs to the individuals assigned to represent it overseas.

Similarities to Lobbying

Corporate diplomacy resembles lobbying in a number of respects. As is the case with Congress, representatives of foreign countries are responding to a multitude of pressures when negotiating with American corporations concerning crude oil purchases, high technology, and other matters of mutual interest.

It is, however, not easy to enumerate these pressures. The American political system is built upon values and beliefs deeply ingrained in its culture. A foreign culture, likewise, will have a political order that reflects its own values and beliefs. To an American, however, that order may not be apparent or even comprehensible, just as our own order is bewildering to foreigners who have not had constant exposure to it.

To understand the sources of pressure on individuals and governments in other countries requires a thorough understanding of the social, political, psychological, and cultural forces that shape decision-making processes in a particular country.

Personal Relationships

Take, for example, the shift from the production of crude oil from concessions to the purchase of crude oil from foreign governments, which has heightened the importance of personal contacts between the firm's representatives and representatives of foreign governments. Here as elsewhere, solid relationships are built on trust, confidence, and a belief on each person's part that the relationship is mutually beneficial.

In face-to-face meetings, it is important that the company representative understand what kinds of values and experiences the foreign representative brings to that setting. For example: in negotiating with Third World representatives it is self-defeating for U.S. corporate representatives to employ the sociological jargon generated by American academics. The clichés are likely to be alien to the local negotiators and their usage by the corporate representative may establish a needless communications barrier. Typically, the individuals in oil-producing countries who meet corporate executives have high status within their own societies. Plainly, they should be treated with the respect and consideration their positions dictate.

As members of an elite, senior officials of foreign states are naturally attracted to the signs and symbols of Western wealth and power. Most likely, they enjoy the technological sophistication and opulence of our society, to which they are exposed by international travel. They may also feel some resentment, since their own status pales in comparison with the power embodied in Western society.

Familiarity with the cultural and personal backgrounds of key individuals is an indispensable aid in negotiations. Through greater knowledge of his counterpart's values and beliefs, the American corporate representative can build a relationship that has value to the firm, potentially much greater than the sums involved in a particular purchase agreement. It is a function of corporate intelligence to provide such cultural and personal backgrounds.

Mexico again is a special and interesting case. Since the Mexican Revolution, nothing of any major importance happens in Mexico without the personal approval or personal knowledge of the President. It therefore becomes most useful for an oil company's representative to have personal relationships with the President of Mexico and the President of Pemex, as well as cultivating close relationships with the country's elite.

Societal Relationships

Inevitably, an American corporate representative and a foreign government official serve as unofficial representatives of their respective cultures. Their interactions reflect to a large extent the goals and expectations of their societies, as well as the corporate and governmental aims they are pledged to fulfill.

A government official in a Third World nation will be personally successful if he can prove useful in meeting his government's promises to its own people. If an American oil company representative is well versed in the social and economic goals of his interlocutor's society, the discussion of crude oil purchases can provide an opportunity for a more far-ranging discussion, moving into other areas where cooperation of mutual benefit may be possible. A great American oil company, through its technical resources, may be able to provide assistance to a government in fields unrelated to petroleum sales; the good will accrued may prove extremely important at a later date. In some cases, this idea could become an extension of the use of business philanthropy, as previously noted.

The Foreign Relations of Great Corporations

The large business corporation is but one of a large number of different types of private organizations that function as private governments. Columbia University is a private government, and so are the Mayo Clinic and the Hughes Tool Company. The Supreme Court itself appears to have recognized that corporations are quasi-governments and in a series of decisions the Court has gradually extended many of the principles of the United States Constitution to the conduct of corporate affairs. Equal opportunity employment regulations are familiar, but many "due process" constraints also apply to the actions of corporations.

Indeed, as discussed earlier, large business corporations have many of the attributes of sovereign states. It is easy to understand why very large organizations like General Motors, IBM, General Electric, AT&T, and Exxon are treated much like nation-states. AT&T, for example, before the divestiture on January 1, 1984, had an annual budget larger than that of most of the members of the United Nations.

The fact that business corporations function like governments of nations in various ways is something many businessmen would rather ignore. Their distaste at the thought is quite understandable; business and government often have opposing interests, and businessmen in general regard government with a strong antipathy. Yet the fact of possessing governmental attributes is undeniable. And one of the least well understood of these quasi-governmental functions of the corporation is its conduct of "foreign relations."

The United States-based corporation must come face to face with the extent to which its fortunes are affected by its foreign relations. The plain fact is that every corporation with extensive overseas dealings is dependent for its out-of-country survival on its ability to function effectively in the international arena. But successful corporate foreign policies do not occur by accident. Moreover, it is not true that the same policies that work well at home will automatically produce profits abroad.

No corporation's home country policies arise out of a vacuum. No company would attempt to conduct its home country policies without a legal counsel, a public relations department, and special representatives in many of the state capitals as well as in Washington. Yet corporate foreign relations are often conducted in the dark. Even companies that have extensive overseas operations, such as Citicorp, Chase, Exxon and IBM, possess little more than an informal foreign office, and they establish their foreign policies in ways that are equally informal. This situation can be improved upon. There is no doubt that an appropriate way could be found to formalize, and to make useful, a corporate foreign office—indeed in some corporations this has already begun. Corporate international affairs have grown in significance at the same time that the corporation has been thrown upon its own resources for survival in the international world.

It is now in the best interests of the corporation to organize its foreign office activities more formally into a company unit or department. In every large multinational corporation this requires conducting a thorough survey of the company's customary—and its needed—foreign office operations; determining those of its corporate goals that can best be furthered through its foreign relations; and then deciding which needs should be served through a central foreign office, and which through foreign branch offices.

This does not mean that American corporations should create their own private state departments, staffed by a diplomatic corps. That sort of government mimicry—which some corporations have succumbed to—is the wrong way to acknowledge the similarities between corporations and governments. But quasi-state problems do arise in private firms. Corporate divisions and subsidiaries do operate in foreign countries and these actions are often ineffectively coordinated. This is true of almost all multinational business.

Sometimes a subsidiary or branch office in a foreign land is far along in a wrongful endeavor before its conflict with the corporation's overall strategy is realized at the executive offices. The history of American business abroad proves this point. A branch operation in a foreign country tends to acquire an autonomy that is hard to question even when the parent company, or the corporate headquarters, strongly suspects that the local branch is erroneously interpreting the country within which it functions. This is a common occurrence. Anyone can think of many other ways that foreign operations go wrong. A "Foreign Office" can provide the necessary coordination.

Recent Changes in World Power and World Economics Affecting All Business Corporations

Size and complexity alone would seem to dictate that large international corporations should formalize their foreign office functions, but there is another reason for doing so. This derives from the basic shift in the dynamics of international relations now taking place throughout the world. This shift can be described simply as the end of the bipolar world. During the period after World War II, the world was dominated by the United States and the USSR, and that fact determined the conditions of doing business abroad. Now, however, foreign business is conducted in a world that contains many power centers, each one of which is subject to shifting influences and hegemonies.

The American and Soviet blocs are still predominant, but both are now faced with restive sources of defiance from within their traditional blocs and countervailing forces of opposition from without. The United States has trouble with its independently-minded NATO allies, and the USSR has similar problems in conciliating Finland, Rumania, and Poland. Elsewhere, Japan, the People's Republic of China, India, the Muslim petromagnates, the sub-Saharan African states, the South American states, Scandinavia, and Southeast Asia, all possess sufficient power to thwart the two giants whenever their own interests require doing so. A recent example of big power weakness was the inability of the complementary diplomatic policies of the United States and the USSR to prevent the Pakistan/Libya entente from acquiring thermonuclear weaponry.

One of the themes of this book merits restatement: The survival strategy of multinational corporations should include the formal creation of a foreign office at the highest executive level to establish explicit foreign policies. Two developments have made this

93

advisable. The first is the expansion of international business operations generally that occurred after World War II, during the period of America's atomic supremacy. The second was the decline of the latter, leaving far-flung corporate operations in an exposed position. The growth of the multinational corporation is well known and widely discussed, but its relationship to the vicissitudes of American world power is less familiar.

Consider what today's international environment means to the American corporation. In the past the business firm could trade on the fact that American power was of a sufficiently massive character, and so widely deployed throughout the world, that business abroad could be conducted under an umbrella of protection and prestige. Terrorism was negligible. In marginal areas of the world, the vicissitudes of revolutionary instability—though present—were risks that could be insured against through defensive increased pricing policies. Under extreme situations, unanticipated confiscations and expropriations could be compensated for by recovery payments from the federal government, which was the reimburser of last resort. The offices of both U.S. consular and intelligence services could be made readily available in a pinch. Under such conditions of combined industrial and political supremacy there was little need for a corporate foreign office.

In the first years after World War II, the prestige that had been created by our magnificent war effort spilled over into the private sector in the form of the presumption that all things American were naturally superior. American firms benefited from an automatic competitive advantage symbolized by the durable Jeep, the flawless DC-3, Zenith radios, and GE appliances. Everything American, from business machines to food products, was taken by the world as its standard of both excellence and economy. Then two changes occurred in the mid-1960s, one economic and one political.

The economic reversal that brought us to our present state had many causes: rising labor costs, welfare state taxes, television marketing, style-obsolescence design practices, more modern facilities in foreign countries, the use of profits for conglomeration rather than plant modernization. These are only a few of the more prominent economic factors that put American firms in adverse competitive positions throughout the world following the 1960s.

All during the Cold War, American industry had been the free world's "company store." In the 1960s, that artificial seller's market was closed down on American firms throughout the world. The jibe that "America is the world's greatest producer of factory seconds" now comes readily to the lips of foreign purchasing agents. World markets are hardening against us.

At the same time, the massive political shift from bipolarity to multi-centered power was taking place. And America has yet to learn how to function in this changed environment of world power. Our situation is clear in talks recently given to overflow university audiences throughout the country by convicted Watergater G. Gordon Liddy. His message: The world treats America as a feeble old lady, easy prey and unable to retaliate. The students came in as skeptics and many left persuaded.

The solution is not for the nation to become a collective G. Gordon Liddy, but rather to recognize that the policies of the past will not serve in the present. This fact will probably not be measurably altered even by the present administration. A show of firmness, or even belligerency, unfortunately will not soften the hard heads of the world: not Ayatollah Khomeini, Quaddafi, or Castro. Western European nations cannot be bullied into resuming their former subservience. We cannot afford to lavish bounties on them as we once did through NATO, and even if we could manage to do so, France and Germany would temper acceptance with lofty protestations of their independence.

Thus, new conditions confront corporate internationalism; the environment for a new era of corporate diplomacy has arisen. Today overseas business must be conducted in an unsheltered environment. A corporate foreign office would be advisable in any case, but now it can be argued that it is a prerequisite to profitability. Those firms most adept at the special kind of corporate foreign relations appropriate to these new conditions will dominate the industrial future of the western world.

The Goals of Corporate Diplomacy

A corporate foreign policy differs in special ways from a national foreign policy. However, its keystone is the fact that it must rest upon corporate interests, just as national diplomacy rests upon national interests. Corporate interests, carefully considered, imply a fundamental set of objectives that can serve as guidelines for company representatives operating outside the United States. These guidelines will consist naturally of two kinds: 1) general rules for the overall conduct of the company's international relations; and 2) subsidiary commitments, goals, and directives designed specifically for each separate country of concern. Together these constitute the company's foreign policy. Generally stated, it would be an extension of the company's commercial interests expressed in terms of its own general philosophy. To produce such a policy requires special procedures of formulation, and also a method of promulgation and observation. A corporate foreign policy must be subject to periodic review and revision. A policy so conceived and administered could become an important factor in a company's long-term success in the world. Five basic corporate objectives are central to the conduct of foreign operations.

1. Economic Goals

The foremost goal of corporate diplomacy is economic: the profitability of the firm's various activities. Of course, profitability, considered generally, is the touchstone of all corporate foreign policy objectives, for all other objectives are ultimately defensible only as they enhance the firm's profitability. However, a significant part of corporate foreign relations deals with money, capital, and profits, i.e., the firm's economic goals in foreign relations. They will vary from country to country. In one, the concern may be with the terms of trade for acquiring locally produced crude oil; in another, the acquisition of a percentage of the shares in a local company with which participation is desired; in a third, the direct conduct of extractive or manufacturing activities. Whatever they are, these economic objectives must be identified with precision, and then made clear and specific for the special conditions the corporation faces in each country of concern.

2. Cultural and Social Goals

The second foreign policy objective derives from the fact that the company's top management has a right to expect its representatives in each country to know and to further the social and cultural objectives of the firm. Hence the firm must have the developed capability, *at the top level,* to establish such objectives

96

on the basis of sound assumptions. One of the primary necessities is to demystify foreign cultural and social environments so the firm can operate with sureness within the countries of its concern.

All foreign countries are to some degree mysterious arenas in which business is done under highly special conditions, many of which are difficult for the outsider to assimilate. The social acceptability, so to speak, of an American firm can be produced only through a special knowledge of the local folkways and by an acute awareness of the kinds of cultural activities most likely to produce favorable responses.

It is also necessary to know exactly what the opposition—the competition—is doing and planning to do in the cultural affairs area. For example, any oil company desiring to operate in Indonesia should know rather exactly what Mobil, Arco, IBM, and International Nickel are doing there or are planning to do there.

The IBM case is most instructive. It has a large cultural activity in Indonesia, which has helped the country by furnishing the government with a computer model for the reconstruction of the great temples of Borobudur. This is a costly gift, and IBM obviously expects to reap considerable benefits from so magnificent a cultural contribution. Any firm in competition with IBM must somehow compensate for the favor IBM is wisely bestowing on the Indonesians.

It is not impossible. Indeed, there are other cultural activities appropriate to Indonesia that would be less costly and most effective. But knowing them and knowing how to accomplish them requires a highly competent foreign office operation. For example, an effective cultural affairs section within a company could produce cost-effective cultural policies enabling the company to compete with less well directed competitors on quite advantageous terms.

3. Foreign Policy Goals

The third objective is political. We know our own country so well that we may forget how important it is, in doing business inside the United States, to possess an accurate knowledge of the power positions of the various political factions who may be able to affect a firm's business operations for good or ill. This is second nature to us in our own country, but it is often ignored

97

when we do business abroad. One reason is that politics is to a nation what a mannerism is to a person—a highly individual characteristic.

All firms with extensive foreign dealings must equip themselves with a capacity for feeling "at home" in the political environment of their host countries. They must be able to assess with confidence the comparative power positions of the various forces that contend against each other inside the country. This involves establishing good relations with the U.S. Department of State in Washington and with its embassies in each country of concern—even though this effort may sometimes seem pointless.

Even more important, however, is maintaining good relations with the foreign offices of the host countries inside each of the firm's areas of operation. Reliable assessments of the present and prospective political stability of each important country is one of the prerequisites of all other foreign business planning. This includes assessments of incipient revolutionary movements and reliable calculations of the extent and type of native terrorist activities.

It is essential as well to prepare careful estimates of the potential for, and the inclination of, each country involved to engage in external military actions. The twists and turns of the power plays and ideological alliances of the host country must be charted assiduously. The chief result of being able to make accurate political assessments of these countries would be to give a company the capacity to estimate its own investment security factors for each of its foreign operations.

(4) Intelligence as a Goal

The fourth objective impinges on all the others. It is the creation of an information and intelligence function, as has been suggested earlier. This is a separate activity because what we demand from this area is a special kind of knowledge that will permit a company to be certain that it can furnish its other foreign office departments with "surprise-free" projections. It is important to note that the intelligence function must be separate from policy-forming departments to keep information from being shaped to pre-established goals—often a source of disaster.

It is not possible to control the future, and organizations cannot arrange matters so that they experience no surprises at all. But they can influence the future. A corporation must not be caught unaware by the unheralded intrusion of events subversive of the profitability of the firm's foreign operations. The types of intelligence to be compiled must be defined by the economic, cultural, and diplomatic units of the firm. It can be acquired in many ways: through the establishment of reliable local contacts, by holding area conferences, by monitoring the media, and by fostering the exchange of information with a wide range of experts from journalism and academe.

Intelligence information may sometimes be strange without being any the less useful. Take the case of Indonesia. The Indonesian government is wooing not only the Western business community but the rest of the world (both countries and corporations) for their investment monies. A testament to that fact is the elegant complex of Western-type hotels in Jakarta. From the hotels, and a few lovely boulevards, one could conclude that Indonesia had taken on the culture of the West, as well as Western ideas of property, intact. This conclusion, however, is not valid. The Western hotels and the like are only a facade. Under the surface is a society interwoven with a set of mystical beliefs almost incomprehensible to the Western business mind. Not just the lower classes but all classes, including generals and top businessmen, believe in ghosts, spirits, white magic, black magic, gurus, and *Dukuns** who can cast spells and influence political decisions. Even General Suharto, the President, "is a mystic who is known to listen to his *Dukuns* before making important decisions."[7] It is important for businessmen with dealings in Indonesia to be familiar with the role of magic in modern Indonesian culture.

(5.) The Goal of Maintaining an Index of Elites

The fifth objective refers to intelligence about significant persons. Here, it is suggested that the firm develop dossiers: firms need production of accurate information about all those persons who might, on their own initiative, affect the firm's future. This involves creating and maintaining a "classified" index of the most important and significant persons in each of the countries involved. These indexed dossiers permit the evaluation of all those persons who, by either positive power or by capacity for

---

* In Indonesia a *Dukun* is an adviser on personal problems, a healer, and a sorcerer—especially the latter.

obstruction, may be in a position to interfere with, or enhance, the company's ability to accomplish its business goals.

These five separate activity areas form the basis on which corporate foreign policies must be designed. The companies that establish such activities on an ongoing basis will be able to create for themselves an impregnable competitive position.

6

Organizing a Corporate Intelligence Function

Iᴛ is the position of this study that an intelligence function should be established within large multinational corporations, and that it should be established as soon as possible. The following discussion will outline what the implementation of this suggestion might require.

Relation to the Chief Executive Officer

As mentioned at the outset, the main purpose of an intelligence function is to serve as an informational aid to the chief executive officer in the execution of his broad responsibilities. This obligation or commitment to the chief executive officer is the top priority. It requires that the intelligence function be geared to the strategic questions of the chief executive officer's choosing, and that it serve to enhance lobbying and diplomatic work as he sees fit.

This does not mean that the director of intelligence works *only* with the chief executive officer. It is likely that the director will have a primary audience and a secondary audience. Working with these corporate executives, the director will develop assign-

101

ments for his department within the guidelines set by the CEO. He will have six major responsibilities:

1. *Obtaining* the general information that is needed
2. *Distilling* out the most important information
3. *Defining* the issues from the information
4. *Analyzing* the issues for his particular company's needs
5. *Recommending* actions to be taken
6. *Briefing* individuals and groups within the company's structure

These six duties define the rhythm of the director's daily life.

He *must,* however, report directly to the chief executive officer. The discussion so far has made the case that 1) intelligence is closely tied to strategic planning, and that 2) lobbying and corporate diplomacy can be enhanced through a well-designed intelligence organization.

These are extremely sensitive areas of corporate activity, and the final say in each area must rest with the chief executive officer. Thus, while particular operations may be carried out in conjunction with, or under the supervision of, other management personnel at the chief executive officer's request, a direct tie to the CEO is essential to a balanced corporate strategy.

Relation to Other Information Systems

There are many offices within a large corporation that generate information of various sorts. The day-to-day economic life of the firm's many affiliates provides essential information, as do public relations and lobbying work currently being conducted.

The collection and analysis of data leading to policy information should be kept distinct from these other vital information systems. This is not meant to segregate policy information in some artificial manner—it is rather a question of the point at which the integration with other kinds of information takes place.

In order for policy information—intelligence—to be most useful to the chief executive officer, it is suggested that a planning office or committee, chaired by the CEO, be the prime organizational site for the merging or integration of these various information sources. This assures the CEO the greatest access to the variety of perspectives that different kinds of activity within the firm provide, a key element in leadership of *any* large organization.

Number of Personnel Needed and Budget

A study on implementation, based on the chief executive officer's specifications, would be a prerequisite to an accurate description of the size of the staff and the exact "fit" of the intelligence function in the firm's organizational chart.

Many factors will affect staff size and proportionate distribution. For example, each region of the world will require different amounts of staff time depending on the extent of a company's current involvements and prospective involvement.

The budget for an intelligence function should be appropriate to its stature as one of the major functions of the company.

Job Descriptions

Staff duties will flow from the actual implementation plan. There will be a need for "area desks" or "area persons," individuals whose chief responsibility will be keeping up to date on a particular country or region of the world. Someone within a particular area of responsibility will:

- —carry out continuing study of the structure of the *power elite* of each country his company is in
- —be familiar with *cultural factors* for that area, and will stay current on major cultural studies
- —do *trend studies* in sociopolitical issues

Appropriate subdivisions would be made as needed.

The Director's Role

The person in charge of the intelligence function must operate in a number of worlds. He must have access to a broad range of people outside the firm, since his division may be asked to develop information in a short period of time on any conceivable subject. As an information specialist, he must be capable of tapping reliable sources in any professional field or research area. Furthermore, he must be good at asking questions that will allow experts in any field to provide useful data without the "excess baggage" that specialists routinely indulge in.

The director must get to know the writers and editors of major sources of information, including the authors of books. This exposure allows him to stay current in important fields, and provides the firm with a secondary advantage: through these contacts, the director will be able to place articles representing the long-range interests of the company in important places.

The head of the intelligence function should also gain the respect of the heads of various area desks of the State Department and the CIA, and other Federal intelligence agencies.

To carry out his responsibilities, the director will need his own secure communications facility, his own cable desk, and his own map room for briefing top officials. (Many corporations, such as Dupont, have had such a map and briefing room for years.) The director must have secure methods for transmitting and receiving information.

Information Structure

Information must be organized to be useful. Within each area subdivision, Essential Elements of Information (EEI) will be identified and gathered. For many years, the notation EEI has been a fundamental concept for intelligence officers in many parts of the world. The implementing of the intelligence function is on one level the development of EEI on various topics and subjects.

A few examples of categories might be:

—Area descriptions
—Natural resources, such as mineral and oil information
—Production resources
—Transportation systems
—Power plants, including all energy facilities
—Social and psychological factors
—Communication facilities
—Terrorism
—The security of key personnel, as well as plant security
—The problem of loyalty of employees, both within and outside the United States

—Economic dependencies
—Economic sanctions
—The political stability of various countries where trading is currently taking place
—Competition, the emerging trends in competition in various countries, and the trend of the law regarding competition
—Credit worthiness of individuals, and various groups
—Technological status including new developments in computer technology
—The acquisition, organization, retrieval, and security of *special information* (via computer banks) for the use of the CEO and certain senior officers
—Developing the highest degree of security for the passing of, and the exchange of, information
—Demographics
—Elites
—Political and economic power centers

How to Acquire Information

In each of the policy sciences, individuals must be found who are sensitized to the company's Essential Elements of Information. As indicated earlier, banking relationships can be extremely useful if they have been established at the highest level between the bank and the company. When necessary, appropriate bank employees may be instructed to cooperate with representatives of the company in reviewing intelligence reports the bank has prepared for internal policy review and evaluation.

This relationship is very different from conventional contacts with bankers and accountants. "Numbers people" have a definite usefulness, but generally speaking, they don't understand social trends. Sometimes at the board or chief executive officer level there will be men of long-term political and social insight, but they do not exist in large numbers and tend to be fairly well known. Most bank officials, and investment bankers, have a rather short-term perception of political and social issues, and respond to these matters only in an immediate and pressing crisis.

The experts in political, psychological, and sociological areas are usually academic scholars, and it is from that community that a group of highly qualified and loyal outside consultants should be established. In certain fields, the company's existing staff can be helpful, since they work regularly with experts in a number of professional fields.

A basic problem must be recognized in regard to work with academics, namely, that such scholars are sometimes hostile to the business community. It is true they will take a fee for performing a particular consulting service, but the inner hostility nevertheless remains.

A full explanation of the phenomenon is not clear, but perhaps it relates to the fact that many young and well-qualified professors have never had a "real" contact or association with the business community and have been educated in a "liberal" environment.

This observation is made only in a cautionary way, not as a firm "rule." Most certainly, a useful group of highly trained scholars, sensitive to the social and political problems of the large corporation, can be developed. Also, the services of ex-politicians in the acquisition of information can and should be developed. Both these groups would be of great usefulness in the overall development of the intelligence function.

Corporate Security, Intelligence Work and Catastrophe Plan

A continuous study concerning the ultimate security of a company's strategic corporate records should be factored into the overall intelligence function. As the nuclear monopoly disappears, an unforeseen attack on the United States is not inconceivable. Since magnetic tapes can be obliterated by explosion or their magnetically encoded data can be erased or rendered unreadable by radiation, there should be more than one repository for such records.

A catastrophe plan should be prepared and regularly updated. In such a plan, various officers and staff within a company's organization would, in the event of a nuclear or conventional military attack on the United States, perform designated tasks essential to maintaining the company's continuity and integrity. Precise roles and instructions would be developed as part of a comprehensive design by the director of intelligence.

This is not a new idea. A number of companies have such plans, although public notice has not been given to them. However, companies with catastrophe plans frequently let them go stale.

Orientation within the Company

Clearly, a firm's possible uses of an intelligence function cannot be predicted totally in advance. It should be clearly noted that a corporate intelligence function is more than just a textbook business operation, and its potential value lies largely in the hands of the chief executive officer.

Senior management officers would need to be oriented to the need for, the range and versatility of, and the possible applications of this new function early in its implementation. And, at an early stage, and at the discretion of the chief executive officer, the board of directors would be introduced to this new corporate policy instrument.

7

Trade Secrets

INDUSTRIAL espionage, according to the distinguished French scientist and author Jacques Bergier,[1] is older than military espionage conducted by nation-states. Since the dawn of history, Bergier writes, men have been extracting technological secrets from one another. Perhaps the earliest example of technological theft occurred during the Stone Age, when a tribe that had not discovered fire sought to steal this epochal breakthrough from those who had developed the burning and heating capability. Flint, used for striking fire, was a parallel technological secret captured by theft. Parenthetically, both fire and flint became known through use of primitive intelligence in what in today's parlance would be called a "reconnaissance."

The process for the manufacture of silk, another early technological secret, was stolen from the Chinese. So zealously did the ancient Chinese guard the secret of silk manufacture that they decreed death by torture for anyone revealing it to outsiders. The theft, ironically, was carried out by a Chinese princess, who, on a trip abroad, concealed some silk worms in a flowered hat she was wearing. Chinese legend has it that she gave the stolen silk worms to her Indian lover. And that was how the secret of silk production was acquired by a trade rival.

In the eighteenth century, industrial espionage enabled the Europeans to purloin another valuable Chinese trade secret: the process for the manufacture of porcelain. The Chinese had been producing high-quality porcelain for centuries. As with the production of silk, knowledge of the porcelain manufacturing process was heavily guarded. Over centuries, industrial spies from the West had been sent to the Middle Kingdom to discover the secret of porcelain technology. A French Jesuit, Father Francis Xavier d'Entrecolles, succeeded in learning the secret porcelain manufacturing technology, which he described in letters dated September 1712 and January 1722, after he had visited the royal porcelain factory "in the secret city of King-tö-tchen." Based on Father d'Entrecolles's description of the manufacturing process employed by the Chinese, and after considerable experimentation by local entrepreneurs, a French factory which became celebrated for its wares was established in Sèvres in 1756. It was not long before an English espionage agent infiltrated the French plant and stole the trade secret, enabling English manufactured china to dominate the porcelain market for decades.

The catalogue of misappropriated technology and trade secrets is extensive. In the march of industry there is scarcely a technological development which has not been stolen by competitors or would-be competitors: the secret for steel production was stolen from the British by the German Alfred Krupp; the secret of rubber was stolen by spies and pirates who repeatedly infringed on Charles Goodyear's basic patent for vulcanization; and representatives of various nations freely pirated Rudolf Diesel's car engine. It is not an exaggeration to say that modern industry is largely wrapped in the mantle of stolen trade secrets.

The corporate spy's mission is to acquire a rival's secret proprietary information—by outright theft, when necessary, or by more subtle, conventional methods, when possible. Whichever method is utilized, industrial espionage is widespread and commonplace throughout the contemporary business world. Owing to the technical nature of their trade secrets, competitive espionage is prevalent and intense in the high-technology industries—in aerospace, electronics, computers, instrumentation, pharmaceuticals, cosmetics and weaponry. In addition, few U.S. industries—large or small, well-known or obscure—are entirely free from economic espionage. One security expert puts it this way: "Little companies steal from big companies. Big companies steal from little companies. Everybody steals from everybody." As Japan, the Soviet Union, Western Europe and the United States vie with increasing intensity for economic supremacy, industrial espionage has reached epidemic proportions.

What Are Trade Secrets?

Trade secrets are as varied as the spectrum of American business.They run the gamut from medical and cosmetic formulae to geological studies pinpointing the location of rare minerals, from computer software to plans for a corporate takeover. A trade secret, in short, can be anything that gives a company a competitive advantage, including its pricing and marketing policies; customer lists; labor relations policies; sales forecasts; long-range overseas investment plans; and plans for the opening of new plants here at home.

The model Uniform Trade Secrets Act,[2] section 1(4), defines the term to mean information, including a formula, pattern, compilation, program, device, method, technique or process that

(1) derives independent economic value, actual or potential, from not being generally known to, and not being readily ascertainable by proper means by other persons who can obtain economic value from its disclosure or use; and

(2) is the subject of efforts that are reasonable under the circumstances to maintain its secrecy.

In recent court actions for alleged theft of trade secrets by former employees,[3] IBM delineated the term "trade secrets" broadly as any information not publicly disclosed by itself, including

—product announcement objectives and strategies
—financial projections
—planned product or services offerings
—inventions
—designs, drawings, blueprints
—software
—product ideas
—concepts
—prototypes
—features
—flow charts
—block diagrams

In a crucial phrase, IBM also included in its description "all ideas . . . related to . . . actual or anticipated business or research

110

and development. . . ." Clearly, IBM's definition of a trade secret is so sweeping that any executive, engineer, scientist or research worker who leaves the company to take another job, or to establish his own computer business, is potentially liable to a suit for alleged theft of trade secrets!

The courts, which ultimately must determine whether trade secrets have been purloined by former employees or by competitors through espionage, in the main rely on standards contained in *The Restatement of Torts,* a legal reference of basic principles that embodies case law developed from the English common law:

> A trade secret may consist of any formula, device or compilation of information which is used in one's business, and which gives him an opportunity to obtain an advantage over competitors who do not know or use it. It may be a formula for a chemical compound, a process of manufacturing, treating or preserving materials, a pattern for a machine or other device, or a list of customers. . . .

The Restatement of Torts says categorically that an "exact definition of a trade secret is not possible." However, it suggests that in determining what is—or is not—a trade secret the courts should take into consideration a number of factors incident to a particular business:

> (1) The extent to which the information is known outside his business; (2) The extent to which it is known by employees and others involved in his business; (3) The extent of measures taken by him to guard the secrecy of the information; (4) The value of the information to him and his competitors; (5) The amount of effort or money expended by him in developing the information; (6) The ease or difficulty with which the information could be properly acquired or duplicated by others.

Lawyers who specialize in trade secrets litigation emphasize two criteria for determining the existence of a trade secret: (1) Is there in existence something that is not generally *known* in the trade or industry? and (2) Is there something which *provides its owner with a competitive advantage?*

The Restatement of Torts also stresses the element of secrecy by noting that "a substantial element of secrecy must exist, so that, except by the use of improper means, there would be difficulty in acquiring the information."

111

Everybody Does It

In the secret world of industrial espionage, the techniques used to misappropriate trade secrets are as varied as imagination, opportunity and circumstance allow.

A competitor wanted to know when Du Pont would complete the construction of its new methanol plant in Beaumont, Texas, fearing that once the plant was in production its own product would be unable to compete successfully. The competitor arranged to photograph the unfinished plant—still roofless—from a hired small plane. Du Pont had not filed for a patent on the chemical process, preferring to keep the method secret. Du Pont's management believed that by an analysis of the photographs of the plant layout—a kind of "reverse engineering"—its competitor could learn the nature of the secret formula for producing an alcohol derivative.

Du Pont sued the aerial photographers, Rolfe and Gary Christopher, who admitted they had been hired to photograph the unfinished plant, but refused to name the party for whom they were spying. The Christophers argued that the air space in which they had flown was "public airspace." They were therefore entitled to photograph objects within the public domain, including Du Pont's plant under construction. Both the trial court and the U.S. Court of Appeals, sitting in New Orleans, rejected this contention. Judge Irving Goldberg, speaking for the Court of Appeals, held that, while anyone is free to apply "reverse engineering" to a product (if it is lawfully obtained) by breaking it down into its component parts, or by chemically analyzing its elements and thereby discovering its secret, "our devotion to freewheeling industrial competition must not force us into accepting the law of the jungle as the standard of morality . . . in our commercial relations." In ruling for Du Pont, Judge Goldberg observed: "This is a case of industrial espionage in which an airplane is the cloak and a camera the dagger. . . . In taking this position we realize that industrial espionage of the sort here perpetrated has become a popular sport in some segments of our commercial community," but he concluded that it is not to be condoned.[4]

The lone inventor has always occupied a special niche in American business folklore. As a recent *Business Week* essay observed, while the myths about him are many, "it is no myth that marketers eager to cash in on his invention frequently treat him shabbily." Large manufacturers and distributors can dictate tough terms, and if the inventor refuses to agree, they are free to dupli- cate his invention by "designing around the patent," an accepted form of commercial piracy. This, in effect, is misappropriating someone else's trade secret.

A blatant deception of a small inventor was practiced by Chesebrough-Ponds, Inc., which pirated his patented breathing apparatus. The particular device was a breath exerciser invented by Harold Hanson, an employee of Laurie Visual Etudes, Inc., a small manufacturer and distributor of records and music publi- cations to whom Hanson had assigned the rights to the invention. The device was intended for use by students of wind instruments, to teach them to inhale and exhale properly. Hanson's physician suggested that the device also had medical uses and could be utilized by bedridden patients who experienced difficulty in breathing.

Chesebrough-Ponds' health division was interested in obtain- ing a licensing agreement to market the breath exerciser because its own device for aiding patients with lung problems—a "blow bottle"—was cumbersome and awkward to use. In the course of the negotiations, the music company, at Chesebrough's request, provided detailed drawings and prototypes of the breath exer- ciser. The Chesebrough research and development staff used this information to design substantially similar devices which were subsequently patented and named Uniflow and Triflo. The prod- ucts were immediate successes. From 1975 through July 1980 gross sales amounted to $13.5 million.

Laurie sued in a New York court, alleging wrongful appropria- tion of a trade secret. During pretrial discovery, damaging inter- nal Chesebrough memoranda were brought to light which disclosed that executives of the health division had not negotiated in good faith and had contrived to misappropriate Laurie's trade secret.

Justice Richard W. Wallach of the New York State Supreme Court ruled that Chesebrough had learned Laurie's trade secret during the licensing negotiations. "The law creates in such cir- cumstances," Justice Wallach said, "a confidential relationship which restricted Chesebrough from utilizing the disclosure for anything other than the purpose of the disclosure themselves." Corporations remain free, the court held, to use public informa- tion about an invention, "but once they enter into discussions and draw on information disclosed, they are barred from copying."[5] In other words, Chesebrough could not pirate Laurie's invention and market a duplicate design.

A South Korean pharmaceutical company, Chong Kun Dang Corp., one of the country's largest drug houses, bought an antibiotic stolen from an Italian subsidiary of Dow Chemical Co. and marketed the drug as if it were the product of its own research and development.

Parenthetically, Third World companies, like the South Korean drug firm, justify similar misconduct on the grounds that only through the acquisition of stolen trade secrets are they able to compete with Western high-technology companies. The perception that Third World corporations are unable to compete with giant multinational companies from the U.S., Western Europe and Japan is belied by the invasion of the lucrative Middle East market by South Korean multinational construction-engineering companies and their skilled labor forces. Competitors from the developed countries have observed with astonishment how swiftly the South Koreans were able to extend their capabilities beyond civil construction and into the more technical and financially attractive engineering areas formerly dominated by major Western and Japanese construction-engineering firms. Indian construction firms have elbowed aside Japanese and Western companies on construction jobs to build roads, railways, power plants and airport terminals—jobs worth about $4 billion ($2.1 billion in Iraq alone, $1.2 billion in Libya)—and have booked $5.1 billion on other jobs. Many Third World multinational companies have astounded the industrialized world by their resourcefulness in exporting technology to labor-intensive environments in such industries as tropical agriculture, aquaculture, textiles, rural construction and housing. Brazilian multinationals have provided technical assistance to Peru in copper mining and Colombia in coal mining. Third World multinationals are increasingly involved in complex industries—for example: Taiwan's in electronics, Singapore's in oilrig construction, Brazil's in light aircraft manufacturing, and India's in chemicals.

The theft of the antibiotic from Dow Chemical's Italian subsidiary was ingenious in its simplicity. A retiree from the subsidiary made a farewell visit to the pharmaceutical laboratory where he had been employed. While visiting with his former co-workers, he appeared to have accidentally dropped his handkerchief into a fermentation vat. Retrieving his handkerchief, the retiree restored it to his pocket and walked out of the laboratory, carrying with him an invaluable trade secret for the production of Rifampicin, an antituberculosis drug. Sopped up by the handkerchief was a sample of the bacterial strain used to produce the antibiotic. In addition to obtaining the formula, the retiree confessed to having previously stolen technical documents describing the process for manufacturing Rifampicin. In sum, the thief had in his possession everything another laboratory would need to duplicate the Italian company's product. Through a Swiss intermediary, the retiree found a ready and willing buyer for his stolen trade secrets in South Korea.

Although the major security emphasis in California's high-technology electronic industry (in the North) and aerospace industry (in the South) has been to prevent theft of secret, proprietary information by the Soviet Union and its East European satellites, U.S. intelligence specialists and West Coast security consultants have long believed that Japanese firms are as much a threat as the Soviets. The June 22, 1982 arrest by FBI special agents of five employees of Hitachi, Ltd. and four from Mitsubishi Electric Corp. on charges of buying secret data stolen from IBM would appear to confirm long-held suspicions that the Silicon Valley is also an arena for Japanese industrial espionage. FBI affidavits allege that Hitachi paid $622,000 for stolen IBM data pertaining to its new superfast 3081 computer, while Mitsubishi paid $26,000.

It seems absurd for two prominent Japanese companies to buy high-technology data stolen from IBM, when Japanese industry—and these two companies in particular—already have a commanding lead in consumer electronics, computers, microchips, and genetic engineering. The motivation for industrial espionage by Japanese companies can be understood in the context of the Japanese compulsion to be No. 1 in computer data processing. In the Japanese business community there is a strong feeling that the FBI and IBM were allowed "to play a dirty trick on the Japanese because of a U.S. government effort to retard Japanese technological development." Both companies and their employees who were arrested have pleaded innocent to the charges, and their lawyers have argued that the FBI improperly "entrapped" the Japanese.

Almost as an anticlimax, Hitachi and two of its employees

pleaded guilty in a U.S. District Court in San Francisco on February 8, 1983 to conspiring to transport stolen IBM trade secrets to Japan. Hitachi was fined $10,000, the maximum on the single count in the indictment, and the two employees, Kenji Hayashi and Isao Ohnishi, $10,000 and $4,000 respectively. Hayashi was placed on probation for five years and Ohnishi for two years. Both were prohibited from conducting any business in the United States on behalf of Hitachi. A piddling $10,000 fine for a company whose annual sales are in the billions of dollars is obviously no financial hardship for Hitachi. The company's real punishment was self-inflicted: a loss of face, which in the Japanese culture is the ultimate degradation.

Of the world's ten largest semiconductor-chip producing companies, five are American, led by Motorola and Texas Instruments. But four are Japanese and of these, Nippon Electric and Hitachi are breathing down the necks of the leading U.S. firms. When Japan renounced war as an instrument of national policy at the end of World War II, it seems her giant corporations fell heir to this mission. Elsewhere we have observed that corporations have assumed many of the attributes of the nation-state. Perhaps global economic warfare between multinational corporations—as in the case of Hitachi and IBM—can now become a substitute for wars between nation-states.

Dr. Robert S. Aries is a classic example of an industrial spy who used his academic profession as a cover for commercial espionage and the acquisition of trade secrets.[6] A naturalized American citizen of French extraction, Dr. Aries was a distinguished chemist who taught at Brooklyn Polytechnic Institute. Many of his students were employed by major drug and pharmaceutical companies. He used his graduate students as industrial spies. They were encouraged, as part of their "real life" involvement, to bring him their employers' trade secrets. According to Merck & Company, Rohm & Haas and Sprague Electric Co., Dr. Aries obtained "secret documents and samples of extreme value" from the vaults of each company.

Merck contended in a court action against Aries that a culture developed in its laboratories, a micro-organism for destroying parasites in poultry (called Amprolium and estimated by Merck to be worth $20 million), was purloined by the professor through one of his students. The theft came to light when Merck was negotiating with a French chemical company for acquisition of the company. During the negotiations Merck learned that Dr.

Aries had licensed the French firm to manufacture a new drug for destroying parasites on poultry, which he claimed to have discovered and which he called Mepyrium. He had provided the company with chemical and production data. On comparing these data with their own materials for the production of Amprolium, Merck's scientists realized that Dr. Aries' Mepyrium was an exact duplicate of Merck's own product.

Merck's management immediately instructed its legal counsel to obtain an injunction to prevent Dr. Aries from any further exploitation of the stolen formula, but in the meantime he had fled to Switzerland. The Swiss refused to extradite him (there is no extradition treaty between Switzerland and the United States). Dr. Aries returned to France, which also declined to extradite him on the ground that, as a French national [sic], he should be tried in a French court in France. While these legal maneuvers were under way, Dr. Aries filed a countersuit against Merck, claiming that the drug company had stolen the trade secret from him!

When Merck's management investigated the breach of security that enabled Dr. Aries to acquire the formula for Amprolium, they learned that one of their employees had been a student of Dr. Aries at Brooklyn Polytechnic Institute. A comparison of the employee-student's handwriting with the handwriting on documents that Dr. Aries had transmitted to the French chemical company showed them to be identical.

Other students had also furnished Dr. Aries with trade secrets from companies where they were employed. In this manner, Dr. Aries was able to obtain a formula for a new oil additive, a trade secret owned by Rohm & Haas, as well as the details of an electrical device used in computers, developed by Sprague Electric Co.

Dr. Aries subsequently abandoned commercial espionage and took up residence on the French Riviera, where one presumes he is enjoying a comfortable retirement.

Corporations have much to fear from the theft of trade secrets by their own employees, whether motivated by misplaced enthusiasm, as with Dr. Aries' graduate students, or greed, as in the case of Eugene Mayfield. Mayfield was a Procter & Gamble employee who offered to sell a marketing plan for Crest toothpaste to P&G's competitor, Colgate-Palmolive Co., manufacturer of Colgate toothpaste, for $20,000. (P&G executives placed a value of $5 million on the marketing plan.)

Colgate's management alerted the FBI to the proposed sale,

and Mayfield's downfall occurred at New York's Kennedy Airport at a rendezvous in a men's room with a Colgate employee. The two conspirators were to use the code names "Mr. Crest" and "Mr. Colgate." An exchange of money for the marketing plan was to take place in adjoining stalls. There were slapstick overtones to the transaction: Mayfield insisted that the buyer hand over his trousers along with the money so that he would be unable to pursue Mayfield out of the men's room. FBI agents were waiting outside and grabbed Mayfield, who later pleaded guilty to a federal charge of interstate shipment of stolen goods.

From this brief recital it would appear that the most cost-effective way to undertake research and development is to steal a competitor's trade secrets. "It is perceived as a low-risk activity compared with the enormous savings of time and money to be gained," writes James H. Pooley, chairman of the lawyers' committee of the American Electronics Association and author of *Trade Secrets.* Thefts of trade secrets now cost American firms up to $20 billion annually, according to August Bequai, a Washington lawyer and counsel to the American Society for Industrial Security.

What Can Be Done?

Many companies are reluctant to acknowledge a loss of trade secrets or to prosecute employee-thieves lest it become common knowledge that the company is no longer in possession of its most valuable assets. "Most executives would rather bury the losses in earnings statements than admit they've lost the family jewels," is the way Belden Menkus, a top security consultant, puts it.

Companies are loath to sue their employees or competitors who have filched trade secrets because court cases can reveal important details of the stolen materials as well as provide potential spies with an inside look at a company's security system. Many companies do not resort to litigation because they are blissfully unaware that industrial spies have stolen their trade secrets.

Is there a cure for the epidemic of industrial espionage? Not really. In the unlikely event that Congress were to enact a law prohibiting industrial espionage, the legislation would soon become another "Prohibition" statute—honored more by its breach

118

than its observance. In a technological era, one company's trade secrets are another's death-knell. It is a harsh reality but certainly one lifeline to survival is corporate spying.

In a technological society in which information—intelligence—means money, growth and profits, companies must learn to cope with those who threaten or steal their trade secrets. But how?

> —By creating an environment in which employees do not become disgruntled and hold grudges against their employers and are thereby tempted to steal proprietary information "to get even"
> —By utilizing sophisticated security measures
> —By a greater willingness to risk the fortunes of litigation to prosecute corporate spies.[7]

8

The Practice of Industrial Espionage

INDUSTRIAL espionage has flourished in America since the birth of our Industrial Revolution—the founding in 1789 of Slater's Mill in Pawtucket, Rhode Island. Samuel Slater had memorized the plans of the layout of an English textile mill, where he had worked as an apprentice. Under the then prevailing English law, the export of factory plans was forbidden, as was the emigration of textile workers. Slater, nevertheless, managed to slip out of the country and find passage to the New World, where he established a textile mill from the plans he had committed to memory.

Samuel Slater's method for the theft of a trade secret is still widely followed. When an executive moves from one job to another, he doesn't have to carry his former employer's secret documents in a briefcase—it's what he carries away in his head that matters. But the route between ex-employer and prospective employer can be a legal minefield. Employers are aggressively laying claim to the information stored in a former employee's mind. "Who owns your brains" when an employee changes jobs, to borrow a provocative phrase from Kevin McManus,[1] is a lively question before the courts.

A prevalent industry practice of luring away a competitor's key employees in order to find out what a rival is doing—or planning to do—is increasingly being challenged in the courts. In the course of an antitrust suit between IBM and Telex Corp., IBM charged that Telex offered IBM executives substantial bonuses to join Telex. IBM, as the leader of the computer industry, is "the trend setter in litigation," observes Steven Brill, publisher of *American Lawyer.*

Is the charge that former employees are attempting to use trade secrets a smokescreen to preserve a monopoly position? In a suit by IBM against three former employees who were accused of attempting to sell trade secrets involving IBM's personal computer, a defense lawyer contended that the so-called trade secrets his clients were accused of peddling were in reality common knowledge in the computer industry, published in other companies' brochures. The alleged trade secret offense, it was argued, was being used by IBM to prevent its former employees from establishing their own business and competing with IBM.

During the 1960s an exodus of managers and engineers from Fairchild Camera and Instrument Corp. in the Silicon Valley drained the company of much of its corporate leadership as a host of new semiconductor companies were established, including such (now) well-known enterprises as Intel, Signetics, National Semiconductor and Advanced Micro Devices.[2] Since 1970, former IBM executives have launched several highly successful computer companies, including Amdahl Corp., which manufactures equipment that plugs into IBM systems. Now, in the 1980s, following these "golden footsteps," dozens of executives are being enticed away from Hewlett-Packard by venture capital money pouring into Silicon Valley. Over the past two years, former Hewlett-Packard managers and engineers have organized at least ten new companies in the minicomputer or personal computer industries, with a few in semiconductors.

In the past, IBM and other computer manufacturers were prone to accept the departure or hiring away of key employees as an integral part of the competitive game. Now, however, computer companies, led by IBM, are taking former employees to court. Thus, Microcomputer Systems Corp. of Sunnyvale, California, was awarded a $2 million judgment against two former employees who had established a competing firm. In another case, Fairchild Camera and Instrument Corp. obtained a temporary restraining order against National Semiconductor Co., who sought to hire away a Fairchild engineer with knowledge of Fairchild's patented isoplanar process.

In a 1982 New York state court action, IBM won a sweeping injunction against two former employees and a company they had organized, for alleged theft of trade secrets. In the consent order and injunction, the defendants were forbidden to use any IBM trade secrets or proprietary, confidential business information. The injunction granted IBM blocks the employee-organized Bridge Technology, Inc. from hiring any IBM employee unless the individual had previously resigned and worked elsewhere for six months. The two former employees against whom the suit was brought agreed to repay a portion of their salaries to IBM.

Continuing its aggressive policy of suing former employees who leave the company to establish their own firms, IBM, on March 17, 1982, brought suit against five of its former employees and Cybernex, the company they had organized, alleging theft of IBM's trade secrets and unfair competition. In addition, IBM also sued the venture capitalists who had bankrolled the former employees, charging they, too, had knowledge of the misappropriation of IBM's trade secrets.

The complaint alleged that the misappropriation involved the principal component of a computer disk storage device known as the "head." The component is used to "read" and "write" data on the disk's surface. The president of Cybernex denied that his company's process for manufacturing thin film heads was based on IBM's trade secrets. In its complaint IBM alleged that it had spent more than $200 million over fourteen years, and thousands of hours by hundreds of employees had been expended, to develop a technologically advanced thin film head. The technological breakthrough that had been achieved, IBM argued, enabled it to produce tiny heads which perform with extraordinary accuracy and reliability and represented a signal improvement over previous "ferrite head" technology both in price and performance. The complaint noted that IBM had taken extensive precautions to safeguard the trade secrets developed at its San Jose division in the Silicon Valley. It observed that the five defendants had been key IBM employees and "comprised a critical element of the core management and engineering teams" working on the thin film head. Cybernex was accused of misappropriating virtually the entire IBM process for making recording heads. Cybernex had set up its San Jose, Calif., production facility in less than eight months and had begun shipping prototypes of its products less than a year after that. IBM charged: "it is inconceivable that an organization could have duplicated IBM's thin-film head production process without access to IBM trade secrets and confidential information, especially in the short period the founder defendants and Cybernex devoted to this effort."

William Klein, a cofounder and president of Cybernex, responds: "About ten companies make this product. We have independently developed what we think is a much better process than most of them have, and many of the people involved never worked for IBM." Moreover, the complaint declared the five defendants had each signed an agreement stipulating that during and following their employment with IBM they would not disclose to anyone outside the company, or themselves make use of, confidential, proprietary information except by written permission.

A suit by Texas Instruments against Compaq Computer, a company founded by several former TI employees led by Joseph Canion, who left TI in 1981, is not unlike the Cybernex litigation. Canion and his colleagues organized Compaq to manufacture and market a personal computer. TI indignantly proclaims this was not another manifestation of American entrepreneurial innovation but plain corporate theft of TI's proprietary information. TI accuses its former employees of stealing company trade secrets and infringing on a number of TI patents. In a countersuit, Compaq alleges that TI's patents were invalid and unenforceable; hence (it contends) there was no patent infringement. Moreover, in its countersuit Compaq argues that TI's complaint that trade secrets were purloined is invalid as "none of the former TI employees were requested to divulge or use any confidential information of TI in their work for Compaq."

In her distinguished recent book *Secrets,* Sissela Bok pinpoints the problem of an employee's loyalty to the company which employed him:

> Such loyalty may be entirely appropriate; but like all practices of secrecy it becomes morally problematic when it brings individuals into the secret who are thereby hampered, injured, or rendered less free. This can happen when employees, sometimes even without prior knowledge or consent, learn facts that make it more difficult for them to leave their place of employment; or when a condition of employment is that any inventions or innovations by the employee become the property of the employer. . . . When any

123

important technological secret is shared, those who share it may thereby be less free. As with the sharing of certain other secrets, they risk bondage, not just bonds, especially since secrets, once learned, cannot easily be unlearned.[3]

Professor Bok cites a suit brought by B. F. Goodrich Company against the former manager of its space-suit division, Donald Wohlgemuth, as an example of the "bondage" she deplores. He had left the company to join a rival firm, International Latex, which had been awarded the major space-suit subcontract for the Apollo program. In a suit seeking an injunction to prevent Wohlgemuth from working in the space-suit field for *any* other company, Dr. Bok quotes a commentator:

> At the appeals court level, the Goodrich brief sought an injunction that would prevent Wohlgemuth's disclosure of *any* information on space-suit technology to *anyone,* prevent his consulting or conferring with *anyone* on Goodrich trade secrets, and finally, prevent *any* future contact he might seek with Goodrich employees.
> These four broad measures were rejected by the Ohio Court of Appeals. . . . The court did provide an injunction restraining Wohlgemuth from disclosure of Goodrich trade secrets. In passing, the court noted that in the absence of any Goodrich employment contract restraining his employment with a competitor, Wohlgemuth could commence work with Latex.[4]

Non-Disclosure Agreements

Companies are increasingly endeavoring to combat copying of products by competitors who hire away their key employees by requiring them to sign non-disclosure agreements.

Among Silicon Valley's most aggressive companies in demanding that its employees sign non-disclosure agreements is Intel Corp., whose key employees during recent years have departed to start up a half-dozen competing firms. Each of Intel's 19,400 employees—from the janitor on up—is required to sign a confidentiality agreement. Intel, according to its general counsel, Roger S. Borovy, has developed a "golden rule of trade secrets": "Don't let your employees do to you what you did to your former boss!" (Intel was formed by former employees of Fairchild Camera and Instrument Corp., itself a spin-off of the Shockley Semiconductor Laboratories.)

When employees leave Intel, its legal department conducts an "exit interview," during which the departing worker is requested to sign a form acknowledging he has "acquired knowledge or had access to trade secrets and proprietary information . . ."

The departing employee's supervisor also attends. "We discuss the areas the employee was and wasn't involved in, and sort of negotiate if there are any issues. This is just sort of a last warning, a reminder," Borovy said.

When key employees join a competitor, Intel sometimes sends a letter both to the employee and his new employer, reminding them of the confidentiality agreement.

These tactics, however, have not deterred key Intel employees from leaving the company to start their own companies. In January 1983, several employees resigned and announced the formation of their own company. All refused to sign the confidentiality or non-disclosure agreement. The leader of the group was Casey Powell, Intel's former general manager of microprocessing. He and the other two leaders of the departing group were responsible for operations that represented about 20 percent of Intel's revenues.

Borovy said he intended to "see what their product line is" before deciding whether to sue Powell and his new company. Powell is now president of the newly formed company, called Sequel, a name which, in the Silicon Valley, brings to mind another spinoff of Intel, Seeq. Two weeks after Seeq was organized in January, 1981, it was sued by Intel. "We concluded that it was inevitable they had to use our technology. They were going to make two of Intel's hottest products," according to Borovy. Among Seeq's founders were Intel's former managers of marketing and engineering. After a year of pre-trial skirmishing, the two sides negotiated an out-of-court settlement in which Seeq agreed to maintain for a year technology processes that were demonstrably different from Intel's and would not hire away any key Intel personnel for a year.

The "first line of defense," says Thomas D. Kiley, vice-president for legal affairs of Genentech, Inc. (a San Francisco-based genetics engineering firm), against losing trade secrets or having to engage in unfair competition law suits, is to foster conditions that discourage key employees from seeking employment elsewhere. Daniel G. Wendin, associate counsel of Apple Computer in Cupertino, California, agrees. "The key is to offer them stock. And have the stock go up!"

Despite the contention of some executives that non-disclosure agreements cannot be enforced, the courts are upholding them. A Massachusetts court, for example, ordered Data Translation, Inc. to cease manufacturing and selling a data acquisition system that Analogic Corp., another small electronics company, claimed was nearly an exact duplication of its own product.[5] Data Translation's president and vice president were former Analogic executives. Analogic contended they used its trade secrets and marketing information in developing Data Translation's competing line of products.

Dirty Tricks

To ferret out a competitor's trade secrets, some companies resort to the corporate equivalent of "dirty tricks." A private investigator tells of a cleaning woman who was hired to separate the trash she collected at the chemical company where she was employed and sell it to a competitor who was searching for its rival's batch formula. It was found among discarded notes.

The president of a public relations firm reports that companies for whom he has worked had their employees pose at times as customers, shareholders, and security analysts to pry information out of competitors. To gain access to a competitor's premises some companies still resort to such time-worn ruses as sending an employee who poses as a "fire inspector" or a "telephone repairman." Printers and lithographers are fertile sources of information about upcoming products and promotions. Executives have been known to "feel out" direct mailers and cataloguers, who have a long lead-time and thus an advance look at what is coming on line, to ascertain what products and promotional plans the competition is contemplating.

Other private investigators have reported the use at conventions of "hostesses" who were primed to solicit certain kinds of information from salesmen and executives.[6]

For corporate Mata Haris there are available "brassieres that will listen" and transmit "any whisper exchanged between wearer and friend." A more advanced design is the "stereo bra," with a separate microphone in each cup that enables the wearer, seated in a bar, to transmit simultaneously conversations from both her left and right. In short, the bar girl who is hired to eavesdrop becomes a veritable broadcasting station.

Jacques Bergier observes that in the United States there are industrial espionage agents who specialize in spotting engineers and technicians "with heavy mortgages on their homes or who are otherwise living obviously beyond their means." Such individuals become easy targets for unscrupulous companies. Like all recruits for an espionage network, once they have accepted a payment for having supplied a piece of innocuous information—a telephone directory of headquarters personnel, for example—they are conditioned to purloin important and vital trade secrets.

Without question, says Raymond F. Forbes, a division marketing manager at Beckman Instruments, "tactics for keeping track of the competition are at times sneaky, may be even immoral or unethical. The line is drawn only when something might be illegal."

It needs to be emphasized, however, that the best source of information regarding trade secrets is neither a hired agent nor a greedy employee, but a loose tongue and a big mouth. Information garnered from a salesman, relaxing at a convention, or from visiting "firemen" being shown the hotspots at Las Vegas, who blab about what their companies are doing in defense work, R&D, or new investments, can be as revealing and obtained at far less expense than the information acquired from a concealed bug, wiretap or hired prostitute.

Legitimate Access to Trade Secrets

Not all trade secrets are acquired by theft, deceit, fraud or dirty tricks—or even employment of covert operations. Trade meetings, scientific seminars and professional junkets provide invaluable opportunities for technically-trained executives to pick the brains of colleagues employed by competitors.

Moreover, for most companies it is unnecessary to resort to subterfuge to obtain a competitor's trade secrets. A wealth of information can be found in published sources—trade journals, professional publications, company annual reports, securities analysts' studies of individual companies, news releases, interviews, promotional pamphlets and speeches by corporate officials. Indeed, the *Wall Street Journal* and the financial-business sections of the major U.S. newspapers are a cornucopia of leads and information for the trained reader. While these sources will usually provide only bits and pieces of information, an experienced intelligence analyst can put them together and discern significant clues regarding a competitor's plans, policies and expectations. The Soviet embassy in Washington is said to ship tons of American publications in the diplomatic pouch for perusal by Moscow industry specialists.

We tend to forget, if most of us ever knew, how much valuable intelligence is available for the asking. In his informative book on international espionage, *The Secret War,* Sanche de Gramont reminds us:

> Soviet defectors have estimated that a Soviet military attaché in the United States is able to obtain 95 percent of the material he needs simply by asking for it. The Government Printing Office supplies at a nominal cost such items as harbor installations of the United States, dimensions and locations of airfields, lists of United States mineral resources, registers of retired officers; in short, practically everything from "how to drive a nail" to "how to build an atom bomb." The Map Information Office of the U.S. Geological Survey, Department of the Interior, is another favorite source, and provides topographic maps of the entire United States. Subscriptions to technical magazines such as *Aviation Week* and *Bulletin of Atomic Scientists* are never allowed to lapse. Soviet diplomats also attend industrial conventions. . . . Publications such as *The Pilot's Handbook* or the eighteen-volume edition on port facilities put out by the Army Engineers would certainly be restricted in the Soviet Union—in the United States they are available to anyone.
>
> In April 1960, Vice Admiral Hyman G. Rickover told Congress's Joint Atomic Energy Subcommittee that a toy manufacturer had produced a model of the Polaris atomic submarine so accurate that "a good ship designer can spend one hour on that model and tell he has millions of dollars' worth of free information."

The notice that came with the $2.98 toy said:

> This ballistic firing nuclear submarine is another of a series of models built in strict accordance with specifications contained in official U.S. Navy Blueprints. We wish to take this opportunity to express our sincere gratitude to the Electric Boat Division of General Dynamics Corporation for generously furnishing complete and accurate data. Without this cooperation, the development of a completely authentic model would not have been possible. This model incorporates all the interior details of the submarine

including atomic reactor, control room galley, crew's quarters and two Polaris missiles. Your model is authentic in every detail and is accurately scaled to 1 foot = 300 feet.[7]

For many companies, their own worst enemy is the executive—not infrequently the CEO or chairman—who is a congenital blabbermouth and incapable of keeping a trade secret under tight security wraps. Consider a news item that appeared in the *Wall Street Journal* for December 17, 1982 on page 25. Argo Systems, Inc. of Sunnyvale, California, with justifiable pride but with a lamentable sense of security, apparently itself announced—presumably in a news release or perhaps in an interview given by its CEO—that it had developed a "receiver technology that can find hidden military signals, even when the transmitter skips rapidly from one frequency to another. The technology, called instantaneous direction finding, enables a receiver to scan a broad range of frequencies at once and automatically reconstruct those coming from the direction of the enemy." To keep battlefield communications secret, most major nations have devised methods to spread a message across the radio spectrum, sending only brief fragments of it over any one frequency. By using this technique, the sender can effectively conceal military transmissions by disguising them as part of the ordinary, unintelligible clutter on the airwaves emanating from commercial television, radio, radar and satellite transmitters. Argo Systems, as the preceding quotation from the *Wall Street Journal* makes clear, has developed a device that is capable of "unscrambling" a disguised military transmission. Obviously, possession of such an instrument can be of supreme importance to a nation hostile to the United States. And, obviously, by blabbing about its discovery Argo Systems has become a target of espionage not only for the KGB but for an army of commercial espionage agents armed with Minox cameras.

Use of Consultants

Outside consultants have created a flourishing industry supplying information-hungry clients with market data, competitors' price changes and general competitive economic intelligence.
Such well-known consulting organizations as Arthur D. Little, Battelle, and Booz, Allen and Hamilton systematically furnish

scientific, demographic, income, age and other data on how a client's product compares with those of its competitors.

Even in the sensitive oil exploration business, Petroleum Information Corp., a Denver-based intelligence service, has succeeded in persuading companies to forego an old industry habit of keeping well data to themselves and of depending on their own intelligence-gathering facilities.

To the ranks of conventional management consultants there has recently been added a growing number of "political risk" consultants whose members are former intelligence officers or former government officials with close ties to the intelligence community. Prominent among these new political risk consultants are Henry Kissinger, former Secretary of State; Brent Scowcroft, a retired Air Force general who was Dr. Kissinger's deputy and later his successor as National Security Adviser; William E. Colby and Richard Helms, both former Directors of the Central Intelligence Agency; and Ray C. Kline, a former CIA Station Chief in Taiwan and the agency's former Deputy Director of Intelligence.

Political risk analysis is a vital component of managerial overseas investment decision-making. It is a function of intelligence assessment. Whether or not a company should invest in Brazil or Taiwan, Mexico or Nigeria, Gabon or the Philippines depends on a number of factors. The country's political stability, the influence of the military establishment in the country's political affairs and economic development, the culture, customs, traditions, ideological predilections, and economic and political sophistication of the regime in power, and especially its attitude towards enforcement of written contracts—these and similar considerations have been the stuff of political risk intelligence assessments. Some managements have developed elaborate criteria to assist them in evaluating the elements of political risk; others depend on an instinctive sense that enables them to detect the direction on the political spectrum in which a country is moving and its hospitality for foreign investment.

The involvement of such "superstars" as Messrs. Kissinger, Colby and Helms in political risk consulting may have introduced into the conventional managerial practice of political risk analysis an element of "influence peddling." Their entree to foreign leaders may be more appealing than their advice, as Peter H. Stone observes in his perceptive article in the *New York Times*

(August 7, 1983). Moreover, the fees of this new breed of management consultant are not cheap; they may start at a few thousand dollars and exceed $100,000 per assignment. (Dr. Kissinger's New York-Washington firm charges $100,000 for a consultation—with or without his personal participation.)

Some of the new political risk consulting firms have added to their intelligence assessments such additional services as "kidnapping negotiations" and "removal" of extortion threats. One such firm advises its clients on how to cope with violence in countries in which they have located their subsidiaries, as well as providing training and protection for overseas branch managers. "We sometimes suggest hardware for companies," said the director.

Comparison Shopping

Competitors are subjected to comparison shopping by some companies in the same way that customers make comparisons between competitive products and merchandise. Many banks—Chase Manhattan is an example—have their employees open accounts in competing banks in order to evaluate their services. Outside organizations are utilized for comparison shopping of a bank's own branches.

Reverse Engineering

Major manufacturers, such as the automobile companies, for years have routinely examined in detail their competitor's models as they appeared in the marketplace. "It's no secret that we buy damn near all our competitors' products and tear them down to the last bolt," a spokesman for General Motors declared. "They're gone over with a fine comb. It's good business."

Breaking down a competitor's product in this fashion is known as "reverse engineering," a technique so common throughout U.S. industry that the courts have generally found the practice to be competitively acceptable and not an assault on trade secrets. The Supreme Court of the United States in *Kewanee Oil Co. v. Bicron Corp.,* 416 U.S. 470, 476 (1974) held that:

> trade secret law . . . does not offer protection against discovery
> by fair and honest means, such as by independent invention, acci-
> dental disclosure, or by so-called reverse engineering, that is by
> starting with [a] known product and working backward to divine
> the process which aided in its development or manufacture.

Reverse engineering has long been utilized by Japanese manufacturers not only to duplicate products manufactured in the
West but as a means for the improvement of their own competing
products.

The Soviets are not far behind the Japanese in utilizing reverse
engineering as a method for the acquisition of Western technology. Moscow's marketing specialists selected as the moniker for
the Soviet's first personal computer the English "Agatha," but
Western wags jokingly refer to the new computer as *Yabloka,*
or "apple" in Russian—which should have been the new computer's rightful name rather than Agatha inasmuch as Apple Computer Inc.'s Apple II was the model used by Soviet computer
engineers as their prototype. Apple II now joins IBM's System/
360 and Digital Equipment Corp.'s PDP series among the products pirated by the Soviets through reverse engineering.

Although there is widespread industrial and judicial tolerance
in the United States for reverse engineering, in our view the
practice constitutes theft of a trade secret.

Freedom of Information Requests to Tap Proprietary Information

Perhaps the most "legitimate" source from which confidential
industry information can be obtained is the federal government,
which for regulatory and contractual purposes requires public
corporations—and even many private companies—to make extensive disclosures regarding their products, finances and operations. Hence, various agencies of the government are repositories
of considerable confidential information, knowledge of which
can be useful to business competitors.[8]

Corporate executives—and, indeed, the KGB[9]—have become adept in extracting some of this confidential information by utilizing the Freedom of Information Act. Although this statute was
enacted in 1966 primarily to assist the media and the public to

learn about the operations of the Washington government, in actual practice the law has been more useful to businesses seeking information about their competitors. Former Food and Drug Commissioner Alexander Schmidt recently disclosed that 90 percent of the requests for FDA documents fall into the category of "industrial espionage."[10] Requests for Freedom of Information data have increased from 2,600 in 1974 to 32,000 in 1979. Of this latter number, 86 percent originated with industry, service companies and attorneys. Only 10 percent of such requests were from individuals, the media and public interest groups—the intended beneficiaries of the law.

Procter and Gamble, the consumer-products company, contends that a competitor gained access in 1980 to one of its valuable trade secrets through a Freedom of Information request to the Food and Drug Administration. At issue was a chemical treatment of operating-room surgical drapes that allowed them to be sterilized safely.

Although Procter and Gamble had submitted two sets of documents to the FDA in seeking the agency's approval of the chemical—including one set for public release with the chemical formula blanked out—the bureaucrats at the FDA released both sets of documents to a P&G competitor who had filed a Freedom of Information request for the data.

With possession of the chemical formula, P&G's rival was, in effect, able to market P&G's chemical treatment for surgical drapes as if it were the product of its own research and development.

Procter and Gamble's plight was not unique. According to a 1980 study by a University of Oregon scholar, 37 percent of Freedom of Information queries submitted to 29 federal agencies (not including the FBI and CIA) were directed to the Food and Drug Administration.

This anomalous situation creates a critical predicament for many corporate managements, especially those in the pharmaceutical industry. Before a marketing campaign can be undertaken, FDA product approval must be obtained. To secure such approval, trade secrets are frequently submitted to the agency in the expectation—illusory, as it turns out—that their confidentiality will be safeguarded. But the competition, with no more cost than a postage stamp, can obtain such confidential, proprietary information by means of a Freedom of Information request and thereby nullify a marketing plan, not to speak of acquiring other valuable economic and financial data.

We believe this inequitable situation prevails in part because the FDA disregards a provision of the Freedom of Information Act which in plain English declares: "trade secrets and commercial or financial information obtained from a person and privileged and confidential" are exempt from disclosure (5 USCA paragraph 552[b] [4]). In part—the greater part—the FDA releases trade secrets because the functionaries who deal with Freedom of Information requests for the release of such data are unaware of the nature and range of corporate trade secrets. In their hands, proprietary and innocuous information are confused. It is not without interest that other countries with Freedom of Information legislation are able to protect confidential, proprietary information submitted to governmental departments and agencies. Sweden, for example, provides protection for certain banking, financial and stock exchange data, labor relations material, price and trade competitive information and other trade activities. Similar protection is provided under Freedom of Information statutes in Holland, France, West Germany and Great Britain.

This predicament could be resolved administratively were the FDA to enact a rule similar to the Securities and Exchange Commission's Rule 0–4, promulgated under the Securities Exchange Act of 1934, which prohibits officers and employees of the Commission from making public confidential information or documents unless specific authorization for their release is obtained from the Commission or it is determined that the release of such information or documents is not "contrary to the public interest." If the SEC is able to protect corporate registrants from unauthorized disclosure of their trade secrets, the FDA could emulate a sister agency and thereby restore respect for its discredited administrative procedures.

Computer Espionage and Theft

The meteoric growth in the use of computer data processing over the past 25 years has opened a new and fruitful area for corporate espionage. In addition to their susceptibility to competitive espionage, computer-stored data, as many companies have learned to their dismay, are extremely vulnerable to theft and manipulation by a new type of corporate criminal—the computer thief. Dana B. Parker, a computer crime expert, states that, of more than four thousand cases of computer-related crime he has documented, 30 percent involved penetration of computer systems for the purpose of manipulating data or to scrutinize secret information.

Computer systems can be invaded by a specialist with no more difficulty than having access to a computer terminal and a telephone. Indeed, computer larceny can be committed, in *Time* magazine's phrase, "from the comfort of [a] living room." As Thomas Whiteside observes in *Computer Capers: Tales of Electronic Embezzlement and Fraud,* penetration of a computer actually presents an intellectual challenge to the computer criminal: "it is a form of breaking and entering in which the burglar's tools are essentially an understanding of the logical structure of and logical flaws inherent in particular programming and processing systems."

Computer security consultants reiterate that no computer as yet has been built that cannot be penetrated. Even the Pentagon's own security-enveloped Worldwide Military Command and Control System computers have been invaded by U.S. military computer specialists, seeking to learn whether the military establishment's computers could be penetrated by a hostile nation's espionage agents. As Dana Parker puts it, "the perfectly secure computer is one you can't use."

Stanley Mark Rifkin, a talented computer analyst in Los Angeles, epitomizes the new breed of computer criminal. Apparently for the sheer mental delight it afforded him, he manipulated the computers at the Security Pacific National Bank into disgorging $10 million. Arrested for the crime and while still free on bail, as if to thumb his nose at the authorities, he was again arrested for attempting to steal $50 million from the computers of Union Bank!

The Soviets were quick to appreciate that computer penetration could extend vastly the shadowy world of industrial and military espionage. By means of a sophisticated penetration, Soviet computer specialists, working at a private research institution in Austria, succeeded in linking their computers to the highly advanced U.S.-built Cray-1, in Britain, and were able to obtain "complex calculations for nuclear weapons design." In 1981, Soviet experts successfully established a computer link to a secret Lockheed facility in Sunnyvale, California, to tap that company's aviation and weaponry trade secrets, and were forced to discontinue the tap only after the CIA had discovered it.

The FBI was successful in exposing a New York City businessman, turned computer criminal, who was using a terminal in his office to burglarize information stored in a competitor's computer in California. By employing a password, obtained illicitly from an employee in the competitor's firm, he was able to tap into a special time-sharing network and read his rival's marketing surveys, budget forecasts and pricing policies—in short to scrutinize the sensitive information that enabled his rival to enjoy a competitive advantage.

Many computers are vulnerable to manipulation through remote diagnostics—a method whereby one computer diagnoses the problems afflicting another. Owing to the prohibitive cost of maintaining technicians in the field for servicing computers that are "down," computer manufacturers diagnose the ailments of their purchaser's computers from their corporate headquarters over a telephone line and provide a prescription telephonically. It is at this juncture that remote diagnostics lends itself to abuse. An unscrupulous computer operator, on his own or acting as an espionage agent, using the cover of a manufacturer's "rep," can use remote diagnostics to scrutinize or extract trade secrets.

Breaking into the data bank of the Federal Reserve Board's computer presents no difficulties—at least for a former E. F. Hutton economist, T. C. Langevin, who tapped into the Federal Reserve's data bank by telephone. He was in search of advance weekly projections of the U.S. money supply, information which was invaluable to him in his job as a forecaster of Federal Reserve Board policy on interest rates. Short-term interest rates often rise or fall on the basis of what the Federal Reserve Board reports, resulting in pronounced swings in the price of stocks and bonds. Hence, anyone with advance knowledge of what the Federal Reserve Board's report is likely to contain is in a position to reap huge profits by buying or selling. Such in essence was Langevin's scheme. It was a model of simplicity in its execution. The brokerage firm's computer has a telephone modem, a device that translates computer bits into signals that can be transmitted over phone lines. The Federal Reserve Board's computer operates in a similar manner. Using the access code of a Federal Reserve Board employee, Langevin put his terminal in touch with the

Fed's data bank and was able to rifle the central bank's files.

Langevin's ruse was discovered a day later. His illegal tap had been recorded on a log maintained by the computer and printed out daily. In scanning the printout, a supervisor discovered that the Fed employee whose access number Langevin had used was on vacation. A trap was set for Langevin. The Federal Reserve Board's computer was rigged to supply fictitious money-supply data and a tracing device attached to the computer telephone line. On his next call, Langevin was caught.[11]

The disturbing implications of this instance of computer theft are all too clear: confidential government information, some of it private data on individuals—income tax files, for example—stored in computer data banks is no longer secure from scrutiny, manipulation or theft by a skillful computer criminal.

Computer Pranksters

Not all computer penetration has theft as its primary objective. Some types of penetration, perpetrated by hackers, as computer fiddlers are known in the trade, take delight in making a computer use language that would cause a longshoreman to blush. When, one day, U.S. Leasing International Inc.'s typically well-behaved computer, whose only language was staid computerese, started talking dirty, the computer specialists knew they had a problem. It stated to one of the company's operators, "The Phantom, the system cracker, strikes again . . . Soon I will zero (expletive deleted) your desks and your backups on System A. I have already cracked your System B. Have fun trying to restore it, you (obscenity)." Some other uncomplimentary, non-printable, anatomically impossible suggestions were made as to what the operator could do with various pieces of computer equipment.

The culprit was a bright 20-year-old computer hacker who had secretly fiddled with U.S. Leasing's computer by telephone from Los Angeles to show off his computer expertise. He was not satisfied with being just a prankster; he had done obvious damage. Important inventory files, which allowed leasing subsidiaries to keep track of their equipment, had been destroyed. U.S. Leasing spent thousands of dollars wiping out the hacker's profanity so as to restore its computer to normal.

Hackers, who enjoy browsing over the electronic byways of

the country, find help from an underground network of electronic bulletin boards suspended in computer circuits around the country. By leaving messages on these bulletin boards, hackers can swap passwords, identification numbers and computer phone numbers to assist them in penetrating company computer systems. One such bulletin board carried detailed instructions for invading a key computer system operated by Pacific Telephone and Telegraph Co. in Los Angeles. "Tap," an underground computer newsletter with a New York City mailing address, also offers tips to hackers on computer penetration. Its March 1983 issue gives the telephone number and other entry details for the penetration of a university's computer.[12]

Computer yahoos, who electronically invade other people's computers, usually for the challenge or delight it affords them, have become an increasing problem for business, in large part as a consequence of the proliferation of home computers and growing computer expertise among amateur users. "People don't realize the extent to which their systems are being broken into," says Clifton M. Garrott, Los Angeles deputy district attorney for electronic crimes, who prosecuted the U.S. Leasing case.

Dubious Business Conduct and Illegal Espionage Operations: A Summary

U.S. business resorts to economic intelligence and uses espionage methods that raise questions regarding their propriety and legality. For its intelligence sources and espionage practices U.S. industry relies on:[13]

1. Published materials and public documents, e.g., court records and government reports
2. Disclosures made by employees and obtained without subterfuge
3. Market surveys and consultants' reports
4. Financial reports and securities analysts' research surveys of individual companies; annual company reports; interviews and speeches by corporate executives
5. Trade fairs, exhibits, and competitors' brochures
6. Analyses of competitors' products (i.e., reverse engineering); comparison shopping; and special consultants' reports
7. Reports by salesmen and purchasing agents

The foregoing methods are considered to be ethical.

8. Employment interviews with individuals who worked for a competitor (during which the discussion touches on the competitor's know-how, manufacturing costs and other proprietary information)
9. Camouflaged questioning and "drawing out" of competitors' employees at technical meetings
10. Direct observation of a device or piece of equipment clandestinely (usually involving surreptitious photography)
11. False job interviews with a competitor's employee (i.e., where there is no real intention to hire)
12. Breach of confidentiality in negotiations for a licensing agreement (in which access to a trade secret is acquired and pirated)
13. Hiring a professional investigator to obtain a trade secret or using prostitutes for the same purpose
14. Hiring an employee away from a competitor to obtain specific know-how or other trade secrets
15. Trespassing on a competitor's property in the course of a clandestine espionage operation
16. Bribing a competitor's supplier or employee to obtain trade secrets
17. Planting an agent on a competitor's payroll for the purpose of securing trade secrets
18. Eavesdropping on competitors (e.g., by wiretapping or bugging)
19. Theft of drawings, samples, documents and similar confidential property belonging to a competitor
20. Blackmail of key employees, who have been deliberately compromised through a sexual indiscretion, in order to obtain trade secrets
21. Penetrating a competitor's computer system to scrutinize, manipulate or extract secret, proprietary information

The foregoing methods (8 through 21) run the gamut from dubious business conduct to outright corporate crime.

9

The Soviet Use of Worldwide
Industrial Espionage

I<small>T</small> is important that American business executives understand that the most effective and unremitting industrial espionage comes not from their business competitors but from a hostile foreign power: the Soviet Union.

The leadership of the Soviet Union has traditionally regarded industrial espionage "as an indispensable component of their own scientific research and development."[1] In carrying out this objective, John Barron writes, "the Soviet Union, largely through the KGB, has succeeded in transforming American research, development, inventiveness and productive genius into a major national resource of the Soviet state."[2]

To appreciate how this singular, brilliantly executed and unparalleled feat has been accomplished, it is essential to comprehend the structure and functions of the Soviet agency primarily responsible for carrying out this extraordinary achievement—the Committee for State Security, universally known by its Russian initials KGB from *Komitet Gosudarstvennoi Bezopasnosti.*

In addition to acting as the Soviet eyes and ears for collecting foreign intelligence, the KGB, like its predecessor organizations from the time of Czar Ivan the Terrible and his *Oprichniki,* also serves as an internal secret police—perhaps its most important activity. Throughout its numerous transformations—it has been known as the Cheka, GPU, OGPU, NKVD, NKGB, MGG and, since 1954, the KGB—the Soviet secret service has been an instrument of intimidation, harrassment, coercion, torture, assassination, subversion, terror, midnight arrests and executions in the notorious Lubyanka prison. The KGB is the most dreaded and feared body in the Soviet Union.

The Structure of the KGB

The KGB is organized into five Chief Directorates, divided into "Services," "Departments" and various numbered directorates. Overseas espionage operations are conducted by the First Chief Directorate, which is reputed to have a corps of a hundred thousand professionally trained officers with military rank. The Second Chief Directorate is responsible for counterintelligence; it provides the muscle that keeps the population of an authoritarian state in line. Its tentacles reach into every city, town, village and collective farm throughout the Soviet Union. Officers from the Third Directorate are assigned to every army unit, down to the company level, for the purpose of detecting signs of incipient dissidence or deviation from the current party line.

An unnumbered Border Guards Directorate—a headquarters unit which is considered to be a Chief Directorate—supplies an estimated three hundred to four hundred thousand troops, with their own tank units, armored vehicle detachments, helicopters, and high-speed patrol vessels, for guard duty along the thirty-seven thousand miles of barbed wire, no-man's land and waterways that mark the sealed borders of the Soviet Union's far-flung empire. The Border Guards are an elite military force, who are honored by a special holiday known as "Border Guard Day." The distinctive forest green uniform of the *pogranichnik*—Border Guard soldier—with its smart garrison cap and conspicuous shoulder boards, distinguishes him from his compatriot in the nondescript uniform of the regular Red Army.

Despite their high-powered weaponry, the Border Guards are not intended to be used to repel an invader—that job is reserved for the regular Soviet armed forces. The real function of the Border Guards is to prevent Soviet citizens from escaping across the borders into the West's open societies.

The KGB's Fifth Chief Directorate is responsible for policing and infiltrating dissident groups. Known as the "dissident" or "ideological" directorate, it is "widely despised among KGB officers" because of the disreputable methods and practices it follows, such as, for example, forcibly confining dissidents to "psychiatric" wards where they are reduced to vegetables. It is worth mentioning in passing that this activity was established by Yuri Andropov during his tenure as chairman of the Committee for State Security. This is the same Yuri Andropov who is being hailed in some quarters as a "closet liberal," an "admirer of American jazz," a man of "Western tastes, with a fondness for whiskey," and with "intellectual discrimination and tolerance"—all of which he managed to accomplish, overnight, as it were, with the enthusiastic cooperation of the U.S. media.

The Eighth Chief Directorate develops cipher and cryptographic systems for both the KGB and the Ministry of Foreign Affairs, and maintains the secrecy of government communications inside the Soviet Union. Personnel of this directorate monitor, intercept and decipher foreign communications, utilizing in this effort satellites, ships, and special installations within Soviet embassies.

The KGB runs the Soviet prisons and forced labor camps—the notorious *Gulags*—and supplies financial and technical aid to Middle East terrorist groups, e.g. Black September. The infamous terrorist "Carlos," sometimes known as "The Jackal" (but whose true name is Ilich Ramirez Sanchez), was trained by and has long been affiliated with the KGB, which not only directs and manages his terrorist activities but on occasion "leases" his services to various Middle East terrorist organizations.

A specially trained unit from the Seventh Directorate continuously maintains surveillance over all major embassies (but particularly the American) and Western diplomats and business executives stationed in Moscow, as well as anyone suspected of being a foreign intelligence officer.

The Ninth Directorate furnishes KGB military detachments that provide security for ports, railroads, factories, communications and nuclear facilities; bodyguards for the leading members of the Soviet hierarchy; and the elite troops that guard the Kremlin.

Since the earliest days of the Russian revolution, secret assassination has been an official instrument of state policy. This function is assigned to a special "Executive Action" unit in Service

"H" of the KGB's First Chief Directorate. This unit has responsibility for planning and carrying out assassinations. It selects and trains assassins; chooses their weapons; and determines whether it will be a conventional firearm, poison gun, knife, grenade, handheld rocket (with the explosive power of an artillery shell), or gas, fired from a special ejector gun (exposing the assassin to the same certain death as the victim unless an antidote pill is swallowed in time to immunize the killer from the effects of the poison). The Executive Action section plans the getaway and, above all, makes certain that the actual assassination is not traced to the Soviet government. Agents assigned to the Executive Action unit are expert in staging fatal vehicle crashes that appear to be accidents. They are specialists in unarmed combat who know how to deliver a fatal body blow. Agents are trained in sabotage and subversion, enabling them to paralyze a country's communications and transportation systems.

Allen Dulles observes in *The Craft of Intelligence,* his authoritative account of the organization and operation of contemporary secret intelligence services, that the KGB "is more than a secret organization, more than an intelligence and counterintelligence organization. It is an instrument of subversion, manipulation and violence, for secret intervention in the affairs of other countries."[3]

Dulles' indictment of the KGB was borne out by an incident that occurred recently in Switzerland. In late April 1983, the Swiss government expelled a Soviet journalist and closed the Bern office of the Soviet news agency Novosti on the grounds it had become a center of subversion and agitation, including organization of anti-nuclear demonstrations. In a protest lodged with the Soviet Embassy, the government said that Alexei Dumov, head of Novosti in Switzerland, directed his staff in Bern to engage in "continued gross interference with Swiss affairs incompatible with journalistic work."

A strongly-worded communiqué charged that these activities ranged from helping to organize rallies for nuclear disarmament to "paramilitary training" of youthful demonstrators. The Swiss government also charged that Novosti advised and supported men refusing to serve in the Swiss army. In both Switzerland and the Soviet Union, conscientious objectors are subject to jail sentences.

"Disinformation" as a technique for spreading false information has been developed by the Soviets into an art form. Responsibility for planning and executing deception operations rests with Service "A" of the KGB's First Chief Directorate. The KGB spreads disinformation through Soviet "journalists," academicians and scientists, by its own operatives posing as diplomats, by planting articles in the foreign press, by the use of clandestine radio stations, and by manipulating foreign communist parties and international front groups, e.g., the various Soviet friendship societies, the Afro-Asian People's Solidarity Organization, and the World Federation of Trade Unions.

One of the latest—as this is written—Soviet disinformation ploys is a worldwide campaign directed against United Nations Ambassador Jeane Kirkpatrick in which Soviet publications maliciously accuse her of such misdeeds as taking political payments from South Africa. That this scurrilous effort will silence Ambassador Kirkpatrick is improbable. To counter Soviet propaganda thrusts such as this U.S. overseas diplomatic missions are now receiving "propaganda alerts" from Washington to inform them of the latest stories spread by the KGB disinformation specialists.

The Russian secret service has a long history of forging documents, having concocted the *Protocols of Zion* over seventy-five years ago, under the Czar, to promote anti-Semitism. The KGB has followed the Czarist tradition, using forgeries to discredit the West, and the United States in particular, to sow discord and suspicion among the Western allies and to drive a wedge between the peoples of the Third World and the industrialized nations. Proposals for forgeries may originate either in KGB headquarters at Moscow Center or in the local KGB *rezidentura*. Depending on its sensitivity and importance, approval for a forgery will be obtained from the KGB leadership, the International Department of the Central Committee of the Communist Party, or the Secretariat of the Central Committee itself. KGB specialists prepare a forgery under the supervision of the KGB's First Chief Directorate. Although any KGB agent or asset may be used to circulate the forged document, the chief of the KGB residency's active measures group controls the operation.[4]

Although the Soviets have developed considerable proficiency in fabricating U.S. government documents, even their best forgeries can be unmasked by expert analysis. Some errors are readily apparent in that the phraseology is stilted, disclosing that the forgery was not prepared by native-born speakers of American English. British spellings may occur in purported American documents, for example the British spelling of "manoeuvre" instead of the American "maneuver." In a forgery of a purported U.S. Department of Commerce memorandum, dated February 18, 1982, the Secretary's name is misspelled. As the Department of State points out, "while these linguistic flaws may not be evident to the target audience, especially in non-English speaking areas, they are important clues in establishing lack of authenticity."

The KGB is not, as is sometimes mistakenly assumed in the West, an autonomous organization. Its interlocking network of intelligence-gathering, espionage and secret police functions is designed to further the political objectives of the Soviet Communist Party. The chairman of the world's largest spy and state security machine is appointed by and is responsive to the party leadership. Although he directed the KBG for fifteen years, and before then, for much of his adult life, had been a henchman of the secret police, Andropov is no ordinary policeman or intelligence functionary. In their masterful political biography, *Andropov: New Challenge to the West,*[5] Arnold Beichmann and Mikhail S. Bernstam make crystal clear that Yuri Andropov is a tough, ruthless, amoral Soviet *apparatchik*—a survivor of Stalin's purges and executions, as well as a participant in their bloody implementation.

How did Andropov manage to obtain control over the key center of Soviet power? It may be reasonably surmised that Andropov succeeded by calling in a pocketful of political IOUs, acquired over more than a decade of having access to the secret dossiers on the Soviet leadership and their families—even Brezhnev's family (his daughter's corrupt activities, in particular). In a word, Andropov had knowledge of where the bodies were buried—and, most importantly, whose bodies they were. But there was more to his reach for total power: with Brezhnev's heir-apparent, Konstantin Chernenko, waiting in the wings to be anointed, it required exceptional—in fact, brilliant—political skill for Andropov to manipulate the diverse, antagonistic factions and power centers residing in the Politburo so as to have himself designated the new *Vozhd*—the leader: General Secretary of the CPSU. This role makes the incumbent nominally first among equals but in reality the supreme ruler of the Soviet Union. The deals made by, and the promises extracted from, Andropov in effectuating his bid for total power will necessarily remain unknown and the subject of speculation by Sovietologists—until one or more of the Soviet leaders disclose them in their memoirs.

Many intelligence experts consider the KGB, next to or along with the Israeli secret service, the Mossad, to be the most effective intelligence organization in existence.[6]

The KGB and Western Technology

The KGB's First Directorate is believed by Western intelligence experts to have some twenty thousand highly-trained specialists whose primary function is to identify the location of and acquire Western (but especially U.S.) technology for use in Soviet weaponry systems and by Soviet industries.

Soviet industry has long depended for its major innovations on Western technology, primarily U.S. technology, obtained at times by legitimate procurement, but more often clandestinely. U.S. Assistant Defense Secretary Richard Perle estimates that 150 Soviet weapon systems, among them the SS-20s aimed at European capitals, are based on Western technology, most of it acquired by theft and deceit, let alone the West's own careless security.

To cite but one example of the military use to which the Soviets put technology obtained from the West: in 1972, a U.S. company, Bryant Chucking Grinder Co., sold 164 precision grinding machines to the Soviet Union over the sharp, but ineffectual, protest of the U.S. intelligence community, who understood all too well that these machines would be used to produce small, high-precision ball bearings which would give the Soviets a more accurate missile guidance system than would have been possible with the use of indigenous Soviet equipment. As a consequence of allowing the Soviets to purchase these grinding machines, the United States was forced to "harden" its missile silos and then to devise the controversial MX basing scheme. In sum, the United States will be obliged to spend billions of dollars to improve its own defenses as a consequence of a blunder of its own making. For Washington's bureaucracy to have allowed the Soviets to acquire these grinding machines was worse than a crime: it was stupid.

Lagging behind the West and Japan in technological innovation, the Soviets are endeavoring to close the gap by a massive industrial espionage operation led by the KGB.

In the United States, the major centers for Soviet espionage are located at:

—the Soviet Mission to the United Nations at 136 East 67th Street in New York City

—the Soviet Embassy at 1125 Sixteenth Street, N.W., in Washington, D.C.

—the Soviet Consulate at 2790 Green Street, San Francisco, California

In addition to its own professionally-trained agents, the KGB draws on the military professionals from *Glavnoye Razvedyvatelnoye Upravleniye* (GRU), the Chief Intelligence Directorate of the Soviet General Staff, who supply military attachés to the Soviet diplomatic missions as well as "illegal" operatives.

Viktor Suvorov (an assumed name of a former high-ranking Soviet officer who defected to the West and now lives in London under the protection of the British Secret Service) writes in his authoritative book *Inside the Soviet Army* that the GRU "carries out espionage on a scale unparalleled in history. It is enough to record that during World War II the GRU was able, with its own resources, to penetrate the German General Staff from Switzerland and to steal nuclear secrets from the United States, and that after the war it was able to induce France to leave NATO, besides carrying out many less risky operations . . . the Head of the GRU has two separate world-wide intelligence organizations, a colossal number of electronic intelligence centres [and] centrally controlled diversionary units." In short, the GRU may well have an intelligence operation which in size and scope exceeds that of the KGB.

Suvorov observes that "the Soviet intelligence services, the largest in the world, search unceasingly for anything new in the field of military equipment. The enormous extent of Soviet activity in this sphere beggars description. Soviet intelligence succeeded in obtaining all the technical documentation needed to produce nuclear weapons, in winning over a number of distinguished scientists and in ideologically recruiting others as agents." Since the war, Suvorov declares, "the Soviet Union has succeeded in copying the American B-29 bomber, the British

Rolls-Royce aircraft engines, American lorries and German V-2 rockets . . . it has stolen plans for the construction of French anti-tank rockets, American air-launched missiles, laser range-finders, stabilisers for tank guns, rocket fuel, special dyestuffs and many, many other highly important products."

Intelligence specialists believe there are between 350 and 400 KGB and GRU officers operating in the United States.

Diplomatic Spies

Owing to the presence of the United Nations and many of its specialized agencies in New York City, the KGB, using the UN as a sanctuary or cover, has the largest concentration of its officers in that city. As of January, 1983, there were 330 Soviet nationals employed in the UN Secretariat, along with 310 members of the Soviet diplomatic delegation. As most of the Soviet nationals were accompanied by husbands or wives, the number of potential KGB agents can be increased by at least another one-half. Utilizing "journalists" and "trade representatives" assigned to the UN, the KGB is enabled to deploy additional operatives.

Finally, there are several hundred East European and Cuban nationals who are employed by the UN or are assigned to it in the guise of diplomats. A large percentage of these satellite officials are professional intelligence officers whose espionage activities are coordinated or directed by the KGB. Ironically, the salaries of the KGB-controlled operatives at the UN and its specialized agencies are paid in part by the U.S. through its annual $2 billion contribution for the upkeep of the UN.

Stanislav Androsov, nominally Counsellor of the Soviet Embassy in Washington, but actually the KGB's Washington *rezident**—the most powerful Soviet intelligence officer stationed in the United States—oversees a network of Soviet and Soviet Bloc agents and technicians estimated at 240 in Washington alone. The mansard roof of the Soviet Embassy bristles with more antennas—used, among other purposes, for intercepting and recording official and private telephone conversations transmitted by microwave—than any other building in the area except the Pentagon.

The Soviet Mission in New York and the Soviet Consulate at

* See Glossary of Espionage Terms.

148

San Francisco also eavesdrop on private telephone conversations. From the San Francisco Consulate the Soviets are able to intercept telephone conversations that take place in the Silicon Valley—the heartland of America's technological research and development.

Senator Daniel Patrick Moynihan, vice chairman of the Senate Select Committee on Intelligence, warns against this ominous invasion of American privacy:

> I cannot stress too strongly that modern technology has given to foreign espionage a new dimension which needs to be understood in this country. The targets of Soviet interception of telephone communications now include our businesses, our banks, our brokerage houses, as frequently as our government agencies. Soviet espionage seeks to penetrate into other aspects of American life—commercial, intellectual, political—as much as it seeks illegal entry into the councils of government. This is precisely why the problem is now one of interest to all Americans in their daily lives—not an abstract problem for intelligence operatives in trench coats.

The Soviet Union spends millions of dollars on dubious business ventures in order to provide cover for KGB field operatives. Soviet embassies and consulates are sanctuaries for KGB and GRU officers who, under the cloak of diplomatic immunity, pursue military and industrial espionage. At least one-third to one-half of the diplomatic staffs of Soviet embassies are believed by intelligence experts to be KGB operatives. In an interview on CBS's "Face the Nation," April 24, 1983, Judge William Webster, director of the FBI, placed the number of Soviet and satellite diplomats in this country at approximately three thousand. Of this number, he said, one out of three (as many as perhaps 1,200) had intelligence responsibilities.

The "Illegals"

These numbers are, however, deceptive. They do not include the concealed "illegals," under the control of Directorate "S" of the KGB's First Chief Directorate. These "illegals" are nationals from the Soviet Union, the East European satellites and Cuba, and native Americans (recruited into KGB espionage networks). For pro-Soviet support, if not for outright espionage, the KGB can count on that not inconsiderable body of American fellow travelers and congenital do-gooders whom Lenin once described as "our idiots." Not infrequently from this group the KGB can recruit idealistic industry spies, who, because of their pro-Soviet sympathies and antipathy to capitalism, will hand over trade secrets of the companies by whom they are employed.

Some six thousand Soviet nationals annually visit the United States. It should be taken for granted that any Soviet citizens who are assigned overseas either work directly for the KGB or will supply that organization with any services demanded of them. Whether a scientist visiting an American university on a cultural exchange program, a member of a trade delegation touring the United States, a teller or credit manager in the New York branch of the Moscow-Narodny Bank, a salesman for Lada cars, a Tass correspondent stationed in Washington who routinely covers Capitol Hill and White House press conferences, or a graduate student enrolled at Columbia University or UCLA—a Soviet citizen abroad should never be regarded simply as a foreign national minding his own business. His business is the KGB's business.

Soviet Use of Agents from Other Countries

It should also be kept in mind that agents from the secret services of Czechoslovakia, East Germany, Poland, Hungary, Bulgaria, Romania, North Korea and Cuba, whose organizations the KGB controls, can be summoned for special assignments. Professional agents from the satellite secret services are not popularly associated with the Soviet Union and are therefore uniquely useful in KGB-directed industrial espionage. Indeed, operatives from the Cuban secret service (of whom there are an estimated three thousand in the United States) can easily blend into the environment of Florida and the Southwest where, in many communities, Spanish is a second—and frequently the only—language and where Spanish traditions are built into the cultural landscape. (It would not be surprising if the Sun Belt held a special attraction for the Cuban General Directorate of Intelligence, acting for the KGB, owing to the explosive influx of high-technology firms. As California has its Silicon Valley, Florida has its "Silicon Beach," in the counties of Dade, Broward and Palm Beach along South Florida's Atlantic Coast. At Boca Raton, for instance, on 850 acres of what was once scrubland there is now an industrial park that serves as headquarters to some of the most sophisticated technological research and production in the world. Here will be found the Siemens Corporation—West Germany's electronics and telecommunications giant—and other major electronics and telecommunications enterprises that include the electronic-telephone-switching plant of Mitel Corporation, the world headquarters of STP and the medical instrumentation firm Datamedix. IBM, the city's largest firm, with 5,500 workers, developed and produces its successful personal computer in its Boca Raton plant.)

The East European secret services were used by the KGB to acquire military-industrial related technologies in such areas as computers, microelectronics, chemicals and nuclear energy. They have worked closely with the KGB and the GRU in arranging illegal diversions of export-controlled equipment.

The crucial role played by the East European secret services as surrogate for the KGB is exemplified by Marian Zacharski, a Polish intelligence officer (who operated under cover as a vice-president of a Polish-American company called Polamco, incorporated in the United States but in reality an arm of a Polish state-owned enterprise) and William Bell (a former project manager, specializing in fire control systems for the Hughes Aircraft Company in Los Angeles). On December 14, 1981, William Bell, an American citizen, and Marian Zacharski, a Polish national, were each sentenced to prison terms (Bell for eight years; Zacharski for life) for their complicity "in one of the most damaging espionage cases uncovered [by the FBI] in this country in over a decade."

Bell testified that he and his wife had met Zacharski and his wife while living in the same Cross Creek Village apartment complex at Playa del Rey, California. Zacharski and Bell became close friends and tennis-playing companions. Bell's recruitment began when Zacharski asked him for a copy of a Hughes employee newsletter and another innocuous company publication. A short time later, the apartment complex in which Bell and Zacharski were renters was converted into a condominium. Bell expressed his concern to his friend over his financial inability to purchase an individual unit. Zacharski offered to help and Bell gratefully accepted a loan of $110,000, which was to be repaid over a three-year interval.

Soon, however, Bell found himself under pressure to supply Zacharski with classified documents. William Bell, an American engineer, a project manager in a defense contractor's plant, became an espionage agent for the Polish secret service, but in reality for the KGB. He began photographing classified documents; meeting Polish intelligence officers in the U.S., Switzerland and Austria; receiving and making telephone calls to foreign intelligence agents; using code names; and accepting payment in gold pieces for the stolen documents. Bell testified to having been paid nearly $170,000.

What was so damaging in Bell's espionage was the nature of the reports passed to the Polish intelligence service for eventual use by the Soviets in their advanced weapons systems. Among the classified reports those of prime importance to the West's security and defense included:

—the F-15 look-down-shoot-down radar system
—the quiet radar system for the B-1 and Stealth bombers
—an all-weather radar system for tanks
—an experimental radar system for the U.S. Navy
—the Phoenix air-to-air missile
—a ship-borne surveillance radar
—the Patriot surface-to-air missile
—a towed-array submarine sonar system
—a new air-to-air missile
—the improved HAWK surface-to-air missile
—a NATO air-defense system

Intelligence experts believe that possession of this classified information will have saved the Polish and Soviet governments hundreds of millions of dollars in R&D costs by enabling them to implement proven designs developed in the United States, and to place weapons systems into operational use in a much shorter time period than if they had come from Soviet or Polish drawing boards. Knowledge of U.S. specifications on current and future weapons systems also enables the Warsaw Pact countries to develop defensive countermeasures.

The Bell-Zacharski relationship is a textbook case on how to accomplish a transfer of technology to a hostile intelligence service. First you have what appears to be a casual, chance *social meeting* that enables an experienced intelligence officer to spot a potential recruit. Next comes a lengthy period—lasting over months—of careful *cultivation* of the prospect, ripening (as it did with Bell and Zacharski) into a close friendship. Then comes a *deliberate sounding out* of the prospective agent to furnish innocuous company information. Then the prospect is *tied-up with a financial loan* (to enable Bell to buy a condominium). Now comes "the moment of truth," when the hostile intelligence officer is ready to turn his prospect into a full-fledged espionage agent: the *request* to produce classified documents or company trade secrets. When these data are supplied and payment therefor is accepted, the American victim is fatally compromised: he has become an espionage agent for a foreign power.

Summary of KGB Activities in the United States

To return to our overview of the KGB's organization: in addition to its direct responsibility for intelligence collection and clandestine activities, the KGB through its *rezident* supervises a parallel organization of "illegals." These are the "deep cover" agents who employ false identities, complete with fictitious personal histories or "legends" that enable them to penetrate deeply into American society. Some within this organization of illegals remain inactive for years, living the lives of ordinary American citizens, until the day they receive their "assignment." The illegals operate from their own headquarters, an illegal *rezidentura,* perhaps an inconspicuous, dingy bookstore or a photography shop in a back alley. The unit the Soviets call the "legal *rezidentura"* has its headquarters in the Embassy and is immune from visit and search by the counterintelligence officials of the country in which it is situated. The *rezidentura,* and such of its operatives as enjoy diplomatic status, are likewise immune from search and arrest. Each *rezidentura*—both the legal and illegal—has its own separate communications with Moscow and takes its orders directly from the KGB headquarters, known as the Center. The arrangement by the illegals for communicating with the Center is frequently their weakest link, as direction finders can, in time, locate a radio-sending apparatus.

Care is taken to keep the legal and illegal organizations separate from each other. Although an illegal apparatus lacks the advantages that diplomatic cover provides for a legal network, those who are part of the illegal organization are likely to attract less attention from the counterespionage services, and its operations will not be automatically disrupted by a severance of diplomatic relations or an outbreak of war. The illegal networks have their own, concealed *rezident* who is prepared to take instantaneous command of the illegal networks in the event of any break in U.S.–Soviet diplomatic relations or war.

No estimate is possible of the precise number of KGB illegals who are buried in the American environment, nor of the number of Americans who have been recruited by the KGB as illegal operatives.

What is, however, crystal clear is that the KGB has at its command a formidable array of personnel for industrial espionage not only in the United States but throughout the industrialized West and Japan.

Changing Styles of Espionage

Since World War II, espionage has changed dramatically. The United States now relies heavily on electronic and ultrasophisticated technical surveillance for much of its global intelligence information, although worldwide, individually-manned CIA stations are still maintained. The CIA's importance as an intelligence-gathering organization has diminished against the capability of the National Security Agency to eavesdrop even on scrambled radiotelephone conversations in Moscow by the Soviet Union's highest leaders as they are driven in their limousines to and from the Kremlin.

The Soviets also have their own "spy-in-the-sky," but traditionally they have been people-oriented for their espionage. For the Soviets, it is the effort of the classical agent on the ground that remains most significant. Even as highly mechanized modern armies still need the foot soldier, so does contemporary espionage need the agent on the ground. "A satellite photograph may show you what a new plane looks like—it gives you its configuration," an intelligence expert points out, "but it won't tell you what's inside the engines and how they operate. For that you need someone to tell you." If an agent on the ground is needed for interpreting technological intelligence, he is indispensable for the acquisition and interpretation of political intelligence.

In espionage operations in the 1980s, there has been less reliance by the KGB on the once glamorous and celebrated illegals—

a Kim Philby of Britain's MI6; a Colonel Rudolf Abel who for nine years, as an obscure Brooklyn artist-photographer, ran a spy network that covered all of North America, Mexico and Central America; or a Richard Sorge, a GRU officer who, for eight years (using his cover as a Tokyo correspondent of the *Frankfurter Zeitung*) ran an espionage network in the Far East that supplied the Soviets with Japan's most secret intelligence, the warning to Stalin of Germany's intention to invade the Soviet Union and his discovery of Japan's plan to attack Pearl Harbor. The latterday heroes—if, indeed there can be said to be any— are the intelligence analysts, the grey men who sit behind government desks in Moscow, Langley, Va., London and Tel Aviv, where they painstakingly sift through tons of material provided by hundreds of different sources from perhaps dozens of countries before they can (if they are lucky) piece together a picture of, say, the locking mechanism on a swing-wing fighter aircraft.

FBI intelligence officials, however, are certain that KGB activity by agents on the ground is on the rise. Edward J. O'Malley, assistant FBI director in charge of the Bureau's intelligence division, says, "it is evident in the ever-increasing resources deployed against us, in the unrelenting effort by the KGB to recruit agents from government, business and science, and the growing voraciousness of the Soviet appetite for science and technology."

Soviet Trading Companies and News Agencies

Obtaining Western scientific and technological information is the special province of the personnel assigned to the eighty or more worldwide Soviet trading companies under the jurisdiction of the Ministry of Foreign Trade and the Soviet Chamber of Commerce, whose first deputy chairman, Yevgeniy Petrovich Pitovranov, is a general in the KGB. Ten of the Soviet's "multinational" companies are located in the U.S. They provide a made-to-order cover for KGB operatives whose assignment is industrial espionage.

Norway, in February 1982, expelled two Soviet trade officials for illegally trying to buy components of the American F16 fighter aircraft, and for attempting to bribe executives in Norwegian firms into purchasing advanced American technology for reshipment to the Soviet Union.

During February 1983, West German security police arrested

a member of a Soviet trade delegation on a charge of industrial espionage. Also in February 1983, the Italian security police arrested a Soviet airline official on a similar charge. And in Sweden, an executive of one of the country's largest high-technology companies declared that the East Bloc had intensified its industrial espionage efforts in Sweden in response to stricter U.S. export-control regulations. "The Soviets are trying harder to obtain technology by covert means now that they can't get it easily any more," he said.

In addition to using Soviet embassies and consulates as cover for its agents, the KGB also stations them on the staffs of the Soviet Union's news agencies, Novosti and Tass. Actually, of the five hundred or more Soviet journalists working overseas, a majority are regular intelligence officers. The Soviet magazine *New Times* is a KGB front.

The offices of the state-owned airline, Aeroflot, are used to camouflage the real work of KGB operatives. Among other Soviet overseas business facilities utilized as a cover for KGB agents are: Soviet Export Films; Russian Lumber Export-Import Co.; Black Sea-Baltic Insurance Co.; Morflot Shipping Co.; Intourist, the official travel agency; Amtorg, the New York City-based purchasing organization; and Soviet commercial delegations on special overseas purchasing missions.

The KGB Exposed: Some Examples

In March 1983, Britain expelled a "journalist" on the staff of the Soviet magazine *New Times* for "unacceptable conduct" (a diplomatic euphemism for spying). At the same time, two diplomats attached to the Soviet Embassy in London, including Colonel Gennady Primakov, the assistant air attaché, were also requested to leave the country. All three were engaged in industrial espionage. These expulsions bring to seven the number of KGB agents recently apprehended in Britain. But that number is minuscule when the expulsion of 105 diplomats and other Soviet officials in 1971 is recalled.

American counterintelligence officials with good reason regard Britain's internal security as the equivalent of a sieve. According to the *Sunday Times* of London, as a consequence of a U.S. threat to cut off high-technology assistance, Prime Minister Thatcher has formed a top-secret committee to halt the theft and smuggling of military technology to the Soviet Union in which Britain, U.S. intelligence officials believe, has the worst record in Western Europe.

In Cologne, West Germany, during February 1983, a Soviet trade official, who was believed to be the *rezident* of the KGB in West Germany, was caught while trying to buy information pertaining to a cryptology machine used by West German intelligence. West German intelligence officials believe that much of the engineering for the new "magnet" high-speed train already has been leaked to the East. Soviet Bloc espionage agents even steal the designs for consumer goods, such as kitchen appliances, in order to produce copies cheaply.

Acting on orders of President Mitterrand, the French government, on April 5, 1983, expelled forty-seven Soviet diplomats and other officials for what the Ministry of the Interior described as "systematic" industrial and military espionage. The French government was responding, as were other European governments, to a marked increase in and intensification of industrial espionage in Western Europe by the KGB. Intelligence experts attribute this activity in Western Europe to the tighter security restrictions on East-West trade imposed by the Reagan Administration.

France has a special interest for the KGB: (a) it is the home of considerable high technology, especially lasers and telecommunications; and (b) it is an independent nuclear force whose sophisticated weaponry rivals that of NATO. An additional reason for the attraction may be the numerous subsidiaries and affiliates of U.S.-based parent companies. By observing the U.S. scientists, engineers and executives who periodically visit their French subsidiaries, the KGB can target them for recruitment or endeavor to place them in compromising situations for purposes of blackmail.

Intelligence experts have observed that France is becoming a trans-shipment point for high-technology goods purchased by Soviet-front companies in the U.S. By using France as a destination, Soviet officials—or those fronting for them—are able to obtain sensitive equipment otherwise barred to Warsaw Pact countries. Within France itself, KGB operatives have acted boldly, almost contemptuously; they have scarcely bothered to conceal their aims. France, after all, in the jargon of the spy trade, was a "picnic."

Of the forty-seven ousted Soviet officials, two were journalists and five were with Soviet commercial organizations in Paris. Of the two deported journalists involved in the espionage network, one was the Paris bureau chief of the official Soviet news agency, Tass. Parenthetically, an obvious reason for the suspicion with which Western reporters assigned to Moscow are regarded by the Soviet secret service is the use which the Soviets make of their own journalists.

A statement released by the Ministry of the Interior said that the French counterintelligence service had "produced evidence of a systematic search . . . by many agents of the secret services of the USSR for scientific, technical and technological information, particularly in the military domain." The newspaper *Le Figaro* reported that Soviet diplomats and other officials who were deported were part of an espionage network that had stolen 30 to 40 percent of France's high-technology secrets! The newspaper quoted a senior official in the Ministry of the Interior as saying the Soviets had collected information on aircraft, missiles and their guidance systems, submarine technology, microelectronics, computer design and programming, new materials, and nuclear weapons, including France's neutron bomb. (The striking successes of Soviet espionage suggest that security by France's corporations and state-owned industries is virtually nonexistent.)

Of the diplomats caught in the French counterespionage net, the biggest fish was Nikolai Chetverikov, nominally the Soviet Embassy's third-ranking diplomat but in reality the KGB *rezident,* responsible for the Soviet espionage network in France. Whether Chetverikov will, in the course of his interrogation, disclose the identities of other KGB agents in France or elsewhere in the West remains to be seen. The best clue as to whether Chetverikov talked may be seen in the future activities of the *Service de Documentation Extérieure et Contre Espionage* and other secret services in the West.

In April 1983, two officials of the Soviet Mission to the United Nations and an assistant military attaché at the Soviet Embassy in Washington were apprehended by the FBI for trying to obtain classified industrial-military information. After invoking diplomatic immunity, they left the country. Both of the officials were accredited to the UN; one was on an academic exchange program, the other was a KGB officer. The attaché was a lieutenant colonel in the GRU.

The FBI said the thwarted espionage attempts included repeated approaches to an aide to a U.S. Congressional representative by Alexandr Nikolaevich Mikheev, an expert on American affairs here on a cultural exchange program, who sought highly classified information. Oleg Vadimovich Konstantinov, the intelligence officer attached to the Soviet UN delegation, was caught attempting to obtain classified data on U.S. weapons technology from an American who was cooperating with the FBI. Lieutenant Colonel Yevgeniy Nikolaevich Barmyantsev of the GRU, the assistant military attaché at the Soviet Embassy, was seized while retrieving eight rolls of 35 mm. film containing information on laser technology, one of America's most sensitive secrets, from a drop at the base of a tree in suburban Maryland.

Joining Britain, France and the United States in the crackdown on Soviet industrial-military espionage, the Australian government, within a day after Washington expelled the three Soviet intelligence agents, ordered Valery Nikolaievich Ivanov, First Secretary of the Soviet Embassy in Canberra, to leave the country. Foreign Minister Hayden said evidence gathered by Australia's counterintelligence service showed that Ivanov was "a professional intelligence officer of the Committee for State Security (KGB)" who had "infringed the conventions applying to the proper conduct of diplomats." Ivanov's actions, Hayden declared, "threatened Australia's national security in a way which could not be tolerated by the government."

As we have previously suggested, Japan, along with Western Europe and the United States, has been a prime high-technology target for KGB espionage. A former Soviet spy in the KGB's covert-action section, Major Stanislav Levchenko, who spied in Japan for the KGB from 1975 to 1979, when he defected to the United States, calls Japan "a paradise for spies." He described Japan as "one of the best locales in the world to steal American secrets and technology." Levchenko says that eight Japanese politicians and journalists and eighteen other Japanese cooperated with the KGB while he served in Tokyo under cover as a correspondent for the Soviet magazine *New Times*. Stanislav Aleksandrovich Levchenko is now a consultant helping the United States Information Agency spot new Soviet propaganda and disinformation efforts. In his informative book on the KGB John Barron devotes several chapters to Levchenko, whom he interviewed extensively. He writes: "Few men understood the KGB better than Levchenko; few, if any, have done as much as Stanislav Aleksandrovich

Levchenko to wound the KGB. He understands that, as a consequence, he will always be a hunted man."

The Japanese government, on June 21, 1983, announced the expulsion of a Soviet diplomat, Arkady A. Vinogradov, a First Secretary at the Soviet Embassy in Tokyo, on the grounds that he had attempted to obtain information about semiconductors from an executive of a subsidiary of Hitachi, Ltd. This was the first time since World War II that Japan has taken action against a Soviet diplomat for engaging in industrial espionage. According to the Japanese counterintelligence service, Vinogradov and a Soviet technician, Boris Kakorin, attempted to obtain classified information and sought to have the Japanese executive set up an industrial espionage firm with Soviet financial backing, upon his retirement from the company. Vinogradov and Kakorin are both considered to be KGB agents.

Agents of Influence

Finally, the most insidious and potentially the most dangerous of the KGB's activities is the exploitation of what the Soviets call "agents of influence." By insinuating a KGB agent into the White House, the State Department, the Pentagon or other strategic governmental agencies, or burying one of its officers on the staff of an important and influential newspaper, the faculty of a prestigious college or university, or in the upper ranks of *Fortune's* five hundred leading corporations, the Soviets seek to influence American opinion or alter existing policies in its favor. To conceal one of its own officers in American society so deeply that, undetected, he can penetrate the leading economic and social institutions as well as the most sensitive government agencies, the KGB is prepared to wait decades—an entire generation, if necessary—and expend untold resources.

It needs to be recalled that, during the 1930s and early 1940s, Soviet agents managed to infiltrate the White House, the State Department, the Treasury Department, the War Shipping Administration, the Veterans Administration, the Department of Justice, Congressional committees, the Office of Strategic Services, the Foreign Economic Administration, the Securities and Exchange Commission, the Social Security Administration, the War Manpower Committee, the War Production Board, the Gov-

160

ernment Printing Office, the Reconstruction Finance Corporation, the U.S. Information Service and the International Monetary Fund. Richard Deacon, an authority on Soviet espionage, observes in his book *A History of the Russian Secret Service* that "the Soviet grip was so tight that neither the FBI nor the CIA has ever been able to eradicate its still powerful influence and networks in the U.S.A."

The beneficial return from having an agent of influence in sensitive government agencies, especially a secret intelligence service, has been dramatized by the British espionage scandals involving H. A. R. ("Kim") Philby, Guy Burgess and Donald Maclean, who formed "the most daring Soviet spy ring of the postwar era." For an agent of deep penetration to head an enemy's secret intelligence service is a fantasy of every hostile secret service. Philby came within a breath of becoming head of Britain's secret intelligence service, MI6. From the senior position he did succeed in occupying in MI6, that of director of the Counter Soviet department, and as the link between MI6 and the Office of Strategic Services, and later the CIA, Philby was privy to the most secret British-American intelligence. He was able to betray virtually every important secret of Western intelligence, a feat of duplicity unequalled in the annals of modern intelligence. In recognition of his incalculable importance as a secret agent of influence, Philby was awarded the Soviet Union's highest decoration, the Order of Lenin, and was made a citizen of the USSR. The other two celebrated British spies, Burgess and Maclean, were not too far behind Philby in the secrets they revealed to their Soviet masters from the Foreign Office and the British Embassy in Washington.

All three were recruited into the Soviet secret service as probationary agents during the 1930s, while undergraduates at Cambridge, when an apocalyptic assessment of the imminent demise of Western capitalism, fostered by Soviet propaganda and by committed Marxists and Communist sympathizers among the Cambridge dons, led many among Britain's idealistic, upper-middle-class university students to embrace communism as mankind's last best hope. This vision of the Promised Land—held by Britain's Communists and many among her intellectuals, especially the youthful idealists enrolled in her universities—needs to be placed alongside the realities as they were perceived in the time of the Great Depression. In Anthony Boyle's words, "Britain had ceased to be the leader among nations; her Empire was beginning to disintegrate; her commerce and industry were stagnant; the rich were poorer; and the army of the unemployed in depressed areas far from the capital waited listlessly and without hope. People of all classes held most politicians of every party in contempt; the politicians responded uneasily by settling for uncourageous half-measures."[7]

Robert Allason, under the pseudonym Nigel West, in his recent book *A Matter of Trust* (*The Circus: MI5 Operations 1945–1977*, in the U.S. edition), suggests that elitists like Burgess, Maclean and Philby, mourning the decline of the empire of their youth, found in the Soviet Union their new empire, and like other religious converts, became more Catholic than the Pope.

Allen Dulles, who was himself immersed in the shadowy world of intelligence/espionage as a spy master in Switzerland during World War II and in the post-war era as a director of the Central Intelligence Agency, may have caught the true character of the Soviet Union's most celebrated spy when he wrote:

> it is to be noted that Philby was no homeless alien, no outsider whose roots were elsewhere, as in the case of so many spies; nor was he blackmailed, trapped, or enticed by prospects of financial gain. He belonged to the privileged and educated class of his own country. All doors were open to him. For reasons which are easy enough to state but still immensely difficult to understand, he chose treason as a way of life. It apparently satisfied his need for adventure, for self-importance beyond the normal. To what extent he was really motivated by ideological convictions after the time of his undergraduate political enthusiasms remains open to questions. I would think not so much as is generally imagined. What seems to prevail in the man's make-up is a grudge against his own background, a feeling which he shared with his fellow traitors, Burgess and Maclean; a deep-seated and twisted hostility directed against all those things toward which ordinary people feel natural loyalties.[8]

Burgess and Maclean (and, later, Philby) fled to the Soviet Union when their treachery was revealed. (Philby was the "third man" who alerted Burgess, and through him Maclean, that the British secret service was about to close in on them. Of the three, only Philby, who is now seventy-one, survives. He is believed to serve the KGB headquarters in Moscow as a consultant.)

The KGB's plans for creating an agent of influence are not

always successful. In his recently published political memoir, aptly entitled *After Long Silence,* Michael Whitney Straight reveals that, as a youthful Communist activist, he was chosen by his Soviet masters to be groomed for a strategic post in the American establishment—a role he did not fulfill. Like Philby, Maclean, Burgess and Blunt, Straight was recruited in the 1930s by the Soviet secret service while an undergraduate at Cambridge, Britain's incubator for hatching elite Soviet espionage agents. Michael Straight kept his secret for twenty-six years, when at long last in 1963—the year Philby fled to Moscow after his long-concealed treason had been conclusively demonstrated—he revealed to the FBI and the British secret services his youthful folly in joining the British Communist Party, and supplied the names of infiltrators such as Anthony (he became Sir Anthony) Blunt, exposed by Straight as the "fourth man" in the celebrated espionage ring that included Philby, Maclean and Burgess. Among the other names he disclosed was that of his Soviet controller, "Michael Green," whom he was able to identify in a group photograph in the possession of the FBI.

Straight declares categorically that he showed "Green" only political analyses he had written himself which had no intelligence significance. To be sure, we have only Straight's word for this. Nevertheless, those who know—or knew—Michael Straight (as did one of the present authors)* believe him and accept his disclaimer.

Despite his initial protestations, Straight accepted his directive to return to the United States, a country he scarcely knew, and to abandon his adopted country, England, and what seemed a brilliant political future that might have carried him as a member of the Labour Party—Straight had already been offered a Labour candidacy in the House of Commons—to the highest political office in the land.

From Moscow's vantage point to have an individual of Straight's background as an agent of influence in Franklin Roosevelt's Washington would have made a good deal of sense. He was born into a patrician family and was amply endowed with inherited wealth. His father, Willard, and his mother, Dorothy Whitney Straight, had in 1912 founded *The New Republic,* a journal of opinion that long set the tone of American liberal thinking. It was not a difficult assumption for the Kremlin to make that

* Peter Nehemkis.

with his brilliant academic record at Cambridge—he had won three "firsts" in economics under Keynes—Michael would gravitate towards the family-owned magazine, as, in fact, he did, becoming its publisher and editor.

Straight was attracted to the liberalism of the New Deal as a moth to an electric light. He numbered among his friends such New Deal luminaries as Tommy Corcoran and Ben Cohen with whom he worked on presidential speeches. Later he became a volunteer member of the State Department. Whether by his own design or the hazards of the Washington job market, Straight never managed to occupy a significant or sensitive post in Franklin Roosevelt's Administrations.

Straight's usefulness, if any, to the Soviet secret service never remotely matched the contributions of his fellow-Cantabridgians, Donald Maclean (who as a diplomat with the British Embassy in Washington was privy to the most secret Anglo-American intelligence and had access to America's atomic secrets) and Guy Burgess (the debauched reprobate who was a purveyor of high-level diplomatic gossip). The KGB could have done as well by reading the *Washington Post.*

Certainly the awesome array of personnel available for Soviet industrial espionage is frightening. But the KGB is not invincible. Missions are blown. Meticulously contrived covers are unmasked. Spies are caught. Moles are discovered. Agents masquerading as diplomats, trade officials, and journalists are exposed. Defectors compromise secret codes, finger agent operations, and identify important KGB operatives. Double agents are programmed to feed Moscow Center, the KGB's headquarters at No. 2 Dzerzhinsky Square, with "disinformation."

It is not only the patient, persistent (and sometimes inspired) work of the West's counterintelligence services, and especially of our own FBI, that nets enemy agents. Cases abound of experienced and well-trained Soviet agents who have given themselves away by their complacency, lapses in judgment, and by ignoring a fundamental rule of the espionage operative: never to draw attention to themselves.

Despite the mystique of infallibility which the KGB seeks to convey, its Moscow Center is run by Russian intelligence bureaucrats and policemen who do make mistakes—mistakes that can be costly to its overseas agents and to the prestige of the Center. John Barron, in his current study of the KGB, has brilliantly documented one such mistake—or it may have been a series of blunders (only the FBI knows and they decline to tell)—that led the FBI to arrest three moles who were deeply embedded in the American environment—Rudolf Herrmann, a gifted Soviet intelligence officer; his wife, Inga, a fanatically dedicated Communist; and their son, Peter, a college student who, as a second generation mole, was being groomed for a role in a sensitive U.S. government agency.

Barron relates how, disclosing the details of his life and training to his FBI captors, Herrmann asked, "Can you tell me how you found out about me?"

> "That you will never know," Joe answered.
> "There is one thing I have to know," Rudi persisted. "Was it because of some mistake I made?"
> "No, Rudi, you were perfect. The KGB was not."[9]

Nevertheless, a spectacular espionage success goes far towards offsetting KGB embarrassments. In *The Falcon and the Snowman,* Robert Lindsey narrates the gripping albeit tragic tale of the betrayal of his country by Christopher Boyce, an emotionally disturbed twenty-one-year-old American youth from a well-to-do family in Palo Verde, California—a college dropout, who was embittered over the Vietnam war and disillusioned with his country's foreign policies, especially with the operations of the CIA. Boyce was employed at TRW as a $142-a-week code clerk. In this capacity he had—incredible as it now seems in retrospect—Top Secret clearance from the Department of Defense, a Strategic-Byeman clearance from the CIA and a Crypto clearance from the National Security Agency, the most secretive agency within the U.S. intelligence community. With these clearances, Boyce had access at TRW "to the nation's most secret cryptographic systems and some of its most secret espionage operations."

The scheme Boyce concocted was for his childhood companion and lifelong friend, Daulton Lee, a narcotics peddler and heroin addict, to carry the classified documents lifted by Boyce from TRW's "Black Vault," where they were stored, to Mexico City, to be turned over to KGB officers at the Soviet Embassy. Daulton Lee would negotiate the amount of payment and split the sum with Boyce. Over a period of months, the KGB obtained the plans for America's satellite surveillance systems, the cornerstone of

America's defense in the nuclear missile era. Senator Daniel P. Moynihan, vice chairman of the Senate's Intelligence subcommittee, in an interview on CBS television's "60 Minutes" (November 21, 1982), said Boyce's spying had rendered the satellite systems "useless to the U.S. because the Soviets could [now] block them."

The KGB's Current Targets

A recent report by a Senate subcommittee of the Government Affairs Committee observed: "The Soviets dedicate substantial resources to highly focused attempts to secure American technology [and] they are becoming increasingly adept in that effort." The report cited "advanced American microelectronics, laser, radar and precision-manufacturing techniques" as examples of high technology surreptitiously acquired by the Soviet Union. KGB successes in purloining Western technology have reduced the West's technological lead from ten years to about two. Every Soviet industry engaged in research, development and production of weapons systems has benefited from the ease with which the KGB has lifted—perhaps plundered is a more appropriate word— Western and Japanese technology. The key areas in which the KGB has scored notable successes in acquiring—by purchase or theft—Western technology are shown in a table, prepared by the CIA and reproduced on pp. 168–169.

According to the CIA, three of the KGB's prime industrial targets are: microelectronics; computer know-how (especially software and supercomputers); and materials technology (particularly advanced composites). Other high-technology areas of special interest to the KGB are: sophisticated medical devices, genetic engineering, new energy technology (e.g., extraction of oil from shale), nuclear fusion, and futuristic weapons such as lasers and particle beams—the "star wars" weapons. The Soviets have accelerated their espionage efforts to acquire new and emerging technologies in areas of very-high-speed-integrated circuit (VHSIC) and very-large-scale-integration (VLSI) technologies for both military and industrial applications from Western and Japanese universities as well as from commercial laboratories.

Prime U.S. targets for KGB technological espionage are the

East Coast's high-tech corridor stretching from Boston to Baltimore, Southern California's aerospace industry and the electronics industries in the Silicon Valley, near San Francisco. The first Consul General of the Soviet Consulate in San Francisco, an hour's drive from the Silicon Valley, was Aleksandr Chickvaidze, a professionally trained engineer who had previously served as director of the State Committee for Science and Technology, the Soviet Union's most prestigious scientific-technological agency. That so high-ranking an official would be assigned to the San Francisco consulate was not a coincidence. The research and development facilities in California, and especially the technological infrastructure of the Silicon Valley, are the backdoor not only into advanced electronics and industrial technology but into the key Soviet target: *advanced electronics military weapons.* (The dramatic success by the Israeli military forces in using advanced U.S. electronics weaponry to destroy Syrian surface-to-air missiles, supplied by the Soviets, is only one example of how crucial such weapons have become. They will be even more critical as new generations of increasingly sophisticated electronic equipment are developed.)

U.S. intelligence experts believe that as many as sixty specially-trained KGB officers are stationed at the Soviet's San Francisco Consulate. Their assignment is to monitor the Silicon Valley for public as well as confidential, proprietary information. Stefan Halper, deputy Assistant Secretary of State for Political and Military Affairs, characterizes the Soviet consulate as a "major espionage center."

The KGB officers assigned to the San Francisco consulate are from the Scientific and Technical Directorate of the KGB's prestigious First Chief Directorate, whose mission is to establish intelligence requirements for all legal and illegal overseas operatives. Of the S & T Directorate, Dr. Harry Rositzke writes in his classic study, *The KGB: The Eyes of Russia:*

> Here in a kind of wholesale human data bank sit hundreds of specialists, each an expert on a single sector of the modern industrial machine, from textile mills to computer hardware. Each specialist knows what Soviet industry knows and what it does not know. Each specialist tries to find out what Western technology knows that he does not. Each directs the S & T collectors abroad on what to go after in his field of competence, evaluates what they produce, and sends follow-ups for amplifying data. The ques-

Selected Soviet and East European Legal and Illegal Acquisitions from the West Affecting Key Areas of Soviet Military Technology

Key Technology Area	Notable Success
Computers	Purchases and acquisitions of complete systems designs, concepts, hardware and software, including a wide variety of Western general purpose computers and minicomputers, for military applications.
Microelectronics	Complete industrial processes and semiconductor manufacturing equipment capable of meeting all Soviet military requirements, if acquisitions were combined.
Signal Processing	Acquisitions of processing equipment and know-how.
Manufacturing	Acquisitions of automated and precision manufacturing equipment for electronics, materials, and optical and future laser weapons technology; acquisition of information on manufacturing technology related to weapons, ammunition, and aircraft parts including turbine blades, computers, and electronic components; acquisition of machine tools for cutting large gears for ship propulsion systems.
Communications	Acquisitions of low-power, low-noise, high-sensitivity receivers.
Lasers	Acquisitions of optical, pulsed power source, and other laser-related components, including special optical mirrors and mirror technology suitable for future laser weapons.
Guidance and Navigation	Acquisitions of marine and other navigation receivers, advanced inertial-guidance components, including miniature and laser gyros; acquisitions of missile guidance subsystems; acquisitions of precision machinery for ball bearing production for missile and other applications; acquisition of missile test range instrumentation systems and documentation and precision cinetheodolites for collecting data critical to postflight ballastic missile analysis.
Structural Materials	Purchases and acquisitions of Western titanium alloys, welding equipment, and furnaces for producing titanium plate of large size applicable to submarine construction.

Propulsion	Missile technology; some ground propulsion technology (diesels, turbines, and rotaries); purchases and acquisitions of advanced jet engine fabrication technology and jet engine design information.
Acoustical Sensors	Acquisitions of underwater navigation and direction-finding equipment.
Electro-optical Sensors	Acquisition of information on satellite technology, laser rangefinders, and underwater low-light-level television cameras and systems for remote operation.
Radars	Acquisitions and exploitations of air defense radars and antenna designs for missile systems.

Source: Central Intelligence Agency, *Soviet Acquisition of Western Technology*, April 1982.

tionnaires I have seen are as precise and detailed as the specifications of an engineering contract or an advanced research and development contract.[10]

As the U.S. is an open society in which all new research and development is usually published, it is not necessary for the KGB officers at the consulate to emulate the shadowy minor characters in a John le Carré international spy novel. Instead, they function more as MBA-trained market researchers, obtaining information by exhaustive literature searches at the Stanford and Berkeley libraries. According to the FBI, the Soviets acquire about three-quarters of their intelligence from documents, publications and other sources freely available to the public. The Soviet Union devotes an enormous effort—involving perhaps as many as a hundred thousand people—to sifting and systematically disseminating unclassified technical data obtained in the U.S., Western Europe and Japan.

The S & T specialists at the San Francisco consulate are highly educated young men, graduates of Soviet universities, with good manners, an excellent command of colloquial American English, and specialized scientific and technological training. Gone are the squat, potato-faced types the Soviet Union sent abroad during the 1950s, reeking of eau de cologne and conspicuous in their baggy, ill-fitting suits. This new breed of agent is garbed in Brooks Brothers pin stripes and a button-down shirt, and gives the impression of being on his way to attend a divisional sales meeting.

Along with their clandestine espionage activities, the S & T specialists at the San Francisco Consulate carry on an active, respectable and legitimate public routine, visiting industrial installations, laboratories, and trade shows, attending scientific conferences, fraternizing with academics at Berkeley, Stanford and San Francisco University, and meeting other experts in their own fields of professional competence. Business executives in and around San Francisco are assiduously cultivated. With unlimited expense accounts, they patronize San Francisco's best restaurants.

The purpose of this ubiquitous activity is threefold: (1) to acquire scientific and technological intelligence; (2) to spot likely recruits; and (3) to identify sources of intelligence for subsequent follow-up.

It should come as no surprise to the reader to learn that Silicon Valley high-technology trade secrets end up in the Soviet Union. To cite only one example: stolen technical data relating to Intel's microelectronic circuits were diverted to East European Bloc countries and trans-shipped to the Soviet Union. Acquisition of existing Silicon Valley companies—the route followed by West European and Japanese multinationals to gain access to micro-electronic technology—is not open to Soviet state-owned enterprises, for ideological reasons grounded in Marxist dogma. And, as the more recent pattern followed by computer, communications and semiconductor companies (who have formed joint ventures and cooperative technology exchanges), is likewise closed to Soviet enterprises, who are in the main copiers, not technological innovators, the KGB operatives must resort to theft, pirating and espionage.

"Manufacturing technology has moved to the top of the Russian [priority] list," says John D. Shea, President of Technology Analysis Group, Inc., a San Jose (Calif.) consultant to the Defense Department. The latest semiconductor fabrication equipment, he explains, could probably cut by half the time it takes for the Soviets to move a new weapon from the drawing board to the battlefield. G. Day Hutcheson, vice-president of VLSI Research, Inc., a semiconductor industry consultant, adds that "Soviet attempts to get this equipment are a real problem—and there is no solution in sight."

Almost 30 percent of all U.S. chipmaking equipment is exported. But once this equipment leaves the United States under a validated export license, it has a "nasty habit" of showing up within a few months on the used equipment market, says Hutcheson. The NATO allies make no attempt to regulate the sale of used equipment. Hence, it is a wide open market for East Bloc buyers. According to the CIA, the Soviets have obtained many hundreds of pieces of equipment, worth hundreds of millions of dollars, through used equipment purchases.

The ease with which Silicon Valley trade secrets can be lifted by foreign and domestic espionage agents is abetted by the Valley's own environment. The life style of its talented, wealthy and egocentric entrepreneurs is casual. (Sandra Kurtzig's ASK Computer Systems, Inc. exemplifies the practice. Started ten years ago on a shoestring, Mrs. Kurtzig's computer software business has grown to $22 million in annual sales, has two hundred employees, and enjoys a reputation as one of the most successful software companies in Silicon Valley. She hews to the Silicon Valley tradition of trying to make ASK a relaxed, casual and "fun" place in which to work. "To work here," she says with a chuckle, "you must be able to drink at the company's Friday beer blast.") Technical élan is considered to be more important than security. Job-hopping by executives and researchers is actively encouraged as a kind of "technological cross-fertilization." Gossip and an exchange of information by and among employees about what individual companies are doing, or planning to do, are a way of life. Competition is fierce. Hence, knowledge of what a competitor has on the drawing board places business intelligence at a premium. FBI Director William Webster characterizes the Silicon Valley environment as a natural breeding ground for "hostile intelligence gatherers." The FBI believes that four out of five Silicon Valley companies are routinely the victims of espionage, targeted by domestic and foreign agents seeking competitive trade secrets, high-technology equipment or technological manufacturing processes. Santa Clara County (Calif.) District Attorney Douglas Southward states that $100 million or more in electronic technology products has been stolen from the Silicon Valley over the past five years.

By "borrowing" U.S. technology, the Soviet Union not only saves time and billions of rubles on R & D programs and attains instant industrial modernization, acquiring proven and trouble-free equipment for its weapon systems, but also is enabled to incorporate defensive countermeasures to Western weapons systems through early development of their own weapons programs. Moreover, through its openly published scientific and technical literature the West (and the U.S. in particular) not only provides Soviet scientists and engineers with an unparalleled opportunity to probe the West's scientific technological programs, but frequently furnishes them with data that can be used to repair and maintain products and equipment acquired illegally or surreptitiously through espionage.

Caspar Weinberger, Secretary of Defense, writes:

> Where [the Soviets] were unable to get either the U.S. or those who participate in the International Control System (COCOM) to yield advanced technology, the Soviets employed a number of clandestine means. Businessmen, engineers, scientists and workers were bribed. Innocent-looking corporations have been created to

172

buy equipment later sent to the U.S.S.R. Diplomats and special visitors have been used to ferret out items of special interest. And when all else fails, intelligence missions have been run.

Continental Trading Corp. of Torrance, California, from the time it was organized in 1975 until it was forced to liquidate in 1982, was one of the "innocent-looking corporations" that bought high-technology equipment which was illegally shipped to the Soviet Union. U.S. government investigators believe that Continental Trading Corp. was at the center of a network of phantom companies that diverted high-technology equipment valued at hundreds of millions of dollars to the Soviet Union, including one entire silicon-chip manufacturing plant and an entire truck engine assembly line, incorporated in the Kama River Truck plant, whose trucks are used by Soviet occupation forces in Afghanistan and by Soviet military units in Eastern Europe opposite NATO forces. There are more than twenty Soviet- and East European-owned firms in the U.S. and more than three hundred in Europe, according to a Senate report, that like Continental Trading Corp. are phantom companies engaged in an illicit traffic in proscribed U.S. equipment and technology.

Whether Anatoli Maluta, a Russian-born, naturalized U.S. citizen, who was sentenced to five years imprisonment for his involvement in Continental Trading Corp.'s illegal activities, was motivated by greed—as Los Angeles U.S. District Court Judge Matthew Byrne, who sentenced Maluta, believed—or was "turned" into a spy by the KGB is an enigma.

Maluta, a UCLA-trained engineer, testified he obtained his job as president of Continental Trading Corp. by answering a classified ad in the *Los Angeles Times.* His prospective employer was a German, Werner Bruchhausen, who, Maluta says, hired him after a 15-minute interview. Maluta's job was to purchase high-technology electronics gear to be shipped to shadow companies who reshipped the equipment to Eastern European Bloc countries or to Soviet enterprises. Although the equipment was ostensibly purchased by Maluta for use in the United States, it was immediately exported, usually without a validated export license and in contravention of the export control provisions of the Export Administration Act. An investigative team, directed by a gifted and imaginative Assistant U.S. Attorney, Theodore Wai Wu of Los Angeles, ultimately established that Maluta made at least three hundred shipments of embargoed semiconductor and other electronic equipment valued at more than $10.5 million.

Maluta claimed there were many others engaged in the illegal diversion of equipment to the Soviet Union. Much of his competition, he said, came from the European subsidiaries of U.S.-based multinational companies, with the remainder from other shadow companies in the U.S. and Europe.

The Soviets can sometimes buy high-technology equipment through intermediaries with "false flag operations." Although U.S. export regulations prohibit the sale of sensitive equipment to the Warsaw Pact nations, the Soviets have found convenient and willing channels among West European businessmen who buy equipment proscribed to the Soviets and trans-ship it to dummy European companies which then re-export it to the Soviet Union. Austria and Switzerland, with relatively lax controls on imports, are favored trading posts. There are at least 120 Austrian companies that have access to American micro-processing and data acquisition systems, in addition to sensors that may not be military products in themselves but have military applications. Until Austria was pressed by the Reagan Administration to tighten its technology transfer policy, the Austrians made no serious effort to police their exports.

Literally dozens of schemes were devised, Maluta has testified, to circumvent U.S. export control restrictions. Frequently, these schemes involved bribing or otherwise compromising purchasing agents and other executives of European firms. In a permissive age, sexual entrapment, to be sure, is no longer as effective as it once was. Nevertheless, a prearranged sexual indiscretion at a "swallow's nest" in a Moscow hotel· or apartment with a KGB "swallow" is still a routine Soviet ploy and plays a role in KGB blackmail. A threat by the KGB to reveal photographs and tape recordings of pillow-talk to an employer, or to a wife and family members, or to publicly release the incriminating evidence to the media (if the compromised executive is sufficiently prominent), has sufficed to blackmail a victim into becoming a docile agent who thereafter does the KGB's bidding.

Maluta claimed legitimate electronic suppliers knew that the ultimate destination of equipment purchased from them was Eastern Europe, as his orders specified 50-cycle electrical current, which is standard in Eastern European countries, whereas 60-cycle current is used in the West.

Maluta was arrested, prosecuted and convicted on thirteen counts of conspiracy, falsification of Customs declarations and unlawful exportation. He was sentenced to five years' imprisonment and fined $60,000.

Dr. Lara Baker of the Los Alamos National Laboratory concluded that Maluta's operations had enabled the Soviets to acquire everything they needed to build an entire semiconductor plant. With Maluta's assistance, "the United States gave up technology, much of which the Soviets could not have obtained elsewhere," Dr. Baker observed. "The Soviets showed no interest in purchasing production equipment that was not state of the art. The sequence in which they purchased things and the quantities indicate the production plant would be of medium size and capable of delivering a high-quality product. . . . High-quality integrated circuits are the basis of modern military electronics. The production tooling and equipment obtained by the Soviets will significantly improve their capability to produce such circuits."

John Barron concludes in his current study of the KGB that "in their meticulously planned operation, the Soviets were careful to procure four of each item they needed. Thus, for some time they will have spare parts for their new semi-conductor plant—made in America, delivered by the KGB and assembled in the U.S.S.R."[11] The Maluta incident, Barron observes, "is merely one example of how the Soviets systematically have looted the American semi-conductor industry to feed their armament industry, which would be faltering technologically without U.S. sustenance."

Maluta's operations raise disturbing questions about the ease with which high-technology equipment can be acquired from U.S. suppliers and diverted to the Soviet Union in disregard of U.S. export regulations. The Maluta incident also poses a critical question as to whether or not the Department of Commerce, which plays a major role in the enforcement of export regulations, is "institutionally" capable of carrying out its statutory responsibilities. A Senate subcommittee believes it is not and recommends that the Department's enforcement duties be transferred to the U.S. Customs Service. In anticipation of an expanded role to cut the flow of high technology to the Soviet Union, the Customs Service's budget has been almost quadrupled, enabling the agency to recruit and provide specialized technical training for additional officers. The number of overseas agents will double to around fifty. Officials say they now have under investigation around a dozen "James Bond-type cases," in which efforts were made to smuggle U.S. technology out of the country. Over a period of fifteen months—from October 1981 to January 1983—the U.S. Customs Service made 1,051 seizures of embargoed strategic equipment illegally exported from the United States, much of which was directed to the Soviet Union or Bloc countries. In response to the Customs Service's increased efforts to stem the torrent of U.S. technology being acquired by the Soviet Union, the KGB has been forced to change its methods and routes, if not its objectives.

If Maluta is to be believed, a social question is raised about the indifference of U.S. electronics suppliers to the ultimate user of their equipment and the purpose of its use. "Trade with the Soviet Union is not trade with an ordinary country," as Secretary Weinberger has observed. "It is used almost exclusively to benefit them militarily." Can U.S. managements in good conscience argue—as some do—that their responsibility ends with the sale of their company's product, and the policies of the U.S. government vis-à-vis the Soviet Union are not their concern?

To illustrate the misuse of official invitations to Soviet visitors to inspect U.S. manufacturing facilities, U.S. intelligence officials offer this shocking example. A group of Soviet aviation specialists were invited by the Department of State to tour the non-secret sections of several U.S. aircraft plants, where they observed 747s, DC-10s and L-1011s under construction. Only later did a defector supply a chilling postscript. The Soviet visitors wore special soles on their shoes to enable them to pick up metal shavings, which were used, it is surmised, by Soviet metallurgists to identify metal alloys needed by the Soviets "to produce their giant troop transportation planes."

FBI Director Webster, whose agency is responsible for U.S. counterintelligence, relates this incident to underscore what he and other high-ranking officials in the Reagan Administration view as a major threat to U.S. national security from the Soviet Union's relentless campaign to "vacuum-clean" American high technology.

Aside from the West's own careless security, the KGB has been able to acquire high-technology secrets by means of a brilliantly coordinated use of its own and satellite intelligence resources. (See Figure 1.)

176

Figure 1
SOVIET AGENCIES INVOLVED IN INDUSTRIAL-MILITARY ESPIONAGE

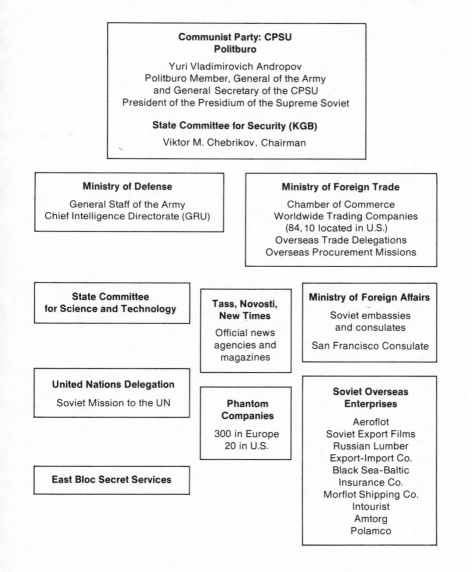

The Problem of Control

Underlying the U.S. official preoccupation with the transfer of technology to the Soviet Union is perhaps the most important question of all: How can the U.S. curb the flow of high technology to the Soviet Union without at the same time seriously damaging

American business? Many U.S. corporations believe that a system of tight controls hurts business and fails to solve the problem of technology leakage. Executives who are directly familiar with the problem advocate decontrolling the sale of virtually all products but imposing draconian restrictions on the export of the manufacturing technology—the machines and processes that make advanced high-technology products possible. This solution also has the support of officials in the Commerce and State Departments as well as Pentagon research and development officials but is opposed by hard-liners at the Department of Defense, and the chief of the hard-liners, President Reagan.

J. Fred Bucy, president of Texas Instruments Co., points out that the Pentagon's critical technologies list "has bastardized the concept of controlling critical technology." Ironically, it was Bucy's own 1976 report—*An Analysis of Export Control of U.S. Technology: A DOD Perspective*—that provided the Defense Department with the rationale for its critical technologies list. The perspective articulated by the task force, chaired by Bucy, was reflected in the Export Administration Act of 1979 (which, as this is written, is before the Congress for renewal). That legislation changed the focus of the U.S. export system from an emphasis on goods to an emphasis on technologies. The provision of the 1979 legislation that most clearly reflected the Bucy committee's report was the section calling for the creation of a "Militarily Critical Technologies List." The objective of the list is to identify "technological elements essential to an advanced military capability, with emphasis on manufacturing know-how, keystone manufacturing equipment, goods which contain sophisticated technology, and maintenance know-how." The list is a classified document and consists of many hundreds of pages.

Bucy, who in a very real sense is the father of the "technologies list," believes "technology is know-how that converts science into products." "It's the detailed processing steps, the ability to make machines that convert theory into practice" that should be controlled, he contends, not the tens of thousands of products that pour out of America's factories. (U.S. export controls apply to more than two hundred thousand products worth more than $20 billion in 1982 export sales.)

In the unlikely event that the Reagan Administration can somehow manage to halt the flow of high technology to the Soviet Union, it would still be confronted with the disarray in export policies among its trading allies. The Europeans believe the U.S. approach to drying up technology transfers to the Soviet Union verges on economic warfare, a route which they are unwilling to take, as they made abundantly clear in the Siberian natural gas pipeline imbroglio.

Disquieting to business executives are White House and Pentagon proposals that could change the way that multinational corporations operate abroad. These proposals call for licensing the transfer of technology between U.S. parent companies and their overseas subsidiaries and preventing access to U.S. technology by foreign nationals who are employed by U.S. overseas subsidiaries. A preview of the confusion and hostility which such proposals would engender was witnessed in the Siberian pipeline controversy when the Reagan Administration prohibited General Electric Co. from selling its turbines directly to the Soviet Union and threatened to impose sanctions on GE's European licensees should they ship any products incorporating U.S. technology to the Soviets for use on the Siberian pipeline. Extension of the embargo to include foreign subsidiaries and licensees of all U.S. companies produced the most critical dispute in the post-war era between the United States and its NATO allies, who regarded this extraterritorial application of a U.S. rule as an infringement upon their sovereignty. U.S. executives are not unmindful of a warning by British Trade Minister Peter Rees that U.S. multinational investors may receive cooler receptions from foreign governments if their overseas subsidiaries and affiliates are seen as vulnerable to restrictions by Washington on exports of U.S.-origin components and technology.

The Reagan Administration's concern with restricting the transfer of technology to the Soviet Union presents a complex social problem: How to staunch the hemorrhage of U.S. technology, important to the Soviet Union for their weapon systems and industrial modernization, without at the same time depriving this country's scientists and research personnel of significant intellectual exchanges with Soviet scientists—limited and infrequent as they are and potentially risky as they may be—and, more important, stifling the free flow of information within the scientific community, which is essential to continued U.S. scientific and technological growth.

There has been a growing concern that the characteristically open scientific community is in practice a channel through which

critical technological-scientific information and know-how flows
to the Soviet Union and other potentially hostile countries. An
open scientific community is perceived as a national security
risk. Former Deputy Secretary of Defense and former Deputy
Director of the CIA Frank C. Carlucci puts the problem this way:

> The [scientific] exchanges to date, in the main, have not been recip-
> rocal. Rather, it is quite apparent the Soviets exploit scientific ex-
> changes . . . in a highly orchestrated, centrally directed effort
> aimed at gathering the technical information required to enhance
> their military posture.

Assistant Secretary of Commerce Lawrence J. Brady is even
more forthright in pinpointing the issue:

> Operating out of embassies, consulates and so-called "business
> delegations," KGB operatives have blanketed the developed capi-
> talist countries with a network that operates like a gigantic vac-
> uum cleaner, sucking up formulas, blueprints and know-how with
> frightening precision. *We believe these operations rank higher in
> priority even than the collection of military intelligence.* . . . This
> network seeks to exploit the "soft underbelly"—the individuals
> who, out of idealism or greed, fall victim to [Soviet] intelligence
> schemes; our traditions of an open press and unrestricted access
> to knowledge; and, finally the desire of academia to jealously pre-
> serve its prerogatives as a community of scholars unencumbered
> by government regulations. Certainly, these freedoms provide the
> underpinning of the American way of life. *It is time, however,
> to ask what price we must pay if we are unable to protect our
> secrets.* [Authors' italics.]

When he served as deputy director of the CIA prior to his recent
retirement, Admiral B. R. Inman urged the scientific community
to exercise greater self-restraint. He urged the scientific community to cooperate with government officials in determining how
to restrict publication of scientific and technological information
that is harmful to the security of the United States when acquired
by the Soviet Union, such as cryptological research, computer
designs and software, electronics, laser technology, crop projections and manufacturing techniques.

The academic and scientific communities, predictably, were
antagonistic to any suggestions of government interference with,
or control over, scientific research and publication, or the right
of universities to invite whomever they desired to visit their cam-

puses. (Even KGB agents masquerading as Soviet scientists?)

This negative reaction, in our judgment, is unrealistic. To begin with, there are already constraints of one type or another on scientific research. Concerned over technology leaks to, and thefts by, the Soviet Bloc, the Pentagon has imposed restrictions on university research projects which it funds. One such restriction is keeping foreign nationals from working on projects the Department of Defense regards as sensitive.

Many academics, however, contend that such restraints should not apply to research undertaken by universities. The Massachusetts Institute of Technology, for example, in 1980 rejected an Air Force contract with restrictions on publication, and the University of California at San Diego in 1982 negotiated the removal of restrictions on publication from an Air Force contract. When the Pentagon informed university contractors of its Very High Speed Integrated Circuits program to keep foreign nationals off the projects (a condition imposed after the contracts were signed), five university presidents protested.

In the commercial area, in which considerable numbers of scientists are employed, scientific research is subject to various types of constraints imposed by companies to safeguard their trade secrets. Scientists employed by private companies have never enjoyed an absolute right of publication. Research papers intended for publication at scientific meetings are customarily reviewed internally to prevent an inadvertent disclosure of trade secrets, and, not infrequently, to prevent disclosure of military secrets. That this practice is followed by the larger companies does not imply that security in the private sector is faultless. Among the smaller companies, the absence of security measures is scandalous.

Companies with defense contracts are subject to security restrictions imposed by the Department of Defense. The Pentagon forced the withdrawal of more than a hundred scientific papers at a San Diego meeting of the Society of Photo-Optical Instrumentation Engineers in August 1982 and "persuaded" researchers in such sensitive areas as laser optics and advanced electronics not to present their papers at scientific meetings. Officials of the Department of Defense assert that the Export Administration Act of 1979 authorizes them to control even *unclassified* scientific information. The Defense Department is in a position to prevent American scientists from presenting papers on virtually any subject at conferences held abroad and can prevent the delivery of papers at U.S. meetings attended by foreign scientists.

Controlling the delivery of scientific papers is not, however, the answer to the problem of halting the leakage of U.S. technology. Most scientists and many government officials believe that restricting communications among scientists will do little or nothing to halt the flow of U.S. technology to the East. "We really can't blame the free flow of information for the hemorrhaging of our technology," declares one highly placed U.S. official. "We really have to blame the Soviet's very active intelligence effort." Judge Webster, director of the FBI, puts it more emphatically, when he says, "I do not think there's been another time in our history when our country has been under such a sophisticated espionage assault."

A recent article by the *Los Angeles Times* correspondent in Peking, Michael Parks, reported (June 19, 1983) that China was establishing a new ministry to "strengthen state security," taking the KGB as its model. Like the KGB, the new ministry is expected to take on, in addition to domestic surveillance, the duties of overseas intelligence collection, including industrial espionage. Perhaps the real significance of this news is that the People's Republic is aiming to become in time a world class intelligence power, whose spies may pose as much of a threat to the West as the KGB's.

In these circumstances it is incumbent on the business corporation to do everything it can to thwart foreign intelligence attacks. The corporation's intelligence function must take on counterintelligence tasks as well. More than profits are at stake: national security and the future of the whole enterprise system.

Part III

Policy

10

The Value of Private Intelligence

PRIVATE intelligence is the means by which non-governmental organizations gather information. If it is to be useful, that information must enable an organization to increase, or at least maintain, its power and/or its profits. But immediate profits and practicality are not the only matters of concern to a corporate intelligence system. For a corporation to survive in the long term it must use intelligence to devise and maintain its corporate value strategy.

The corporate value strategy is a structure that is needed by the executives of an organization to understand both the complex issues that confront the organization and its position vis-à-vis those issues. An important corollary role of the value strategy is to persuade others using different values of the validity of the organization's position.

The corporate value strategy must accommodate the values of the corporation and the values of the communities in which the corporation operates. Value strategies are subsumed in the broader subject of ethics. Prior to the current U.S. economic difficulties, business newspapers, periodicals and commentators, and professors at leading graduate schools of business frequently mentioned and discussed business ethics. Professors of the new courses in ethics were quoted frequently, and the ethical dilemmas businessmen face were elaborated.

Professor L. L. Nash wrote in the *Harvard Business Review* an insightful article, "Ethics Without the Sermon," about the difficulty of ethical issues for business executives. The article proposes "a process of ethical inquiry that is immediately comprehensible to a group of executives and not predisposed to the utopian, and sometimes anticapitalistic, bias marking much of the work in applied business philosophy today."[1] Regrettably, the anticapitalistic bias is too evident today in academia and other influential sectors of society. We will return to this topic later.

Even though one currently sees some articles on the subject, to a degree the current concern with economic challenges has overshadowed the discussion of ethics. This is only a temporary phenomenon. The current and future ethical climate is particularly precarious for the business community because of the amount of international work it conducts, for often international commerce requires a business person to resolve the dilemma of conflicting ethical systems. And business will become still more international in the future, for the business community is closely tied to the globalization of economic relations that is currently under way. By its nature, the work of polycorporations requires an ability to respond to diverse cultures and practices, and to develop profitable relationships in countries many of which sorely need the management skills, technical processes, and capital resources that the modern corporation can mobilize.

To consider just one issue as an example: in many cultures, attitudes toward facilitative payments—payments to an individual to accomplish a specific task—are very different from our own. In most cases, our government now considers these payments to be "bribery," and bribery is, of course, considered to be illegal. Is it ethically wrong for a businessman from the United States to make such payments in a country where they are not only acceptable but deemed necessary? Our present law suggests that it is better to impose our own value system on these culturally different countries, and to refuse to conduct business until such nations reform their traditional methods. Is this the preferred ethical position?

This problem is not limited to just a handful of corporations. Federal law, currently barring a wide range of such payments, requires reporting procedures for others, so the questions raised may be academic at present. But some analysts believe this law is damaging the ability of U.S. firms to compete in international trade and investment, and there is growing attention to the problems presented by the legislation. Certainly, no foreign business will feel bound by United States law in its overseas negotiations, nor will the employees of foreign governments where investment might occur. The sole bearer of the costs of this legislation is the U.S. business community, and, by extension, the American people. We do not wish in any way to suggest that the current law be disregarded, but it is vital that we as a society address the difficult questions that underlie this moral posture.

Here private intelligence is needed to determine the true ethics and will of the people, not just those of the current legislative spokesmen for the people. Where these values are counter to the corporate value strategy, private intelligence must gather information that will enable the corporation to argue persuasively for the acceptance of its position. Alternatively, the corporation could gather intelligence that will enable it to persuade its constituency—its board and its major shareowners—that the ethics of the community are proper and good for the long term prosperity of the corporation, and, indeed, the corporate value strategy should be modified to conform to them.

The business community must live with difficult questions on a day-to-day basis. A corporate value strategy helps to bring order to the chaos this situation can foster. To recognize the complexity of the situation, it is useful to consider ethical positions on very similar issues. Again using the example of facilitative payments, we see that the law deems them bad, an antisocial act. Yet there is virtually a total lack of opposition to the use of payments by agents of our national intelligence services to secure information deemed vital to "the national interest." Is the same act ethical in the intelligence context of a nation-state and unethical in a business setting? Is business less in the "national interest" than espionage carried on by the state?

How we as a society answer questions of this dimension will help decide the future. And, these questions cannot be taken independently, for they are too complex and too time-consuming if the foundations must be totally rebuilt each time an issue is raised. Even more dangerous, the questions are too easily answered with logic that can be inconsistent when several issues are compared, and this can put an individual or a corporation in an untenable position. Answers to ethical questions must be supported by a consistent and solid value strategy.

Values Defined by Externalities

A value strategy is based on one's perception of the tangible and intangible environment in which one exists. An optimistic appraisal of our current global situation places us roughly halfway through a period of rapid transition where man has been confronted by a dramatically changed social environment. Seen in this light, humanity is moving from a fairly wretched situation two hundred years ago toward a new age some two hundred years hence, in which we will control more of the forces of nature and live a more secure existence. The change over this four-hundred-year period will thus be as dramatic as that of the thousand-year period preceding it, a span of time that witnessed the spread of the agricultural revolution around the globe and ended with the birth of the Industrial Revolution.

At the midway point in this industrial era, we have witnessed the emergence of the super-industrial economies, in which enterprises large enough to affect both the physical and societal environment play an important role. Soon we will be at the post-industrial stage of our economic development, in which scientific advance and economic development will make the task of producing the necessities of life—for some societies, at least—a minor one. Eventually, it is predicted by some optimists, all countries will develop the potentials of the post-industrial society.

These changes have been and will continue to be traumatic. Many members of society cannot cope easily with change, and when it is rapid, it is all the more discomforting. One of the manifestations of change that are of great concern today is the decline of the quality of private life. This finds social expression in many ways. White collar crime, nonviolent crimes against organizations and individuals, divorce, drug abuse, alcoholism, and child abuse are only some of the forms this malaise takes. The poor performance of our school systems is also symptomatic, and a danger signal for the future. The search for meaning is reflected in the rise of evangelical movements, cults, and a growing incidence of devil worship, ritual exorcisms, and other demonic obsessions.

The Value of Private Intelligence

Even with these destructive traumas that have the potential to destroy society, institutions, such as business and religion, have endured through many historical eras. They have endured because in eras of change, their value structures have enabled them to respond to the challenge of these changes with a newly revised sense of direction appropriate to the times. Rather than clinging to claims of orthodoxy and legitimacy, these institutions have reordered their objectives and priorities while remaining true to their fundamental values. In this era, too, when change occurs at a speed never heretofore experienced in the history of mankind, there is a need for new responses. We cannot look back to small-town American life for our vision of the future—ours is an increasingly urban world, particularly in the developing countries of Asia, Africa and Latin America. Moreover, the lifestyle, personal mobility and social expectations of many Americans will no longer be satisfied by the patterns of life that were acceptable to the workers of an earlier era: thus, an accommodative solution to our need for a successful transition to the future must begin with a realistic assessment of popular needs.

Private intelligence must be used to assay the society in which an organization operates so as to determine the existing value structures and the evolving stage of adaptation required by the polycorporation.

Role of Institutions

Major institutions not only enable themselves to accommodate change, they play transnational roles in human history, and this may be an important element in meeting the needs of a new global society. In business, trade relations in ancient times brought together disparate cultures, and allowed them to learn from each other. In our own era, the multinational corporation is the key actor in the continuing globalization of our economic order. Religions have also crossed national and cultural boundaries since earliest times, and have adapted to a great variety of situations successfully: the Roman Catholic Church, for instance, was probably the first great multinational organization, and its continued importance in so many of the world's societies suggests a flexibility that will be the key to its survival in the future.

How does all this relate to private intelligence and the corporation? There are two principal ties. First, the corporation is a cooperative effort of people. Second, the corporation serves a segment
of the people of the society. To remain viable, a business organization must know the values and the needs of the people who compose it and the values and the needs of the people of the societies
it serves. Then, to meet the challenge of change, business and
other institutions of society will have to cooperate effectively to
reinvigorate all aspects of the private sector.

In an article about ethical education in the *New York Times,*
Rabbi Balfour Brickner of the Stephen Wise Free Synagogue
wrote:

> . . . students [should] think more and harder about why some-
> thing is suggested as an ethical value, from what source an ethical
> stance might derive, and what, if anything, ought to oblige us to
> abide by any set of values. For example: When truth-telling is
> universally ignored, what are the social consequences? What hap-
> pens to a society in which trust is destroyed by theft or justice
> not seriously pursued? If thievery is profitable, why shouldn't one
> be a thief, especially when everyone, including the highest offi-
> cials, steal?
>
> Clergymen are not the only ones who can, or should, struggle
> with the problems of the sources and meanings of values. Imagine
> teams of our most distinguished lawyers, business leaders, profes-
> sors from schools of business administration, preparing and teach-
> ing curricula for junior and senior high school students that would
> explain and justify, from their respective viewpoints, the moral
> bases for the law or the rules of their businesses or professions.
> Lawyers would be asked to justify the ethical foundations on which
> their theories of right or wrong are established. Businessmen
> would describe the ethical dilemmas they face and explain the
> ethical principles used in resolving them. Case histories could be
> used from business schools to explore ethical solutions to real situ-
> ations. Imagine the effect such information might have on young
> people whose experiences teach them only that caveat emptor still
> applies, that it is only the damned fool who tells the truth or does
> not cheat.[2]

Rabbi Brickner indicates how various institutions of society
must cooperate if we are to overcome the traumas of change,
but unfortunately, in many ways, the public postures of these
institutions seem diametrically opposed. For example, academic
and religious institutions focus on intellectual and spiritual matters, and maintain the teaching of doctrine and tradition. Though

they have a financial dimension, these organizations stand apart from the commerce and industry that dominate the lives of most people. In a sense, business organizations begin where academic and religious concerns stop, deriving their vital energy from the desire to increase the wealth and substance of the society. How can institutions so different in character meet this enormous challenge together?

The answer to that question resides at the core of our institutions: their value structure. As Rabbi Brickner wrote, what are the social consequences when truth-telling is universally ignored? The consequences would not occur only in the schools, the churches and the synagogues. Clearly, there would be a seriously adverse impact on all other sectors of society, including all aspects of commerce.

Though the forces of history continually shape institutions, each major institution of society stretches back in awesome dimension to eras and generations that we can only faintly recall. At the center of this historic strength is a common faith in the potential of the individual. Though each describes this potential in very different terms, the message is nonetheless the same: there is dignity in man, men are to respect each other as they would be respected themselves, and within the association of men something meaningful and significant can occur in an individual's life.

The Belief in Progress

A hallmark of American society has been the traditional belief in the idea of progress. We have believed that, as individuals, we will progress to a better life. We have believed that our progeny will progress to a better life because of what we have done for them, or because of the opportunities we have made available to them. And we have believed that future generations of our society will be better off because of the things we are doing to improve civilization.

Professor Robert Nisbet in his book *History of the Idea of Progress* questions whether this fundamental value of Western civilization is in jeopardy, for there is doubt today that progress is worth seeking, indeed, there is doubt that progress is possible. In his book, Professor Nisbet summarizes how the idea of progress evolved and became perhaps the central pillar of our ethical structure. He discusses the developing disillusionment with religion, science, and knowledge. Among the writers he cites is the distinguished molecular biologist Gunther Stent. Professor Nisbet writes:

> Stated briefly, Professor Stent's argument is that already a withdrawal from and a waning of interest in science, technology, and economic growth is to be seen, especially among youth drawn from the middle class. This is illustrated in his view by the character type we epitomize in the words "hippie" and "beat." The continued development in currently "backward" countries will only lead in time to the same kind of disillusionment with "progress" in all of these countries that is now so vivid in the West. There will be a spreading desire all over the world for escape from the work ethic, the disciplines of technology, and the stigmata of affluence. Gradually but surely, more and more peoples will make their way along "the road to Polynesia," that is, toward a society in which simplicity, naturalness, and tranquil ease will be the highlights. Not all technology will be lost, Stent believes; at one end of social spectrum will be a minority of people still interested in running technology that gives comfort.[3]

There is nothing dramatically new about this concept. We have heard this argument before, though seldom articulated so well. Indeed, the idea is much older than the contemporary articles we read; in fact, Professor Nisbet quotes Lucretius: "Yet if a man would steer his life by true reasoning, it is great riches to a man to live thriftily with calm mind, for never can he lack for so little."[4] Why then are we concerned enough to make this an issue here? And how does it relate to the value strategy of corporations?

The American Work Ethic

Perhaps the keystone of the American system is the traditional work ethic. The work ethic, in turn, is based on key elements of Western culture, among them the idea of progress. Today, there is more than casual questioning of that idea. Indeed, there is a pervasive attack on it. In America today, in all sectors of society, there is profound loss of confidence in the nation's leaders. There is loss of confidence in our institutions.[5] And now, the foundation of the economic system is facing serious challenge. This challenge is predicated upon a practical as well as a moral critique of modern capitalism. Consequently, the value system that has been the philosophical foundation for most United States business corporations is being affected by this period of major change in society.

Many American workers would have said in the past, "I am working so that my family and I will have a better tomorrow." They knew they were sacrificing some pleasure in the present (such as leisure time with their families), but the benefits to be enjoyed in the future were considered to be worth it. Executives, managers, clerical employees, factory workers, laborers—all ranks would have voiced the same concept.

Today, one hears employees talking instead about the pleasures of the present. Office and factory workers find little promise in the future, and the quality of their work and the level of their productivity show this. The vision of a future where one will be doing the same physically taxing and/or oppressively boring work one is doing today causes many workers to seek escape in cults, alcohol, marijuana, and other drugs. It has been noted that this desire for escape affects junior and senior executives as well as non-management workers. Executives forego promotions so they can have time with their families. Promising managers leave corporate ranks to pursue non-business pleasures. Escapism is not new, but the pervasiveness of it is. During a walk on Wall Street in the morning, noon hour, or afternoon, one's nose will be assaulted by the distinctive aroma of marijuana. One observes people of notable serenity, and it seems more likely that their inner peace is the result of artificial agents rather than an intellectual discipline. Their emphasis is on satisfaction in the present.

If tomorrow will not be better than today, why work hard today? Why work a twelve-hour day? Why sweat, physically or intellectually, to do the job better, or simply with minimal diligence, if the rewards in the present are not adequate, and there may be no reward in the future? If the effort will detract from one's pleasure in the present, it simply is not worth it.

The corporation has the challenge of providing incentives to get "an honest day's work." There are many studies on job enrichment and other strategies, but they are not our concern. This issue was cited to illustrate the necessity, to use Professor Stent's phrase, for that "minority of people still interested in running technology that gives comfort," that is, the corporations that are responsible for society's economic well-being, to maintain a private intelligence system that will enable them to (1) be alerted early to changing aspects of society, and (2) to either combat those changes intelligently or adapt efficiently to them, while also mounting an adequate moral and economic defense of the capitalistic system upon which our institutions are founded.

Other important issues could be cited. Among them is the concept of property. Property is a traditional value fundamental to the value structure of business corporations.[6] Yet today there is discussion among responsible people, leaders of other sectors of society, as to who really owns the productive capacity of society.

The Constituencies of a Corporation

Corporations affect and provide incentives to people in many sectors of society. Clearly, entrepreneurs, executives, and employees all expect rewards—traditionally these rewards were based on a value system that assumed good performance today would result in a better future. As we have previously discussed, this value system is undergoing dramatic change. Investors have value systems that justify commitments of their capital. So do communities in which corporate facilities are located. Customers' value systems are the raison d'être for the existence of a business. What happens if these value systems are not observed correctly by a corporation and are not satisfied appropriately by it?

There is no question that corporations which do not have intelligence systems to gather and analyze the value systems of their constituencies will go the way of dinosaurs. Those corporations will not have the ability to recognize the evolution of their environment, and they will cling to manifestations of old values that are no longer valid. By manifestations of values, we mean the behaviors that result from an ethical position. For example, if one believes in equality, and one attempts to treat all people equally, it still may be "socially acceptable" and acceptable to one's conscience to employ women only as secretaries and clerks, for one defines them as a special subset of "all people." But as one comes to see that the value structure around "equality" encompasses equal job opportunities for women, certain types of

194

behavior must be modified. This perception may spring from within, as a truth revealed, or the awareness of it may come in the form of a new societal awareness or even as a new law.

To a large extent, all of us are captives of our experience. It is understandable that we may fail to recognize nascent change. But dissonance and the probability of failure increase when one refuses to acknowledge change and act appropriately. A challenge to all of us is that change may seem to conflict with one's values, but on reflection one may find, as have the enduring institutions of society, that the fundamental value strategy remains firm. Only the behavioral manifestations need to be modified. While the appropriate action often is self-modification, sometimes, as we will discuss later, appropriate action may be to try to persuade others that the emerging trend is injurious to society, and should be reversed.

11

Corporate Strategy and Ethics

THE power and self-justification of modern U.S. business corporations and most of the institutions of "establishment" society are based on values of Western culture. As discussed earlier, an important element in their philosophical foundation, if not the dominant source of its support, is the idea of progress. Another important element is the concept of private property. If these important values are changing, then what are the implications to the institutions which embody them? What are the implications to the individuals for whom these institutions are important vehicles to satisfy their personal goals? And how do these factors relate to a corporate intelligence system?

Leaders of successful organizations must be able to modify the behavior and goals of their organization so as to be in concert with the new environment. This adaptation is viable when it is based on a solid value strategy. But when the value system is compromised, when there is no common sense of direction, then there will be distress and disorientation for members of the organizations. Some common symptoms of that distress and disorientation are visible today; they include the pervasiveness of materialism, the emphasis on immediate gratification, the preoccupation with the self, the increased use of chemical agents to achieve artificial states of well-being, the rise of exotic cults, and white collar crime.

196

To suggest that the answer to these social problems is merely a question of leadership, or the ability to adapt successfully to change, is a gross oversimplification. The core of the problem is the dilemma in which a business executive is confronted by a thorny ethical issue. How does one who is accustomed to dealing with "real" issues begin to tackle amorphous, intangible issues? How does one know when he is right and others are wrong about complex value judgments? Indeed, how does he come to be comfortable with his own beliefs? Where does he find time to deal with ever-present ethical issues? Professor Nash, whose article on ethics was cited earlier, suggests twelve questions that will help analyze the ethics of a business decision:

1. Have you defined the problem accurately?
2. How would you define the problem if you stood on the other side of the fence?
3. How did this situation occur in the first place?
4. To whom and to what do you give your loyalty as a person and as a member of the corporation?
5. What is your intention in making this decision?
6. How does this intention compare with the probable results?
7. Whom could your decision or action injure?
8. Can you discuss the problem with the affected parties before you make your decision?
9. Are you confident that your position will be as valid over a long period of time as it seems now?
10. Could you disclose without qualm your decision or action to your boss, your CEO, the board of directors, your family, society as a whole?
11. What is the symbolic potential of your action if understood? If misunderstood?
12. Under what conditions would you allow exceptions to your stand?[1]

When a person is sure of his values, he has a compass to withstand the storms of change. But, if one's certainty is based on obstinacy rather than a rational evaluation of the values, then undoubtedly he will be misdirected. Both honesty and adequate information are essential. Private intelligence is the means to gather the requisite information. Again quoting Professor Nash:

> Dealing with the immediate case of lying, quality discrepancy, or strained labor relations—when the problem is finally discovered—is only a temporary solution. A full examination of how the situation occurred and what the traditional solutions have been may reveal a more serious discrepancy of values and pressures, and this will illuminate the real significance and ethics of the problem. It will also reveal recurring patterns of events that in

isolation appear trivial but that as a whole point up a serious situation.

Such a mechanism is particularly important because very few executives are outright scoundrels. Rather, violations of corporate and social values usually occur inadvertently because no one recognizes that a problem exists until it becomes a crisis. This tendency toward initial trivialization seems to be the biggest ethical problem in business today.[2]

Private intelligence enables leaders to identify possible modifications to existing values and newly emerging values; it indicates when corporate behavior is no longer appropriate; and it helps to evaluate modes of adaptation to change. If it is to be effective, private intelligence must be guided by a corporate value structure. The value structure gives direction to the intelligence-seeking activity, provides a screen to segregate relevant information from the mass of other data, and it provides a context that gives significance to the information. It is a decision structure that enables one to determine where an issue fits in the ethical context, facilitating the ability to make decisions quickly without the need for extensive analysis of each individual issue.

Values Legitimatize Action

As discussed previously, values help to resolve ethical dilemmas. Situations of ethical ambiguity can result in great anguish for the decision-maker and other participants. This anguish, as suggested earlier, can take the form of escapist behavior. It can also take the form of virtually catatonic inability to make a decision and inability to take appropriate action. A common manifestation of this is the businessperson who refuses to face an important decision, but instead procrastinates, hoping the situation will resolve itself.

These dilemmas are not confined to the business sector. A significant illustration comes from medicine. Hospitals have used philosophers to give instruction in medical ethics to students. In itself, that is not remarkable, for society and medical procedures have grown more complex during the centuries that have passed since the time of Hippocrates. But some hospitals are now adding philosophers to their staffs, or are engaging them as consultants, to counsel practicing physicians and nurses about "the often conflicting ethical, legal and moral issues that can confound the keenest medical minds."[3] "For example, does a living fetus that has been aborted have a right to survive even though the abortion was clearly intended to destroy it? Should a hospital permit surgery so that a severely deformed infant can survive an otherwise fatal intestinal obstruction? Should a hospital authorize kidney dialysis for an elderly patient who is near death?"[4] What should be done if a middle-aged alcoholic who is dying from a destroyed liver and heart disease is using major quantities of whole blood, and a shortage of supply develops? Should "more deserving" people be given priority?[5]

Lawyers are trained to avoid the "slippery slope," that is, they do not make an argument that if it is taken just an inch further appears to stay the same, but inch by inch finally becomes another issue. One might start with an example of truly intellectual, non-erotic art, but where does one mark the line that separates it from pornography that is designed to arouse carnal longings? Without an ethical framework, one quickly slips to the bottom of the slope, where one is forced to use the lowest common denominator.

Issues involving value structures are noted not only for their complexity, but often for the diametrically opposed solutions that are advocated by those who are involved in the issue—and even by observers. A sound value system is needed to steer the businessman through the maze of considerations. That system, with information provided by private intelligence, will help develop an action plan that is ethically acceptable and also congruent with an executive's goals. But that is not the end of his problem. He also must deal with the solutions proposed by others. Those solutions cannot be dismissed. If those who suggested other solutions are a friendly audience, they probably share much of the executive's value structure, and they are likely to accept the solution with minimum explanation of how it ties to the corporate and their own value strategies. If the audience is influential, and if it is hostile to the values used by the executive, then a more vigorous program is needed to convince them of the soundness of the executive's position—or to neutralize their opposition.

It is probable today that most decisions with consequences external to the corporation will be challenged by advocacy groups. The less these groups understand the value position of the corporation, the greater the probability that they will be unable to accept the corporation's decisions. Because value decisions are difficult to make, frequently corporation personnel do not feel comfortable defending them—most probably because they are not sure themselves. This leads to an even greater communications gap between business and adversary groups. As stated earlier, an important benefit of a sound value system is that it gives confidence to the decision-maker. It also helps explain and justify action to others.

Other Value Strategies

Businessmen are concerned with tangibles: the quantity of goods produced, the number of products sold, the value of inventory, the dollar value of sales, the number of employees, the percentage of customers buying a new product. Business people are engaged in the production of economic goods and services. Why then should they bother with intangible and difficult questions about values?

The answer is simple. They have no choice. Business is involved with the distribution of goods and rewards. Business decisions affect the material standard of living of virtually the entire society. Moreover, business decisions affect, tangibly and intangibly, the lives of employees, suppliers, customers and shareowners—indeed, society itself. All business decisions are, at bottom, based on values.

Individuals who work for a corporation no longer have the "grey flannel mentality" that was typical twenty or more years ago. Employees today want a measure of satisfaction in the present that was not demanded before by the American work force. They insist upon acceptable working conditions, and work rules, or they flee to other companies, especially if they are highly skilled people who are in great demand, such as computer specialists. If they believe they are being treated unfairly, and they have no employment alternatives, they do a minimal job, or they sabotage their employer's operations, or they steal from him because "he deserves it."

The role, rights and responsibilities of the individual are key components of the value structure. The concept of the nature of the individual affects the design of the corporation's internal organization. The obvious problem is that these values and attitudes can adversely affect the productivity of the American economic machine. And this affects the material well-being of the American people. But the problem is not limited to employees. Shareowners, customers, residents of communities adjoining corporate facilities, and "interested citizens" all are making claims on corporations. The net effect of these claims is to reduce the efficiency of the corporation. In effect, these groups are the new competition of a business.

Traditionally, competition came from other corporations who were engaged in the same or a similar business activity. Today, corporations compete with anyone or any group who feel they have a justifiable claim on the resources of the corporation. In some cases, unjustifiable claims are made by groups who believe they will benefit from the publicity or notoriety of their action, or believe they will gain some other indirect advantage, perhaps personal power for the leaders.

Professor P. L. Berger published an informative article, "New Attack on the Legitimacy of Business," in the *Harvard Business Review*. The synopsis of the article states:

> When people genuinely believe in the "rightness" of certain social arrangements, those arrangements are experienced as proper and worthy of support—that is, as legitimate. And when institutions like the modern business corporation are seen as legitimate, they not only function more smoothly but are also better able to help realize a society's most cherished goals. American business once enjoyed this kind of implicit social charter. It does not today.[6]

Professor Berger discusses the evolution of the changed attitude of society toward business:

> The greatest animus came [during the 1970s] not from organized labor, long the sharpest critic of business, but from the once-friendly pillars of establishment culture—the elite universities, the intelligentsia, and the national media.
>
> Conventional wisdom on the most prestigious campuses pronounced capitalism a cosmic evil, America a sick society precisely to the degree that it was capitalist, and every businessman a rapacious oppressor. National television eagerly gave air time to reports about major companies that despoiled the environment and endangered public health and safety in the mad pursuit of profits. And when not portrayed as villainous polluters, America's corporate giants were shown to be allied to corruption at home and tyranny abroad.

Whatever the lasting influence of this antibusiness sentiment
on public opinion, it certainly had the immediate effect of putting
businessmen on the defensive. But this was not all. Angered and
puzzled by the altered cultural climate outside their organizations,
they discovered an even more disconcerting change within—not,
of course, the overt hostility just described but a lessening of commitment and dedication among their younger colleagues. The reliable "organization men," whom William Whyte had criticized so
sharply some 20 years before, had become rather hard to find.[7]

Professor Berger's perceptive thesis is that the members of a
new social class, if not responsible for the situation, certainly
are fostering it. "To put the point bluntly," he writes, "if many
Americans today challenge the legitimacy of business, more than
likely they are getting something out of it. And what might that
be?" En route to answering that question, he introduces the "new
class." As an example, he uses the concept of the knowledge industry, which "includes all those who engage in the production
and distribution of what passes for knowledge in a society."[8]
Among the members of the new class are the professors at
the elite universitites, the "masses of lesser pedagogues," the
non-business and non-technical professionals of the media, coun-
selors, and government bureaucrats "with jurisdiction over
quality-of-life issues."[9] "In interest, culture, and politics the new
class in America tends to be antagonistic to business and a threat
to its legitimacy. Whether that legitimacy survives—and, if so,
in what form—hinges on the outcome of new-class efforts to aug-
ment its power in American society."[10]

He notes that, "the new class has long taken its cultural cues
from the upper crust of elite intellectuals, who—as part of what
Lionel Trilling spoke of as the 'adversary culture' in America—
have been contemptuous of business and all its works for at least
a century." And, he adds:

> Do not forget that a high proportion (almost certainly the major-
> ity) of the new class is either publicly employed or heavily depen-
> dent on public subsidies. No wonder, then, that the new class is
> generally disposed to a "statist" orientation which, in the context
> of American society, necessarily implies antagonism to private,
> market-oriented business interests.
>
> Take a very clear case the ongoing debate over the environment.
> Environmentalism is a virtually pure instance of a new-class
> movement, and its beachheads within the government bureau-
> cracy—the EPA in particular—are largely held by new-class indi-

202

viduals. It is, obviously, in the interest of these people to allege that business, if left alone, would do terrible harm to the environment because the allegation directly legitimates their own activities.[11]

We would like to share one final insightful quote from Professor Berger's article:

> Virtually without exception, every increase in the power of the new class has been legitimated in terms of the welfare of the poor. And the poor, especially the black poor, have consistently given political support to the new class in its various redistributionist policies, and they have indeed benefited from them. But as an increasing number of black intellectuals have recognized, these benefits come at a high price. The price is dependency—dependency on government and especially on the new-class bureaucrats and professionals who administer the redistributionist machinery of the welfare state.[12]

One might consider Professor Berger's comments interesting, but perhaps a little exaggerated. To do that, however, would be, in our view, a mistake. Let us consider what happened recently in Santa Monica, California. In 1981, Ruth Goldway, a woman who has very "new class" ideas, was elected mayor. It was alleged that among the mayor's supporters were Jane Fonda and her husband, Tom Hayden. The flavor of Mayor Goldway's program was reflected in an article by her husband, Derek Shearer, director of urban studies at Occidental College, a member of the Santa Monica Planning Commission, and co-author of "Economic Democracy: Challenge of the 1980's." The following are excerpts from his article "Popular Planning," which appeared in the *New York Times:*[13]

> As the economic renaissance promised by Reagonomics fails to appear, calls for economic planning will be heard from leading businessmen and politicians. Will such planning, when it inevitably comes, be participatory? . . .
> Santa Monica's city government, elected in 1981 on a platform of economic democracy, is striving to be an exemplar of locally controlled planning. The City Council and other officials believe that President Reagan's "new federalism" should be built on principles of participation, not royalism. For example, the city required one developer to include 100 units of affordable rental housing, a day-care center, a public park, and incentives to use public transit. In another development, a proposed 12-story office building

203

downtown was reduced to three stories in which offices, apartments, and food stores are mixed. . . .

Some national planning will be necessary. The Federal Government should take an equity position in key industries—for example, steel, cars, energy, finance—and then require board representation for union and community leaders. . . .

Local democratic planning would begin with neighborhood-based programs that provide residents with technical help to come up with an assessment of the goods and services needed by their community. This might include public amenities like parks and street repairs, and private needs like particular kinds of stores or, simply, jobs for the unemployed.

Most important, cities would obtain capital to plan for new jobs and neighborhood improvements from municipally owned banks that would loan funds and provide equity for development projects. . . .

The city development bank might also make loans to small-scale manufacturing businesses in, say, new technology, but insist that the firms be organized as employee-owned enterprises, have profit-sharing plans, or at least employ Santa Monica residents.

If Professor Berger is correct about the attitudes of the new class, as we believe he is, and if Ruth Goldway* and her husband Derek Shearer are representative of the new class, then leaders of business will have formidable challenges in the future. It seems very clear that the coming discussion will center on the validity of the values that underpin business decisions and actions.

Sources of Help

By itself, business will have a difficult time trying to convince other sectors of society that its values are more valid than those of the "new class." A solution is to engage the cooperation of institutions whose goals are in concert with those of business. The value traditions and global experience of both business and religion provide a solid basis for future cooperation, but it must also be recognized that there are potential areas of conflict. The success of their efforts to build a future in which both continue to play a viable role in society will depend in large part upon their ability to overcome potential problem areas.

* Ms. Goldway was defeated in her bid for reelection in 1983 to the Santa Monica City Council.

Some religious groups, it should be acknowledged, appear to advocate an equalization of wealth theory, an attitude that is obviously antithetical to the modern business corporation and the private enterprise system. Business cooperation with religious groups of that coloration is automatically untenable, just as religious cooperation with business organizations that espouse atheism or the dehumanization of workers would be impossible.

Cooperation between religion and business must start from the recognition of common centers of gravity in the private sector of society and an acceptance of the differences in the operational codes by which each functions. Much has been made of various forms of white-collar crime in recent years, and certainly the society needs to concern itself with the maintenance of standards that apply equally to all. This is the essence of a concept of justice, upon which a system of law and order must be based. But the questions of conscience that must be legitimately raised should not overshadow the broader trends and grave dangers that face all private institutions, or the very basis for raising questions of conscience will disappear. Both individualism and the belief in individual responsibility upon which ethical codes are built require an underlying system of private associations, in which the notions of individual duties and rights are constantly reinforced.

Religious institutions cannot refuse to work with business institutions on the grounds that business institutions are tainted by materialism that leads to corruption. Religious institutions themselves have not been spared occasional periods of internal corruption and reform. All institutions are subject to the problems of human frailty, and none should be expected to maintain a perfect or consistent record. Just as a chain is only as strong as its weakest link, so, too, are institutions faced with the limitations that human imperfections impose.

Rarely does the business sector work directly with religious institutions. The separation of church and state in the United States has been extended to the separation of church and business corporations, perhaps because many corporations are governments, mini-states, in their own right. However, business and the church share numerous goals, for business in many ways is society's material expression of its spiritual goals. Business corporations and the church also share a common concern: the ever-encroaching powers of government, extended in part

205

through the growth and the activities of the "new class." The policy against direct philanthropy undoubtedly is too strong to alter, even if one could argue that it should be changed. But it should be obvious to the business and the religious communities that business corporations are the source of most of the congregation's wealth, and the congregation is the source of the church's wealth. Consequently, by aiding the congregation, business can provide religious institutions with the economic means to consider and define a value structure appropriate to our changing society. Business leaders can urge religious leaders to use these resources for this purpose—for the good of society.

There are three main institutions that compete with U.S. business corporations: business corporations of other nations, social activist groups, and government bodies. In the past, government controls were exercised principally at the U.S. Federal and state levels, but as the example of Santa Monica shows, government controls are increasing at all levels.

Business corporations of nations that enjoy a "work orientation" will be more productive and will compete more efficiently and successfully than U.S. corporations, and their advantage will grow if U.S. corporations become bound by inefficient social values, particularly as those values are expressed in government regulation. Students of business will recognize immediately the pernicious consequences that result from the loss of market share.

Social-activist organizations advocate redistribution of wealth, resources, and power in ways that will turn the business corporation into a new, less-efficient entity with fewer incentives for its members. Often, in the United States, legislation is the means by which these groups achieve their goals. As Professor Berger stated, and as Mr. Shearer illustrated, the new class is working from positions of power from within the government. Overseas, there is a growing evidence of the debilitating effect of terrorism—which may be the medium of expression of revolutionary organizations or, perhaps, the result of sponsorship by a central authority. Government competes with business corporations and the public for society's resources. It has the advantage of its legislative and administrative powers which it can use to seize those resources. The government also has its own "social-activist" goals, and it can be the agent of change for "social activists," as noted above. The government is able to increase its power in the long run only if it has the support of the public. Disturbingly, public support of the government has been increasing at the same time public support of business has been declining. The outcome may be acceleration of the trends which portend the emasculation of the individual in our society. This trend is pernicious to all.

Value Strategy and Philosophy

Reversal of the trend is not possible in the absence of an open and forthright defense of the capitalistic system upon which the modern corporation depends for its philosophical supports. The loss of belief in progress mentioned above corresponds to a similar loss of belief in the idea of economic growth under capitalism. In fact, for almost a quarter of a century after World War II, growth was cited as the most serious illness of capitalism. Numerous commentators spoke of the "limits to growth" and, in view of the costs of economic growth, many concluded that an end to expansion was necessary. This proposition, coupled with the general assault upon the idea of capitalism, has an extremely negative impact on the corporation and all of its ventures. The economic globalization fostered by the multinational corporation will be dramatically curtailed with the political triumph of the anti-growth philosophy.

In order to avoid these consequences, the corporate value strategy must embrace an effective economic and moral defense of capitalism. This defense of the enterprise system is crucial to a determination of the ethical context of contemporary issues facing the corporation. Only by understanding the broader philosophical concerns of our system can business leaders formulate a value strategy that will refute the accusations of the "adversary culture."

As Jean-François Revel observed in *The Totalitarian Temptation,* the critics of the capitalistic philosophy formulate their attack on dual arguments. First, they maintain that capitalism fails as an economic system in that it simply does not "deliver the goods." This proposition is the most easily discounted since, Revel notes, "no serious economist would deny the long-term increase in both over-all production and average per-capita income."[14] Thus, unless one disregards all statistics, it is obvious that capitalism has solved the problem of production. The second argument against capitalism is that it is profoundly immoral. This belief is the problem that businessmen encounter in their efforts to work with religious leaders. A thorough examination of the moral critique of capitalism, however, will enable fair-minded religious leaders to resist the simplistic temptation to denounce business as materialistic and insensitive to human concerns. In fact, as Revel observes, capitalism is, at worst, morally neutral.[15] Its primary objective is not the subjection of the workers but rather production. In producing the goods and services necessary for improving the lives of the populations of the capitalist states, capitalism can actually have a very positive moral impact. If one grants the moral neutrality of the system and rejects claims that it requires "injustice," then it is possible to see the capability of capitalism to generate numerous moral "goods" in addition to material goods. By overcoming the problem of production, the corporation has enabled people not only to enjoy a more comfortable life, free from the fear of hunger and impoverishment, but it also provides people with an opportunity to contemplate matters of a non-material nature: art, literature and numerous other cultural activities.

It is also possible to explore the question of the nature of the individual within the framework of an examination of capitalism. Such an endeavor supports the idea of the worth of the individual and his right to demonstrate initiative and ingenuity in the marketplace or in any other field of activity. In addition, it can be maintained that a study of the humanitarian aspects of this system supports the proposition that the welfare of the poor can also be related to the success of business in the sense that all of society benefits from the overall success of the business community. In formulating a value strategy that encompasses these views, business can do much to counter the effects of an unfavorable political climate while simultaneously refuting the moralistic pretensions of the redistributionist "new class."

Conclusion

Institutions, not individuals, will conquer the future. Increasingly, the complexity of modern society presents barriers that an individual working independently cannot overcome. The influence of individuals tends to wane rather quickly due to the rapid and pervasive change of modern society, but the power of institutions tends to endure after the time that logic indicates it should end, for the momentum of an institution often sustains its power.

The value systems of institutions merit study. They have (or should have) a strategy imbedded that states or implies goals and the tactics to achieve those goals. These values are the basis for the internal organization of the institution; consequently, they affect the efficiency with which the institution serves society. The values affect a wide audience, for they are projected outward onto the population served by the institution, influencing those people. The value systems are the anchor for individuals in times of stress and, simultaneously, the beacon that marks goals to be achieved.

Business executives must understand the values they are using to make decisions and formulate policy. Business executives must also understand the values of the societies they serve.

Managers must have private intelligence systems to determine whether their values are being expressed in ways appropriate to the values of the people who are employed and served by the corporation.

Values are critical to the continuance of business corporations as vital components of society founded on the precepts of capitalism. They enable complex ethical decisions to be made more efficiently. They provide confidence in one's direction and legitimatize action. It is essential that the business sector identify the values it wants to maintain and the values it wants to establish. Then, business leaders can help convince society of the worth of those values. The business sector must use its resources to help society develop and maintain a valid, workable value structure—a structure of values that will inspire—and help provide a work ethic that is in concert with the true needs of society.

The business corporation is a vehicle by which human and material resources are converted to goods and services. It is a means for the distribution of wealth. It is the instrument through which most members of modern society attain personal goals—both psychic and tangible.

The values that are used to direct the corporation have clear implications. If the emerging values (or lack of values) replace traditional values, then the probable results will be lower productivity, less efficient conversion of resources, a lower material standard of living, and repositioning of the United States among the nations of the world. If people settle for less than their best because they lose the incentives they prize, or if people turn from the traditional incentives offered by business organizations and no new incentives are offered, the material well-being and relative wealth of the society will be lowered, and this probably will lower productivity still further, which in turn will lower real wealth again, and the cycle will repeat itself over and over until some great force interrupts it—or until the affected nations ceases to exist.

As this happens, or if it is allowed to happen, business corporations will lose stature in society, and their prerogatives will be transferred to other institutions.

In addition to the tangible material consequences, the impact on the individual cannot be overlooked. There are numerous studies on self-expression-through-work. For many employees there is self-identification or self-definition via the job and/or the employer. Employees spend about 50 percent of their waking hours, five days a week, at their jobs. Moreover, many employees carry in their minds during work, on the way to and from it, and during leisure activities, a multitude of hopes and concerns about their jobs and careers. This extensive commitment of the individual to an activity demands that the activity be appropriate to the individual's value structure.

Businessmen have a responsibility to share their abilities to help society decide wisely how its productive resources will be used. Private intelligence must be used to collect information that will enable executives to make rational, pragmatic decisions about evolving value systems and the needs of society, and then communicate their findings to society at large. Business people, of course, share values with others in society. In addition, business people have unique tools to identify the pragmatic implications of values. An important role of business should be to help society make choices when values and behaviors are not in concert, and when values suggest mutually exclusive or conflicting behaviors.

Political activism, which includes persuading the public as much as lobbying elected and appointed officials, can be used to promote a sound value structure. To operate successfully in the political sphere—that is, so as to promote the profit and power

210

of the business corporation—businessmen must understand the internal environment of the corporation and its external environment—that is, the society that the corporation serves. The only way to gain that understanding is through sound private intelligence.

12

The Ultimate Dilemma

The greatest influence for good or evil is not man at all. It is a machine: the computer.

—*Time* magazine

THE Intelligence Age is like a Chinese character that can be read to mean either "promise" or "danger."

The promise lies in the computer—an intelligence machine that is already transforming our daily lives and offers a promise of further revolutionizing the way we conduct our businesses. Medical research, aerospace technology, outer space exploration, deep-sea mining, genetic engineering and a gamut of esoteric activities heretofore thought of as "science fiction" are now commonplace, thanks to or because of the computer.

The danger lies in the misuses to which this intelligence machine can be put—through our apathy and careless indifference or by the design of evil men.

It should be kept in mind that the leading computer experts in this country reiterate again and again that at present there is no computer in existence which cannot be penetrated by foreign espionage agents, by representatives of organized crime, by "consultants" who have been retained to spy out a competitor's trade secrets, or by pranksters who frequently are geniuses in their computer expertise.

Computer invasion makes it possible for the electronic burglar to effect an illegal transfer of bank funds. Such attacks on private information enable the corporate criminal or an espionage network to seriously damage not only the commercial banking system, but to invade personal privacy—to cite only one example, the income tax records and other information supplied to the U.S. Internal Revenue Service that are stored in central computers.

The Kennedy, Johnson and Nixon presidencies, among others, revealed with startling clarity the disquieting insight that constitutionally elected occupants of the White House were not averse to spying on their fellow-citizens. Should it ever be the tragic misfortune of the American people that a despot seized control of the White House, unconstitutionally or constitutionally, the computer, with its enormous storage and retrieval-of-information capabilities, would become a tool of extraordinary power for intimidating and controlling an entire society.

Some social critics contend it will not be necessary for the Man on Horseback to appear in order for our liberties and rights of privacy to be eliminated or drastically curtailed; they believe that a computerized society has already done so. One thoughtful and concerned critic, David Burnham, has sounded the alarm in his ominously informative book, *The Rise of the Computer State.*[1]

It is Burnham's conviction—and the evidence he marshalls in support of his belief is impressive and persuasive—that the vast pools of information collected and stored on individuals by banking, finance, credit, insurance, hospital, medical, taxation, educational and telecommunication networks constitute an assault on the individual's privacy that has brought a realization of George Orwell's grim prophecy: Big Brother's enormous computer data banks and retrieval systems now control the individual citizen's destiny.

The great intelligence conflicts throughout history have invariably involved struggles between an omnipotent state and a citizenry fighting to protect its individual freedoms, including (to paraphrase Mr. Justice Brandeis) the right to be left alone. Even at the height of the Roman Empire a great intelligence conflict was waged by the Roman secret service (the *frumentarii*) against

213

the citizens of Rome who resisted—some with their lives—attempts to invade their privacy.[2]

A modern, although rather minor, example of invasion of privacy is the widespread acquisition of unlisted, classified and top secret telephone numbers. The latter two types of telephone numbers are usually listed in a carefully restricted directory. Nevertheless, by bribery or blackmail, or just plain theft, such classified telephone directories can be acquired. A plain unlisted telephone number, assigned to a private citizen, is generally released to local police or other law enforcement officials. And, on occasion, a telephone operator or a supervisor has been known unwittingly to release an unlisted number when confronted by a contrived ruse presented by an unscrupulous caller. In contemporary American society, anyone with a telephone can be reached, legally or illegally, and his privacy invaded. In this example, modern technology further demolishes the wall of privacy, for the automatic dialing machine with a computerized program of affluent (or demographically pertinent) telephone exchanges will relentlessly call listed and unlisted numbers until it delivers its recorded message.

An invasion of privacy through the release of private telephone numbers or a discriminating machine appears picayune in comparison to the resultant devastating effects when confidential statements—made to an attorney, a doctor or minister—about one's personal tax, sexual or family problems are seized by agents of the federal government.

Your files are under study, the federal government informs you, not because *you* are under suspicion for any wrongdoing; it's your lawyer or doctor or clergyman who is suspected.

Professor Alan Dershowitz, a distinguished member of the Harvard Law School faculty, described an incident[3] which occurred in a San Diego, California, lawyer's office, when government agents from the Department of Justice, FBI, IRS, and the Drug Enforcement Agency occupied it for three days while they examined *confidential client files,* and then proceeded to carry them away to be pored over at leisure. Clients, entering what they assumed to be the sanctity of their lawyer's office, were shocked on being requested to identify themselves.

This was not, Professor Dershowitz observes, an isolated episode in which the sanctity of a lawyer's premises and the confidentiality of his files were trampled on by agents of the federal government; it is part of a pattern that is repeated in other parts of the country.

Not without relevance is the Biblical saying "The truth shall set ye free," which still has profound implications for the citizens of an Intelligence Society. If we are to protect ourselves against encroachments on privacy by a misuse of intelligence systems, we need to begin by discarding the mythological baggage that intelligence is a "sinister" and essentially "evil" activity.

Corporations in particular have a compelling need to advance the idea—not only to their own shareholders and other constituencies but to the public at large—that an intelligence function, properly organized and supervised, is an essential component for effective managerial decision-making.

It is deeply unfortunate that even our leading graduate schools of business have neglected to include the vital subject of corporate intelligence and espionage in their formal curricula, although the topic is sometimes dealt with peripherally in such conventional management courses as, for example, marketing, international business law, business and society and (some) computer science and technology seminars.

In our view, there is an urgent need to adopt the attitude of one of the earliest intelligence theorists, the philosopher and general Sun Tzu, who observed that the intelligence agent, when properly trained and professionally motivated, is a man of high character and integrity; and the information (intelligence) he acquires, frequently at the risk of his own life, may be a "matter of life and death, a road either to safety or ruin."[4]

It is our belief that there is a pressing need for the establishment of an amply endowed and creatively staffed foundation whose *long-term* goal—we emphasize "long-term" as the task may well require an effort over an entire generation before there are any perceptible signs of change—is a reversal of the current, unfortunate American attitude toward intelligence and espionage.

In the 1980s, the issue is not whether we should unplug computers or apply sledge hammers to their silicon chips (as the Luddites did to manufacturing machinery during the early nineteenth century in the misguided belief that machinery diminished employment), but how we can make information collecting and processing—intelligence—work for the betterment of our society.

We engage in the acquisition of intelligence to improve the

survival capability of government and the profits/survival of business. Policy, whether of business or government, is only as good as the information (intelligence) upon which it is based: "Only with global intelligence can decision-making be global," in the pithy phrase of our colleague Professor George A. Steiner.[5]

These objectives are both reasonable and feasible. Their attainability is a demonstrable fact. Business intelligence, effectively developed and applied, strengthens business enterprise and enlarges the range of goods and services which it can deliver. By strengthening business enterprise, private intelligence can act as a counterbalance to governmental intelligence. As business, the mainstay of the private sector, is enriched by the intelligence function, the vitality of an open and free society is likewise enriched. Each supports the other.

Business intelligence can also complement government intelligence.

The role of governmental intelligence-collection is generally viewed as extensive and all-encompassing. The most severe critics argue that governmental intelligence operations are a threat to individual liberty. The more restrained and moderate critics and commentators suggest that the intelligence functions of government go too far. But rare is the voice that proclaims the government does not do enough to satisfy its minimum intelligence requirements!

Yet a case can be made—and we trust earlier chapters have done this—that the government should do more to protect the U.S. corporation from espionage and theft of its technological trade secrets by foreign governments and corporate rivals.

IBM is a case in point.

The FBI did not learn through its own intelligence channels about the clandestine activities of Hitachi and Mitsubishi when, in 1982, they were attempting to obtain proprietary information belonging to IBM. The FBI learned about the Japanese endeavors when informed by IBM's management. Actually, it was the FBI's preoccupation with the theft and counterfeiting of electronic parts rather than with industrial espionage that led it to establish a "sting" operation which ultimately resulted in the indictment of employees of these two prominent Japanese companies.

The protection of IBM's security became the concern of the United States because it had implications for this country's world standing in the contest for economic hegemony. The U.S. government in this case was prepared to defend not only its own national interests but also the interests of IBM, one of this nation's leading corporate citizens.

What might have happened had the attempted theft of IBM's trade secrets occurred *outside* the territorial borders of the United States? It would have been incumbent on the CIA to act. However, let us suppose the CIA had not felt free to act on behalf of IBM. The victim would have been left to shift for itself.

It is, therefore, important for corporations with overseas interests not to neglect the development of instrumentalities to safeguard their legitimate business interests and proprietary information which might well be the target of private or foreign governmental adversaries. In some respects, as we have already noted in chapter 9, the KGB of the Soviet Union is a greater espionage threat to technology companies than their private corporation rivals. The KGB is ruthless, dedicated, and able to deploy an awesome array of intelligence resources against specific companies.

U.S. corporate technology is desperately required by the Soviets for their weapons systems and the modernization of their industrial plant. Without U.S. technology, the USSR will be unable to close the gap between itself and the West, a gap that has already been substantially narrowed through both clandestine and "legitimate" acquisition of the technology of the West and Japan.

Clearly, the Soviets also hope to limit the profitability of the polycorporation and its economic and social influence in the Third World. As long as polycorporations, especially those based in the U.S., remain vital instruments for the transfer of technology and Western management practices and are sources for training and employment, the Soviets are handicapped in their efforts to win friends and influence Third World governments. For the hard and harsh reality is that the Soviet Union's economic model is a dud: when the rhetoric is peeled away, Soviet communism is revealed as a fraud. Hence, Soviet propaganda constantly reiterates that the polycorporation is an instrument of imperialism and class exploitation that retards development in Africa, Latin America and Asia. In their efforts to discredit the polycorporation, the Soviets are not inhibited by the obvious failure of the Kremlin's policy to create instrumentalities to compete with the polycorporations of Japan and the West. Nor, for example, are the

Soviets deterred by the obvious economic failure of Ghana which, under Nkrumah, tied itself to Moscow.[6]

Unable to compete directly with the polycorporation in the developing world, the Soviets have launched an assault on the overseas branches of the polycorporation through Soviet-sponsored and financed terrorist attacks. Numerous terrorist organizations, especially those based in the Middle East, have availed themselves of Soviet assistance in funding, weaponry and direction to attack U.S. business installations. As a symbol of Western corruption and decadence, the business executive is deemed by the fanatical terrorist to be as valuable a candidate for extermination as a politician.

International business can protect itself against both Soviet and Soviet-inspired terrorist assaults by developing a greater sense of the need for security, employing sophisticated security devices, providing better training in protection for its overseas representatives, and, most important, utilizing an effective intelligence system to ferret out hostile intentions—*before they are put into operation.*[7]

Just as the government can help corporations, so too can corporations help the government. It is important to appreciate that the corporation's employment of an intelligence function has a wider application than the enhancement of the firm's profitability. The use by the corporation of the intelligence mechanism can also serve the cause of preserving world peace in an increasingly dangerous world.

Today, numerous specialists concur that the prospects for nuclear war are increasing. The analogy most frequently cited is the incident that occurred at Sarajevo in 1914 when Gavrilo Princip assassinated Archduke Franz Ferdinand, the Hapsburg heir to the throne of the Austro-Hungarian empire, thus triggering World War I. Jerome B. Wiesner, former presidential science advisor, says: "You can think of a hundred ways in which nuclear war might start, and it could still start in a thoroughly unpredictable way."[8]

Can the corporation's own intelligence system contribute to the cause of peace? Plainly, in our judgment it would be neither anomalous nor untoward for the corporation to devote itself to serving that cause—in its own self-interest as well as for more altruistic reasons.

Business and government intelligence analysts frequently study the same information. The prevailing tendency is for government to rely on its own assessments and situation estimates, and for business to rely on those business generates. In the *formal* sense, the specialists who work for different employers do not regularly communicate with each other or exchange their respective intelligence assessments. However, in an *informal* sense it is probably true that some communication between intelligence analysis in government and the private sector takes place.

A popular misconception assumes that government intelligence projections and assessments are superior to those prepared in the private sector. Our own studies do not support this view—in fact, the opposite is quite often true. The government intelligence analyst may have put together a correct assessment of a foreign political situation, but his superior—frequently because of political considerations—is a prisoner of preconceived *policy* objectives into which the analyst's assessment does not fit. So it is ignored or dismissed.

David Sullivan points out that because of adherence to the then-prevailing political "line," the CIA failed to project accurately the growth of Soviet defense spending, although sufficient information was available.[9]

The collapse of the Iranian government early in 1979 provides another dramatic example of an inaccurate political assessment by U.S. military intelligence and the CIA. As one of the authors of this book wrote elsewhere:

> Five months before the Shah fled to Cairo, CIA reports gave his regime a clean bill of health. Even in the heat of the social unrest that led up to his decision to leave, the intelligence community was unable to make an accurate assessment of the situation. University professors went to Tehran and came back telling the U.S. government that the Shah had no chance for survival; George Ball, the brilliant former Under Secretary of State—now an investment banker—and a prime example of a "business Statesman," wrote a report for the White House . . . urging U.S. support for a transfer of power within Iran long before the abortive Bakhtiar regime was created. . . . U.S. intelligence failed in Iran because it was focused on the wrong information sources.[10]

It must be added that U.S. business intelligence in Iran was as faulty as that of our government. Despite billions of dollars invested in Iran, "The business community did not factor into their decision-making structure in Iran a method of assessing independently the political risks."[11]

Those engaged in intelligence activities for the government

are much more likely to be the prisoners of a preconceived political policy than are the intelligence analysts employed by a corporation. This is not because business is devoid of political inclinations; it is owing to the paramount interest of business in producing goods and services rather than generating a "political" product. It is also easier for the corporation to rapidly alter the arrangements used in acquiring intelligence because it is not a captive of a legislative process requiring lengthy debates and political considerations incident to achieving changes in direction by governmental agencies. Hence, it is arguable that business intelligence analysts can more readily adapt themselves to the requirements of a rapidly changing situation—either operationally or analytically—in order fully and accurately to assess overseas developments.

This process should enable the business intelligence specialist to make sound judgments and accurate projections, and to formulate policy guidelines that avoid the mistakes in political assessment that lead to international conflicts between nation-states.

Over the past fifty years of development the U.S. corporation has taken on many of the characteristics of a nation-state. The large corporation, which we have called the polycorporation for the reasons given in chapter 4, has evolved into a vastly complex private government whose functions range from the economic to the diplomatic.

Although the great modern corporations do not have their own military and naval forces, such as were under the management and direction of the East India Company, they exercise a pervasive control over economic resources which influence the attitudes and policies of nation-states, especially those in the Third World. In this respect, the modern global corporations are "actors" in the changing political drama of our time.

The modern multinational corporation, the polycorporation, is an *important actor* on the world stage. When its message is effectively articulated, it is listened to—at home and abroad. The lobbying and diplomatic resources of the modern corporation, when used intelligently and professionally, can carry greater weight and have greater influence than many chief executive officers realize.

The importance of intelligence must not be overlooked. It has been a vital factor in the affairs of man since the beginnings of recorded history. The nation-state, from its inception, has used, developed, and expanded intelligence functions. Within the na-tion-state, too, the intelligence function has become a profession, fed by science and technology, and its practitioners are bound together by a spirit of the fraternity of its members. Since the Middle Ages, the fabric of business has been interwoven with a reliance on privileged information in conjunction with com-mercial espionage. Although today's corporation still relies on privileged or proprietary information, it has vastly expanded its espionage function.

To be sure, the intelligence function is not reflected in the for-mal organization of the modern corporation's management activ-ities. Nevertheless, the reality is such that all large business organizations engage in intelligence activities and frequently utilize intelligence specialists. Whether consciously or uncon-sciously, the intelligence function is an integral part of the twentieth-century management process of the entire private sector.

It can be argued philosophically that, in an open and free soci-ety, all information of whatever nature should be freely available, without restrictions, to everyone. Realistically, however, this has never been true, and is unlikely to be applicable in the foreseeable future.

The rise in our society of an intelligence function is a clearly perceptible trend. As we see it, intelligence and espionage opera-tions within the government and outside it will continue not only to grow but in all probability to flourish. If one were to argue that this is not healthy, we would still conclude that there are no remedies capable of controlling or reducing this development. The obvious recourse—to pass extremely complicated legislation against surveillance—is likely to produce a statute honored more in the breach than in the observance.

Without question, in our judgment, the large multinational (or polycorporation, as we call it) should establish well-conceived, effective, professionally-staffed intelligence units within its man-agement structures. It goes without saying that close and effective supervision by the chief executive officer of his company's intelli-gence unit is a *sine qua non* for its effective and useful opera-tions—operations that are beneficial to the corporation's own policies and the chief executive's own decision-making.

The intelligence operation is a prerequisite to sustained and successful polycorporate operations. The intelligence unit is essential to ensure profitability and survivability in a hostile world.

And finally we believe, as the preceding discussion in this book has made clear, that a well-organized and properly supervised intelligence function will enable corporate leaders to play a significant role in the preservation of world peace.

APPENDIX

Uniform Trade Secrets Act

§ 1. [Definitions]

As used in this Act, unless the context requires otherwise:

(1) "Improper means" includes theft, bribery, misrepresentation, breach or inducement of a breach of a duty to maintain secrecy, or espionage through electronic or other means;

(2) "Misappropriation" means:

   (i) acquisition of a trade secret of another by a person who knows or has reason to know that the trade secret was acquired by improper means; or

   (ii) disclosure or use of a trade secret of another without express or implied consent by a person who

      (A) used improper means to acquire knowledge of the trade secret; or

      (B) at the time of disclosure or use, knew or had reason to know that his knowledge of the trade secret was

         (I) derived from or through a person who had utilized improper means to acquire it;

         (II) acquired under circumstances giving rise to a duty to maintain its secrecy or limit its use; or

         (III) derived from or through a person who owed a duty to the person seeking relief to maintain its secrecy or limit its use; or

      (C) before a material change of his position, knew or had reason to know that it was a trade secret and that knowledge of it had been acquired by accident or mistake.

(3) "Person" means a natural person, corporation, business trust, estate, trust, partnership, association, joint venture, government, governmental subdivision or agency, or any other legal or commercial entity.

(4) "Trade secret" means information, including a formula, pattern, compilation, program, device, method, technique, or process, that:

    (i) derives independent economic value, actual or potential, from not being generally known to, and not being readily ascertainable by proper means by, other persons who can obtain economic value from its disclosure or use, and

    (ii) is the subject of efforts that are reasonable under the circumstances to maintain its secrecy.

§ 2. [Injunctive Relief]

(a) Actual or threatened misappropriation may be enjoined. Upon application to the court, an injunction shall be terminated when the trade secret has ceased to exist, but the injunction may be continued for an additional reasonable period of time in order to eliminate commercial advantage that otherwise would be derived from the misappropriation.

(b) If the court determines that it would be unreasonable to prohibit future use, an injunction may condition future use upon payment of a reasonable royalty for no longer than the period of time the use could have been prohibited.

(c) In appropriate circumstances, affirmative acts to protect a trade secret may be compelled by court order.

§ 3. [Damages]

(a) In addition to or in lieu of injunctive relief, a complainant may recover damages for the actual loss caused by misappropriation. A complainant also may recover for the unjust enrichment caused by misappropriation that is not taken into account in computing damages for actual loss.

(b) If willful and malicious misappropriation exists, the court may award exemplary damages in an amount not exceeding twice any award made under subsection (a).

§ 4. [Attorney's Fees]

If (i) a claim of misappropriation is made in bad faith, (ii) a motion to terminate an injunction is made or resisted in bad faith, or (iii) willful and malicious misappropriation exists, the court may award reasonable attorney's fees to the prevailing party.

§ 5. [Preservation of Secrecy]

In an action under this Act, a court shall preserve the secrecy of an alleged trade secret by reasonable means, which may include granting protective orders in connection with discovery proceedings, holding in-camera hearings, sealing the records of the action, and ordering any person involved in the litigation not to disclose an alleged trade secret without prior court approval.

§ 6. [Statute of Limitations]

An action for misappropriation must be brought within 3 years after the misappropriation is discovered or by the exercise of reasonable diligence should have been discovered. For the purposes of this section, a continuing misappropriation constitutes a single claim.

§ 7. [Effect on Other Law]

(a) This Act displaces conflicting tort, restitutionary, and other law of this State pertaining to civil liability for misappropriation of a trade secret.
(b) This Act does not affect:
  (1) contractual or other civil liability or relief that is not based upon misappropriation of a trade secret; or
  (2) criminal liability for misappropriation of a trade secret.

§ 8. [Uniformity of Application and Construction]

This Act shall be applied and construed to effectuate its general purpose to make uniform the law with respect to the subject of this Act among states enacting it.

§ 9. [Short Title]

This Act may be cited as the Uniform Trade Secrets Act.

§ 10. [Severability]

If any provision of this Act or its application to any person or circumstances is held invalid, the invalidity does not affect other provisions or applications of the Act which can be given effect without the invalid provision or application, and to this end the provisions of this Act are severable.

§ 11. [Time of Taking Effect]

This Act takes effect on _____, and does not apply to misappropriation occurring prior to the effective date.

§ 12. [Repeal]

The following Acts and parts of Acts are repealed:
(1)
(2)
(3)

Notes

CHAPTER 1
The New Magic

1. R. Gordon Wasson, Albert Hoffman, and Carl A. P. Ruck, *The Road to Eleusis: Unveiling the Secret of the Mysteries* (New York: Harcourt Brace Jovanovich, 1978), 11 and 56–57. At the heart of the authors' examination of this important phenomenon of ancient Greece is ethnomycology, the study of the role of mushrooms. The key to the Eleusinian Mysteries was the "sacred mushroom" which served as a hallucinogenic device for entry into the sacred world of Eleusis.

   In his study *The Delphic Oracle,* Professor Joseph Fontenrose, Professor of Classics Emeritus at the University of California at Berkeley, observes that the Pythia at Delphi spoke clear and coherent responses directly to the client and was not frenzied or in a state of trance as possession. Professor Fontenrose's research leads him to conclude that at Delphi there were no ambiguous oracles nor extraordinary predictions of the future as commonly supposed. These belong, he asserts, to legend and pseudo-history. See Joseph Fontenrose, *The Delphic Oracle* (Berkeley and Los Angeles: University of California Press, 1978).
2. *Ibid.*
3. Richard Eells, *Global Corporations: The Emerging System of World Economic Power* (New York: Free Press, 1976), 11–18.
4. *Wall Street Journal,* June 3, 1982, 25. See also Neil H. Jacoby, Peter Nehemkis, and Richard Eells, *Bribery and Extortion in World Business: A Study of Corporate Political Payments Abroad* (New York: Macmillan, 1977).
5. For a careful examination of a different conclusion, see Ira M. Millstein and Salem M. Katsh, *The Limits of Corporate Power* (New York: Macmillan, 1981). Here the authors identify different forces circumscribing the discretionary power of the large corporation.

6. *New York Herald Tribune* (Paris), June 7–8, 1980, 11.
7. "Le KGB en Suisse," *24 Heures* (Zurich), February 9–10, 1980, 29–33.
8. James Bamford, *The Puzzle Palace* (Boston: Houghton Mifflin, 1982), 370–72.
9. Max Ralis, "Workers' Social Perceptions," in *The Soviet Worker,* ed. Leonard Schapiro and Joseph Godson (London: Macmillan, 1982), 231–50.
10. *New York Times,* May 6, 1982, A10.
11. *New York Times,* June 24, 1982, A1, D1, and D5.
12. Beardsley Ruml, *Tomorrow's Business* (New York: Farrar and Rinehart, 1945), 51, 58.
13. *Wall Street Week Transcripts,* #1144, April 30, 1982.
14. *GIST* (Bureau of Public Affairs, Department of State), December, 1980, 1.
15. Adolf A. Berle, Jr., *The 20th Century Capitalist Revolution* (New York: Harcourt, Brace and Company, 1954), 172.

CHAPTER 2

The Evolution of Intelligence

1. Richard Deacon, *The Chinese Secret Service* (New York: Ballantine Books, 1974), 26–30.
2. Allen W. Dulles, *The Craft of Intelligence* (New York: Harper and Row, 1963), 14–15.
3. Sun Tzu, *The Art of War,* edited and with a Foreword by James Clavell (New York: Delacorte Press, 1983).
4. Deacon, 48–51.
5. Kurt Singer, *Three Thousand Years of Espionage* (New York: Prentice-Hall, 1948), viii–ix.
6. Dulles, 16–18.
7. Singer, 31–34.
8. Corey Ford, *Donovan of OSS* (Boston: Little, Brown and Company, 1970), 121–305, and Richard Dunlop, *Donovan: America's Master Spy* (New York: Rand McNally, 1982), 295–475.
9. Andrew Patterson, Jr., a professor of chemistry at Yale University, is also a mine warfare historian who through his studies of this subject became interested in the history of the nomenclature of classified information. He has consented to share the results of his research in order to support this study.
10. Andrew Patterson, Jr., "Confidential: The Beginning of Defense-Information Marking" (Copyright by Andrew Patterson, Jr., 1980), 9–14.
11. Patterson, 16–21.
12. Patterson, 95–98.
13. Patterson, 96–102.
14. Herbert O. Yardley, *The American Black Chamber* (New York: Bobbs-Merrill, 1931). The book was reissued in 1981 with a new introduction by David Kahn (New York: Ballantine Books). Also in 1981, the Espionage Intelligence Library published a facsimile of the original edition. Herbert O. Yardley is both an important and a controversial figure in the history of American intelligence. James Bamford

in *The Puzzle Palace* devotes many pages to Yardley (5–27) and establishes his historical position, not unfavorably. On the other hand, Ronald Lewin in *The Other Ultra* (London: Hutchinson, 1982), 19, writes: "Herbert Yardley . . . first penetrated the Japanese code system on a massive scale. Unfortunately, he lacked the fine quality essential in code breakers who serve governments: loyalty."

15. Patterson, 152–59.
16. Lyman B. Kirkpatrick, Jr., *The U.S. Intelligence Community* (New York: Hill and Wang, 1973), 22–39.
17. John Toland, *Infamy: Pearl Harbor and Its Aftermath* (New York: Doubleday, 1982), 3–12. It should be noted that Toland argues in this book that the failure of the warning to arrive on time was not the responsibility of intelligence operatives, but rather the result of a political decision to allow the Japanese to launch a dramatic surprise attack that would mobilize the nation in support of the war effort.
18. Robert F. Ellsworth, "Quick Fixes in Intelligence," in *National Security in the 1980s,* ed. W. Scott Thompson (San Francisco: Institute for Contemporary Studies, 1980), 173–78.

CHAPTER 3
Intelligence Today

1. Alain Besançon, *The Soviet Syndrome* (New York: Harcourt Brace Jovanovich, 1978), 59–68.
2. Robert F. Ellsworth, "Quick Fixes in Intelligence," in *National Security in the 1980s,* ed. W. Scott Thompson (San Francisco: Institute for Contemporary Studies, 1980), 173–78.
3. Richard Deacon, *A History of the British Secret Service* (London: Granada, 1969), 413–18.
4. Francis Dvornik, *Origins of Intelligence Services* (New Brunswick, New Jersey: Rutgers University Press, 1974).
5. David Burnham, "Computer Security Raises Questions," *New York Times,* August 13, 1983, 7.

CHAPTER 4
Corporations and the Intelligence Function

1. Michael Novak and John W. Cooper, editors, *The Corporation: A Theological Inquiry* (Washington, D.C.: American Enterprise Institute, 1981), 38–39. See also Seymour Martin Lipset and William Schneider, *The Confidence Gap* (New York: Free Press, 1983).
2. *Ibid.,* 220.

CHAPTER 5
Elements of Intelligence Strategy:
Diplomacy and Survival

1. Sherman Kent, *Strategic Intelligence* (Princeton, N.J.: Princeton University Press, 1949), 76.

2. Robert W. Miller and Jimmy D. Johnson, *Corporate Ambassadors to Washington* (Washington, D.C.: American University Center for the Study of Private Enterprise, 1970).
3. Congressional Quarterly's *Guide to Congress,* 2nd. ed., Washington, D.C., 1976.
4. Walter Laqueur, "Foreign News Coverage: From Bad to Worse," *Washington Journalism Review,* June 1983, 32.
5. *The Federalist,* No. 10.
6. Miller and Johnson, *Corporate Ambassadors to Washington.*
7. Brian May, *The Indonesian Tragedy* (Singapore: Graham Brash [PTE] Ltd., 1978), 38.

CHAPTER 6
Organizing an Intelligence Function
No notes

CHAPTER 7
Trade Secrets

1. Jacques Bergier, *Secret Armies—The Growth of Corporate and Industrial Espionage* (New York: Bobbs-Merrill, 1975).
2. 14 U.L.A. 539 (1979). The Model Uniform Trade Secrets Act at the end of 1982 had been adopted by five states: Indiana, Kansas, Louisiana, Minnesota, and Washington. The Act is reproduced in the Appendix.
3. See Telex Corp. v. IBM, 367 F. Supp. 258 (1973); and Telex Corp. v. IBM, 510 F. (2d) 894 (1975), cert. denied 423 U.S. 802 (1975).
4. E.I. Du Pont de Nemours & Co. v. Christopher, 431 F. (2d) 1012, 166 USPQ 421 (5th Cir., 1970), cert. denied 400 U.S. 1024, 168 USPQ 385 (1971).
5. Laurie Visual Etudes, Inc. v. Chesebrough-Ponds, Inc., 105 Misc. (2d) 413, 432 N.Y.S. (2d) 457 (1980).
6. For Dr. Aries' *modus operandi,* we have borrowed from Jacques Bergier's *Secret Armies: The Growth of Corporate and Industrial Espionage,* 74–75; and Stanley H. Lieberstein, *Who Owns What Is in Your Head?* (New York: A. Howard Wyndham Company, 1979), 62–64. We gratefully acknowledge our indebtedness to both authors.
7. For the corporate executive who desires to review his firm's trade secret protection program an invaluable reference manual is James Pooley's *Trade Secrets: How To Protect Your Ideas and Assets* (Berkeley, California: Osborne/McGraw-Hill, 1982).

CHAPTER 8
The Practice of Industrial Espionage

1. See Kevin McManus, "Who Owns Your Brains?" *Forbes,* June 6, 1983, 168–79. See also Stanley H. Lieberstein, *Who Owns What Is In Your Head?* (New York: A. Howard Wyndham Company, 1979).
2. On the brain drain that left more Fairchild talent outside the company than inside, see Dirk Hanson, *The New Alchemists—Silicon*

Valley and the Microelectronics Revolution (Boston: Little, Brown and Company, 1982), 112. This superb study contains a wealth of information on the modern Silicon Valley "alchemists" who have found in the former orchards of Santa Clara and San Jose the new "gold" of the silicon chip.

3. Sissela Bok, *Secrets: On the Ethics of Concealment and Revelation* (New York: Pantheon Books, 1982), 145.
4. See Michael S. Baram, "Trade Secrets: What Price Loyalty?" *Harvard Business Review* 46 (November–December 1968), 66–74.
5. Analogic Corp. v. Data Translation, Inc., 371 Mass. 643, 358 N.E. (2d) 809 (1976).
6. A former senior officer of the CIA, Miles Copeland, writes that the espionage services of the Great Powers use prostitutes, male and female, "only for the purpose of getting prospective agents into compromising positions—never to obtain information." Miles Copeland, *Without Cloak and Dagger—The Truth About the New Espionage* (New York: Simon and Schuster, 1974), 153.
7. Sanche de Gramont, *The Secret War* (New York: G. P. Putnam's Sons, 1962), 19–20.
8. Among U.S. governmental agencies which require submission of technical information that may involve a company's trade secrets are: the Securities and Exchange Commission; the Federal Trade Commission; the Department of the Interior; the Department of Agriculture; the Food and Drug Administration; the Office of the Surgeon General; and the Department of Health and Human Services.
9. As asserted by the Director of the FBI, William Webster, in an interview with Ted Koppel on ABC television, "Nightline."
10. See Robert O. Blanchard, "Status Report on the FOIA—First the Good News," *The Quill* (January 1977), 22–23.
11. See *Newsweek,* January 17, 1983, p. 54.
12. Erik Larson, staff reporter for the *Wall Street Journal,* in a page 1 article for the issue of April 13, 1983, described the incidents (and others) used in the text. See also "Thrills and Lax Security Cited in Computer Break-Inn," *New York Times,* August 14, 1983, 30.
13. Adapted from Jacques Bergier, *Secret Armies—The Growth of Corporate and Industrial Espionage* (New York: Bobbs-Merrill, 1975).

CHAPTER 9
The Soviet Use of Worldwide Industrial Espionage

1. John Barron, *KGB—The Secret Work of Soviet Secret Agents* (New York: Bantam Books, 1974), 31.
2. John Barron, *KGB Today—The Hidden Hand* (New York: Reader's Digest Press, 1983), 196.
3. Allen W. Dulles, *The Craft of Intelligence* (New York: Harper and Row, 1963), 86.
4. U.S. Department of State, "Soviet Active Measures: Focus on Forgeries," April 1983.
5. Arnold Beichmann and Mikhail S. Bernstam, *Andropov: New Challenge to the West* (Briarcliff Manor, New York: Stein & Day, 1983).
6. The Mossad is not strictly comparable to the KGB in that it does not combine the functions of counterespionage and foreign intelli-

gence collection as does the KGB. The Israeli counterintelligence activity is the responsibility of the Shin Beth. External military intelligence collection is vested in Aman, which also is responsible for industrial intelligence. The Mossad can properly be compared with the British DI6 (formerly MI6) or the CIA. Of all the Israeli secret intelligence services the Mossad is the most feared in Israel and the most respected abroad. See, for an exhaustive study of the Israeli secret services, Richard Deacon, *The Israeli Secret Service* (New York: Taplinger, 1977).

7. Anthony Boyle, *The Fourth Man* (New York: The Dial Press/James Wade, 1979), 133.
8. Allen Dulles, in his introduction to Edward R. F. Sheehan's account of Philby's espionage, "The Rise and Fall of a Soviet Agent," in *Great True Spy Stories,* ed. Allen W. Dulles (New York and Evanston: Harper & Row, 1968), 50.
9. John Barron, *KGB Today—The Hidden Hand,* 360–61.
10. Harry Rositzke, *The KGB: The Eyes of Russia* (Garden City, New York: Doubleday, 1981), 66–67.
11. John Barron, *KGB Today—The Hidden Hand,* 216.

Chapter 10
The Value of Private Intelligence

1. L. L. Nash, "Ethics without the Sermon," *Harvard Business Review* (November–December 1981), 80.
2. Rabbi Balfour Brickner, article in the *New York Times,* March 7, 1982, E19.
3. Robert Nisbet, *History of the Idea of Progress* (New York: Basic Books, 1980), 342–43.
4. *Ibid.,* 41.
5. Seymour Martin Lipset and William Schneider, *The Confidence Gap* (New York: Free Press, 1983).
6. Richard Eells and Clarence Walton, *Conceptual Foundations of Business,* 3rd. ed. (Homewood, Illinois: Richard D. Irwin, 1974).

Chapter 11
Corporate Strategy and Ethics

1. L. L. Nash, "Ethics without the Sermon," *Harvard Business Review* (November–December 1981), 81.
2. *Ibid.,* 83.
3. "Hospitals Turn to Philosophers on Life Issues," *New York Times,* March 19, 1981, 1.
4. *Ibid.*
5. *Ibid.*
6. "New Attack on the Legitimacy of Business," *Harvard Business Review,* Sept.–Oct. 1981, 82.
7. *Ibid.,* 83.
8. *Ibid.,* 86.
9. *Ibid.,* 87.
10. *Ibid.,* 88.

11. *Ibid.,* 88.
12. *Ibid.,* 89.
13. "Popular Planning," *New York Times,* March 16, 1982, A23.
14. Jean-François Revel, *The Totalitarian Temptation* (Garden City, New York: Doubleday, 1977), 152.
15. *Ibid.,* 180–81.

CHAPTER 12
The Ultimate Dilemma

1. David Burnham, *The Rise of the Computer State* (New York: Random House, 1983).
2. Francis Dvornik, *Origins of Intelligence Services* (New Brunswick, New Jersey: Rutgers University Press, 1974), 106–9. (Francis Dvornik dedicates this book to General William J. Donovan, who urged the writing of a history of intelligence services.)
3. In an article written for the *Los Angeles Times,* June 12, 1983, Pt. IV, 3.
4. See Sun Tzu, *The Art of War,* edited and with a Foreword by James Clavell (New York: Delacorte Press, 1983).
5. See George A. Steiner, *The New CEO* (New York: Macmillan, 1983), 64.
6. See W. Raymond Duncan, ed., *Soviet Policy in Developing Countries* (Waltham, Massachusetts: Ginn, Blatsdell, 1970), 83.
7. See Claire Sterling, *The Terror Network* (New York: Berkley Books, 1982); and Christopher Dobson and Ronald Payne, *The Terrorists* (New York: Facts on File, 1979).
8. *New York Times,* June 24, 1982, A10.
9. See David S. Sullivan, "Evaluating U.S. Intelligence Estimates," in *Intelligence Requirements for the 1980s: Analysis and Estimates,* ed. Roy Godson (Washington, D.C.: National Strategy Information Center, 1980), 69–70.
10. See Richard Eells, *The Political Crisis of the Enterprise System* (New York: Macmillan, 1980), 69–70.
11. *Ibid.,* 70.

A Glossary of Espionage Terms

Agent: An individual who acts under the direction of an intelligence agency or security service to obtain, or assist in obtaining, information for intelligence or counterintelligence purposes.

Agent of Influence: A suborned or ideologically committed individual who occupies a sensitive position in an adversary's opinion-molding institutions or governmental agencies from which he is able to influence public opinion in favor of the Soviet Union. (Politicians, journalists, political commentators, trade union leaders, administrative and legal assistants to members of the Congress, academicians, and senior business executives are occupations that lend themselves to use by an agent of influence.)

Asset: An informant or source who supplies intelligence.

Backstopping: A CIA term for providing appropriate verification and support of cover arrangements for an agent or asset in anticipation of inquiries or other actions which might test the credibility of his or its cover.

Bag Job: In the U.S., a search of a suspected spy's residence to obtain incriminating information.

Basic Intelligence: Factual, fundamental, and generally permanent information about all aspects of a nation—physical, social, economic, political, biographical, and cultural—which

234

is used as a base for intelligence products in support of planning, policymaking, and military operations.

Bigot List: Using the term bigot in the sense of narrow, this is a restrictive list of persons who have access to a particular, and highly sensitive, class of information.

Black: A term used to indicate reliance on illegal concealment of an activity rather than on cover.

Black Bag Job: Warrantless surreptitious entry, especially an entry conducted for purposes other than microphone installation, such as physical search and seizure or photographing of documents.

Black List: An official counterintelligence listing of actual or potential hostile collaborators, sympathizers, intelligence suspects, or other persons viewed as threatening to the security of friendly military forces.

Black Propaganda: Propaganda which purports to emanate from a source other than the true one.

Blown: Destroyed, as when an agent's identity has been discovered.

Bug: A concealed listening device or microphone, or other audiosurveillance device; also, as a verb, to install the means of audiosurveillance of a subject or target.

Bugged: Containing a concealed listening device.

Case: An intelligence operation in its entirety; the term also refers to a record of the development of an intelligence operation, how it will operate, and the objectives of the operation.

Case Officer: A staff employee of the CIA who is responsible for handling agents.

Center: KGB headquarters at 2 Dzerzhinsky Square, Moscow.

Clandestine Intelligence: Intelligence information collected by clandestine sources.

Clandestine Operations: Intelligence, counterintelligence, or other information collection activities and covert political, economic, propaganda and paramilitary activities, conducted so as to assure secrecy.

Code: A system of communication in which arbitrary groups of symbols represent units of plain text. Codes may be used for brevity or for security.

Code Word: A word which has been assigned a classification and a classified meaning to safeguard intentions and information regarding a planned operation.

Collection: The acquisition of information by any means and its delivery to the proper intelligence processing unit for use in the production of intelligence.

Come Home: "Coming in from the cold," as in John le Carré's novel, describes an agent's withdrawal from active espionage.

Communications: A method or means of conveying information from one person or place to another; this term does not include direct, unassisted conversion or correspondence through nonmilitary postal agencies.

Communications Center: A facility responsible for receiving, transmitting, and delivering messages; it normally contains a message center section, a cryptographic section, and a sending and receiving section, using electronic communications devices.

Communications Intelligence (*COMINT*): Technical and intelligence information derived from foreign communications by someone other than the intended recipient. It does not include foreign press, propaganda, or public broadcasts. The term is sometimes used interchangeably with SIGINT.

The Company: The CIA.

Compromise: A known or suspected exposure of clandestine personnel, installations, or other assets, or of classified information or material, to an unauthorized person.

Conditioning: Political agitation caused by the effective use of disinformation (see below).

Confusion Agent: An individual dispatched by his sponsor to confound the intelligence or counterintelligence apparatus of another country rather than to collect and transmit information.

Consumer: A person or agency that uses information or intelligence produced by either its own staff or other agencies.

Control: Physical or psychological pressure exerted on an agent or group to ensure that the agent or group responds to the direction from an intelligence agency or service.

Controller: An agent's direct supervisor or case officer.

Corporations: Communist parties of foreign countries.

Counterespionage: Those aspects of counterintelligence concerned with aggressive operations against another intelligence service to reduce its effectiveness, or to detect and neutralize foreign espionage. This is done by identification, penetration, manipulation, deception, and repression of individuals, groups, or organizations conducting or suspected of conducting espionage activities in order to destroy, neutralize, exploit, or prevent such espionage activities.

Counterintelligence: Activities conducted to destroy the effectiveness of foreign intelligence operations and to protect information against espionage, individuals against subversion, and installations against sabotage. The term also refers to information developed by or used in counterintelligence operations. See also counterespionage.

Courier: A messenger responsible for the secure physical transmission and delivery of documents and material.

Cover: A protective guise used by a person, organization, or installation to prevent identification with clandestine activities and to conceal the true affiliation of personnel and the true sponsorship of their activities.

Covert Action: Any clandestine activity designed to influence foreign governments, events, organizations, or persons in support of United States foreign policy. Covert action may include political and economic action, propaganda and paramilitary activities.

Covert Operations: Operations planned and executed against foreign governments, installations, and individuals so as to conceal the identity of the sponsor or else to permit the sponsor's plausible denial of the operation. The terms covert action, covert operation, clandestine operation and clandestine activity are sometimes used interchangeably.

Critical Intelligence: Information or intelligence of such urgent importance to the security of the United States that it is transmitted at the highest priority to the President and other national decision-making officials before passing through regular evaluative channels.

Cryptanalysis: The breaking of codes and ciphers into plain text without initial knowledge of the key employed in the encryption.

Cryptography: The enciphering of plain text so that it will be unintelligible to an unauthorized recipient.

Cryptology: The science that includes cryptanalysis and cryptography, and embraces communications intelligence and communications security.

Cryptomaterial: All material—including documents, devices, equipment, and apparatus—essential to the encryption, decryption, or authentication of telecommunications.

Current Intelligence: Summaries and analyses of recent events.

Cut-out: A CIA term referring to a person who is used to conceal contact between members of a clandestine activity or organization.

Dead Drop or *Dead-Letter Box:* A hiding place where an agent can deposit or collect messages and material.

Deception: Measures designed to mislead a hostile person or entity by manipulating, distorting, or falsifying evidence to induce a reaction prejudicial to his or its interests.

Defector: A person who, for political or other reasons, has repudiated his country and may be in possession of information of interest to the United States Government.

Dirty Games: Insidious work, such as blackmailing a foreign official or business executive to force him into espionage against his own country.

Disinformation: Spreading of false propaganda and use of forged documents to confuse counterintelligence or to create political unrest or scandals. Originally a Soviet term, but now in general use.

Dissemination: The distribution of information or intelligence products (in oral, written, or graphic form) to departmental and agency intelligence consumers.

Double: An agent working for two sides at the same time.

Evaluation: The process of determining the value, credibility, reliability, pertinency, accuracy, and use of an item of information, an intelligence product, or the performance of an intelligence system.

Executive Action: Any violent action including assassination or sabotage, or, in Britain, arrests. The Soviets call it *mokrye dela* (wet stuff).

Exploitation: The process of getting information from any source and taking full advantage of it for strategic or tactical purposes.

Flaps Well Down: An old phrase still used in Britain, describing an agent who is worried about his future and lying low. Applicable to KGB agents in most West European countries, especially France.

Grey Propaganda: Propaganda which does not specifically identify a source.

Guidance: The general direction of an intelligence effort, particularly in the area of collection.

Illegal: An agent with "deep cover," who is infiltrated into institutions of another country and poses as a citizen. The agent is supplied with a fictitious identity or "legend," including such documents as a birth certificate, social security number, copies of back IRS tax payments and other papers that a U.S. citizen would be expected to have in his possession.

Imagery: Representations of objects reproduced electronically or by optical means on film, electronic display devices, or other media.

Indications Intelligence: Intelligence in various degrees of evaluation which bears on foreign intentions regarding a course of action.

Infiltration: The placing of an agent or other person in a target area within the hostile territory or within targeted groups or organizations.

Informant: A person who wittingly or unwittingly provides information to an agent, a clandestine service, or police. In reporting such information, this person will often be cited as the source.

Information: Raw, unevaluated data at all levels of reliability and from all kinds of sources, such as observation, rumors, reports, and photographs, which, when processed, may produce intelligence.

Informer: One who intentionally discloses information about other persons or activities to police or a security service (such as the FBI), usually for a financial reward.

Intelligence: The product resulting from the collection, collation, evaluation, analysis, integration, and interpretation of all collected information.

Intelligence Collection Plan: A plan for gathering information from all available sources to meet an intelligence requirement.

Intelligence Cycle: The steps by which information is assembled, converted into intelligence, and made available to consumers. The cycle is composed of four basic phases: (1) *direction:* the determination of intelligence requirements, preparation of a collection plan, tasking of collection agencies, and a continuous check on the productivity of these agencies; (2) *collation:* the exploitation of information sources and the delivery of the collected information to the proper intelligence processing unit for use in the production of intelligence; (3) *processing:* the steps whereby information becomes intelligence through evaluation, analysis, integration, and interpretation; and (4) *dissemination:* the distribution of information or intelligence products (in oral, written, or graphic form) to departmental and agency intelligence consumers.

Intelligence Data Base: All holdings of intelligence data and finished intelligence products at a given department or agency.

Intelligence Estimate: An appraisal of intelligence elements relating to a specific situation or condition to determine the courses of action open to an enemy or potential enemy and the probable order of their adoption.

Interrogation: A systematic effort to procure information by direct questioning of a person under the control of the questioner.

Interview: The gathering of information from a person who knows that he or she is giving information, although not often with awareness of the true connection or purposes of the interviewer. This is generally an overt collection technique, unless the interviewer is not what he or she purports to be.

Legal: An intelligence officer who holds a legitimate or "legal" embassy post or is attached to another legitimate organization, e.g., a trade delegation or purchasing mission, or acts as a journalist for a news service or magazine. Tass correspondents are frequently intelligence officers.

Minus Advantage: An unsuccessful project that leaves those who planned it worse off than before.

Music Box: Radio transmitter.

Musician: Radio or wireless operator.

Neighbor: A complementary intelligence service, e.g., the GRU are neighbors of the KGB as are any of the satellite intelligence services. Essentially a Soviet term. But see *Uncle* below.

N.T.:   No trace, as when an agent is asked for information on someone and is unable to comply.

Overt Intelligence: Information collected openly from public or open sources.

Picnic: A place or country where espionage operations are easy to carry out. (West Germany is considered to be a picnic for the Soviets. Until the recent action by the French government in expelling forty-seven Soviet officials, France was considered to be a picnic. So, too, is Japan. Some intelligence experts believe the U.S., despite the Reagan Administration's harsh rhetoric, is a picnic for Soviet agents.)

Plumbing: A term referring to the development of assets or services supporting the clandestine operations of CIA field stations—such as safehouses, unaccountable funds, investigative persons, surveillance teams.

Political Intelligence: Originally, covert operations arranged, coordinated and conducted so as to plausibly permit official denial of United States involvement, sponsorship or support. Later this concept evolved to include the strategy of high officials and their subordinates communicating without using precise language (which would reveal authorization and involvement in certain activities and would be embarrassing and politically damaging if publicly revealed).

Product: Finished intelligence reports disseminated by intelligence agencies to appropriate consumers.

Production: The preparation of reports based on analysis of information to meet the needs of intelligence users (consumers) within and outside the intelligence community.

A Glossary of Espionage Terms

Proprietaries: A term used by CIA to designate ostensibly private commercial entities, capable of doing business, which are established and controlled by intelligence services to conceal governmental affiliation of intelligence personnel and/or governmental sponsorship of certain activities.

Reconnaissance: A mission undertaken to obtain, by observation or other detection methods, information about the activities and resources of foreign states.

Referentura: Section of a Soviet embassy used exclusively by KGB and GRU officers. A *referentura* is barred to any Soviet diplomat—even the ambassador—unless he also happens to be a KGB or GRU officer.

Regrooming: Training in the culture and language of the country in which an agent is to be assigned.

Rezident: Soviet term for a KGB officer who is the head of an overseas intelligence apparatus and who is stationed in a Soviet embassy. Equivalent to a CIA station chief.

Rezidentura: Soviet term for the headquarters of the KGB station chief. Usually located in a Soviet embassy. Illegal operatives have their own *rezidentura,* separate and apart from the legal *rezidentura.*

Safe House: A secure, unbugged meeting place.

Sanitize: The deletion or revision of a report or document so as to prevent identification of the intelligence sources and methods that contributed to or are dealt with in the report.

Scientific and Technical Intelligence: Information or intelligence concerning foreign progress in basic and applied scientific or technical research and development, including engineering R&D, new technology, and weapons systems.

Security Measures: taken by the government and intelligence departments and agencies, among others, for protection from espionage, observation, sabotage, annoyance, or surprise. With respect to classified materials, it is the condition which prevents unauthorized persons from having access to official information which is safeguarded in the interests of national defense.

Sheep Dipping: The utilization of a military instrument (e.g., an airplane) or officer in clandestine operations, usually in a civilian capacity or under civilian cover, although the instrument or officer will covertly retain its or his military ownership or standing. The term is also applied to the placement of individuals in organizations or groups in which they can become active in order to establish credentials so that they can be used to collect information of intelligence interest on similar groups.

Shoe: A false passport.

Shoemaker: A forger of false passports.

Signals Intelligence (SIGINT):   The general term for the foreign intelligence mission of the NSA/CSS: SIGINT involves the interception, processing, analysis, and dissemination of information derived from foreign electrical communications and other signals. It is composed of three elements: Communications Intelligence (COMINT), Electronics Intelligence (ELINT), and Telemetry Intelligence (TELINT). Most SIGINT is collected by personnel of the Service Cryptologic Agencies.

SIS: The British DI6 (formerly MI6), equivalent to the CIA. The letters stand for Secret Intelligence Services.

Source: A person, thing, or activity which provides intelligence information. In clandestine activities, the term applies to an agent or asset, normally a foreign national, being used in an intelligence activity for intelligence purposes. In interrogations, it refers to a person who furnishes intelligence information with or without knowledge that the information is being used for intelligence purposes.

Special Agent: A United States military or civilian who is a specialist in military security or in the collection of intelligence or counterintelligence information.

Spook: Vernacular for a spy. A U.S. term.

Sterilize: To remove from material to be used in covert and clandestine actions any marks or devices which can identify it as originating with the sponsoring organization or nation.

Surveillance: Systematic observation of a target.

Surveillance Hot and Cold: Cold surveillance is secretive and intended to go unnoticed by the target, whereas hot surveillance is open tailing or bugging of an individual for purposes of harassment or intimidation.

Swallows: Girls used by the KGB for sexual entrapment. The indiscretion by a Western diplomat or business executive—usually taped and photographed—is used to blackmail the victim into becoming an operative for the KGB.

Swallows' Nest: An apartment or hotel used for sexual entrapment by KGB swallows. The quarters are equipped with concealed cameras and audio equipment to obtain photographs and to record pillow-talk subsequently used for blackmail.

Tactical Intelligence: Intelligence supporting military plans and operations at the military unit level. Tactical intelligence and strategic intelligence differ only in scope, point of view, and level of employment.

Target: A person, agency, facility, area, or country against which intelligence operations are directed.

Target of Opportunity: A term describing an entity (e.g., governmental entity, installation, political organization, or individual) that becomes available to an intelligence agency or service by chance, and provides the opportunity for the collection of needed information.

Task: A term connoting the assignment or direction of an intelligence unit to perform a specified function.

Terminated with Extreme Prejudice: Killed.

Turn Around or Turn: To recruit a spy to work against his own agency or government.

Uncle: Term used by Soviet satellite intelligence services to denote their KGB overseers.

Walk-In: A defecting agent.

Watch List: A list of words—such as names, entities, or phrases—which can be employed by a computer to select out required information from a mass of data.

Wet Stuff: An executive action where blood is intended to flow. A Soviet term.

Select Bibliography

ALEXANDER, GARTH. *The Invisible Chinese: The Overseas Chinese and the Politics of Southeast Asia.* New York: Macmillan, 1973.

ALLON, YIGAL. *Shield of David: The Story of Israel's Armed Forces.* London: Weidenfeld and Nicolson, 1970.

ALSOP, STEWART. *Sub Rosa: The OSS and American Espionage.* New York: Harcourt, Brace and World, 1964.

Analogic Corp. v. Data Translation, Inc., 371 Mass. 643, 358 N.E.(2d)809 (1976).

ANSOFF, H. I. *Business Strategy.* New York: Penguin Books, 1969.

———. *Corporate Strategy.* New York: Penguin Books, 1968.

ASTON, SIR GEORGE. *Secret Service.* New York: Cosmopolitan Book Corporation, 1930.

BACKMAN, JULES, editor. *Business Problems of the Seventies.* New York: New York University Press, 1973.

BAKELESS, JOHN. *Spies of the Confederacy.* Philadelphia: Lippincott, 1970.

BAMFORD, JAMES. *The Puzzle Palace.* Boston: Houghton Mifflin, 1982.

BARAM, MICHAEL S. "Trade Secrets: What Price Loyalty?" *Harvard Business Review* 46 (November–December 1968), 66–74.

BARKER, SIR ERNEST. *Social Contract: Essays by Locke, Hume, and Rousseau.* Fair Lawn, New Jersey: Oxford University Press, 1960.

BARNET, RICHARD J., and Müller, Ronald E. *Global Reach: The Power of the Multinational Corporations.* New York: Simon and Schuster, 1974.

BARRON, JOHN. *KGB—The Secret Work of Soviet Secret Agents.* New York: Bantam Books, 1974.

———. *KGB Today—The Hidden Hand.* New York: Reader's Digest Press, 1983.

BENN, S. I., and PETERS, R. S. *The Principles of Political Thought.* New York: W. W. Norton, 1959.

BERGIER, JACQUES. *Secret Armies—The Growth of Corporate and Industrial Espionage.* New York: Bobbs-Merrill, 1975.

BERLE, ADOLF A., JR. *The 20th Century Capitalist Revolution.* New York: Harcourt, Brace and Company, 1954.

Select Bibliography

BERMAN, JERRY, and HALPERIN, MORTON, editors. *The Abuses of the Intelligence Agencies.* Washington, D.C.: Center for National Security Studies, 1975.

BESANÇON, ALAIN. *The Soviet Syndrome.* New York: Harcourt Brace Jovanovich, 1978.

BLACKSTOCK, PAUL W. *Agents of Deceit.* Chicago: Quadrangle Books, 1966.

———. *Intelligence, Espionage, Counterespionage, and Covert Operations: A Guide to Information Sources.* Detroit: Gale Research Company, 1978.

———. *The Strategy of Subversion: Manipulating the Politics of Other Nations.* Chicago: Quadrangle Books, 1964.

BLANCHARD, ROBERT O. "Status Report on the FOIA—First the Good News." *The Quill,* January 1977.

BLUM, RICHARD H., editor. *Surveillance and Espionage in a Free Society.* New York: Praeger, 1972.

BOK, SISSELA. *Secrets: On the Ethics of Concealment and Revelation.* New York: Pantheon, 1982.

BOWEN, WALTER S., and NEAL, HARRY. *The United States Secret Service.* Philadelphia: Chilton Company, 1960.

BOYLE, ANTHONY. *The Fourth Man.* New York: The Dial Press/James Wade, 1979.

BRAMSTEDT, E. K. *Dictatorship and Political Police.* Chicago: Quadrangle Books, 1966.

BRECHT, ARNOLD. *Political Theory.* Princeton, New Jersey: Princeton University Press, 1959.

BROWN, SEYOM, et al. *An Information System for the National Community.* Santa Barbara, California: Rand, 1969.

BRZEZINSKI, ZBIGNIEW. "The Diplomat is an Anachronism." *The Washington Post,* July 5, 1970.

BURNHAM, DAVID. *The Rise of the Computer State.* New York: Random House, 1983.

CARLTON, DAVID, and SCHAERF, CARLE, editors. *International Terrorism and World Security.* New York: John Wiley & Sons, 1975.

CARROLL, JOHN M. *The Secrets of Electronic Espionage.* New York: E. P. Dutton, 1966.

CHANDLER, STEDMAN, et al. *Front-Line Intelligence.* Harrisburg, Pennsylvania: The Infantry Journal Press, 1946.

CHASE, HAROLD. *Security and Liberty: The Problem of Native Communists.* Garden City, New York: Doubleday, 1955.

CLINARD, MARSHALL B., and YEAGER, PETER C. *Corporate Crime.* New York: Free Press, 1980.

COHEN, IRA S. *Realpolitik: Theory and Practice.* Encino, California: Dickerson Publishing Company, 1975.

COPELAND, MILES. *Without Cloak and Dagger—The Truth About the New Espionage.* New York: Simon and Schuster, 1974.

CORSON, WILLIAM. *The Armies of Ignorance: The Rise of the American Intelligence Empire.* New York: Dial Press, 1977.

COTTER, RICHARD. "Notes Toward a Definition of National Security." *Washington Monthly* 7 (December 1975).

DEACON, RICHARD. *The Chinese Secret Service.* New York: Ballantine Books, 1974.

———. *A History of the British Secret Service.* London: Granada, 1969 and 1980.

———. *The Israeli Secret Service.* New York: Taplinger, 1977.

Select Bibliography

DE GRAMONT, SANCHE. *The Secret War: The Story of International Espionage Since World War Two.* New York: G. P. Putnam's Sons, 1962.

DEUTSCH, KARL. *Nationalism and Social Communication.* Boston: Massachusetts Institute of Technology Press, 1953.

DOBSON, CHRISTOPHER, and PAYNE, RONALD. *The Terrorists.* New York: Facts on File, 1979.

DONNER, FRANK J. *The Age of Surveillance: The Aims and Methods of America's Political Intelligence System.* New York: Alfred A. Knopf, 1980, and Vintage Books, 1981.

———. "How J. Edgar Hoover Created His Intelligence Powers." *Civil Liberties Review* 3, February/March 1977.

———. "Intelligence on the Attack: The Terrorist as Scapegoat." *Nation* 226, May 20, 1978.

DOWNES, DONALD. *The Scarlet Thread: Adventures in Wartime Espionage.* London: British Book Centre, 1953.

DULLES, ALLEN W. *The Craft of Intelligence.* New York: Harper and Row, 1963.

DUNCAN, RAYMOND W., editor. *Soviet Policy in Developing Countries.* Waltham, Massachusetts: Ginn, Blatsdell, 1970.

DUNLOP, RICHARD. *Donovan: America's Master Spy.* New York: Rand McNally, 1982.

DVORNIK, FRANCIS. *Origins of Intelligence Services.* New Brunswick, New Jersey: Rutgers University Press, 1974.

EELLS, RICHARD, with an Introduction by George W. Ball. *Global Corporations: The Emerging System of World Economic Power.* New York: Free Press, 1976.

———. *The Political Crisis of the Enterprise System.* New York: Macmillan, 1980.

EELLS, RICHARD, and WALTON, CLARENCE. *Conceptual Foundations of Business.* Third Edition. Homewood, Illinois: Richard D. Irwin, 1974.

E. I. Du Pont de Nemours & Co. v. Christopher, 431 F. (2d) 1012, 166 USPQ 421 (5th Cir., 1970), cert. denied 400 U.S. 1024, 168 USPQ 385 (1971).

ELLIFF, JOHN T. "The FBI and Domestic Intelligence." In *Surveillance and Espionage in a Free Society,* edited by Richard Blum. New York: Frederick A. Praeger, 1973.

———. *The Reform of FBI Intelligence Operations.* Princeton, New Jersey: Princeton University Press, 1979.

ELLSWORTH, ROBERT F. "Quick Fixes in Intelligence." In *National Security in the 1980s,* edited by W. Scott Thompson. San Francisco: Institute for Contemporary Studies, 1980.

FARAGO, LADISLAS. *War of Wits: The Anatomy of Espionage and Intelligence.* New York: Funk and Wagnalls, 1954.

FAYERWEATHER, JOHN. *International Business Management: A Conceptual Framework.* New York: McGraw-Hill, 1969.

The Federalist, No. 10.

FELIX, CHRISTOPHER. *A Short Course in the Secret War.* New York: E. P. Dutton, 1963.

FONTENROSE, JOSEPH. *The Delphic Oracle.* Berkeley and Los Angeles: University of California Press, 1978.

FORD, COREY. *Donovan of OSS.* Boston: Little, Brown and Company, 1970.

FREDMAN, H. B. *Field Intelligence, Data Inputs, and Tactical Operations*

Requirements. Washington, D.C.: Research Analysis Corporation, 1965.

GABOR, DENNIS. *Inventing the Future.* New York: Alfred A. Knopf, 1969.

GIERKE, OTTO. *Political Theories of the Middle Age.* London: Cambridge University Press, 1958.

GLASS, ROBERT R., and DAVIDSON, PHILLIP. *Intelligence is for Commanders.* Harrisburg, Pennsylvania: Military Service Publishing Company, 1952.

GODSON, ROY, editor. *Intelligence Requirements for the 1980's: Analysis and Estimates.* Washington, D.C.: National Strategy Information Center, 1980.

————. *Intelligence Requirements for the 1980's: Elements of Intelligence.* Washington, D.C.: National Strategy Information Center, 1979.

GORDON, THEODORE J. *The Future.* New York: St. Martin's Press, 1965.

HALPERIN, MORTON, et al. *The Lawless State: The Crimes of the U.S. Intelligence Agencies.* New York: Penguin Books, 1976.

HANSON, DIRK. *The New Alchemists—Silicon Valley and the Microelectronics Revolution.* Boston: Little, Brown and Company, 1982.

HARRIS, RICHARD. "Reflections: Crime in the FBI." *The New Yorker,* August 8, 1977.

HEUER, RICHARD J., JR. *Quantitative Approaches to Political Intelligence: The CIA Experience.* Boulder, Colorado: Westview Press, 1978.

HILSMAN, ROGER. *Strategic Intelligence and National Decisions.* Glencoe, Illinois: The Free Press, 1956.

HOFFMAN, PAUL. "The Cryptocensors." *Science Digest,* July, 1972.

HUNTFORD, ROLAND. *The New Totalitarians.* Briarcliff Manor, New York: Stein & Day, 1980.

INSTITUTE FOR THE FUTURE. *Corporate Associates Program* (CAP). Menlo Park, California (ongoing service).

IRONS, PETER. "American Business and the Origins of McCarthyism: The Cold War Crusade of the United States of Commerce." In *The Specter,* edited by Robert Griffith and Athan Theoharis. New York: New Viewpoints, 1974.

JACOBY, NEIL H. *Corporate Power and Social Responsibility.* New York: Macmillan, 1973.

JACOBY, NEIL H.; NEHEMKIS, PETER; and EELLS, RICHARD. *Bribery and Extortion in World Business: A Study of Corporate Political Payments Abroad.* New York: Macmillan, 1977.

JASTROW, ROBERT. *The Enchanted Loom.* New York: Simon and Schuster, 1981.

JOESTEN, JOACHIM. *They Call It Intelligence: Spies and Spy Techniques Since World War Two.* New York: Abelard-Schuman, 1963.

JONES, R. V. *The Wizard War.* New York: Coward, McCann & Geoghegan, 1978.

KAHN, DAVID. *Hitler's Spies: German Military Intelligence in World War II.* New York: Macmillan, 1978.

KAHN, HERMAN, and WEINER, ANTHONY. *The Year 2000.* New York: Macmillan, 1967.

KALDOR, MARY. *The Disintegrating West.* New York: Hill and Wang, 1978.

KENT, SHERMAN. *Strategic Intelligence.* Princeton, New Jersey: Princeton University Press, 1949.

Kewanee Oil v. Bicron Corp., 416 U.S. 470, 476 (1974).

KIRKPATRICK, LYMAN B., JR. *The Real CIA.* New York: Macmillan, 1968.
———. *The U.S. Intelligence Community.* New York: Hill and Wang, 1973.
KNORTZ, HERBERT. *The Multinational Corporation: An Economic Institution.* New York: ITT Corporation, no date.
KRIEGER, LEONARD. *The German Idea of Freedom: History of a Political Tradition.* Boston: Beacon Press, 1957.
LAKEY, GEORGE. *Strategy for a Living Revolution.* San Francisco: W. H. Freeman and Company, 1973.
LAKOFF, STANFORD A. *Private Government.* Glenview, Illinois: Scott, Foresman and Company, 1973.
LANGGUTH, A. J. *Hidden Terrors.* New York: Pantheon, 1978.
LAQUEUR, WALTER. "Foreign News Coverage: From Bad to Worse." *Washington Journalism Review,* June 1983.
Laurie Visual Etudes, Inc. v. Chesebrough-Ponds, Inc., 105 Misc. (2d) 413, 432 N.Y.S. (2d) 457 (1980).
LEVERKUEHN, PAUL. *German Military Intelligence.* London: Weidenfeld and Nicolson, 1954.
LEWIN, RONALD. *The Other Ultra.* London: Hutchinson, 1982.
———. *Ultra Goes to War.* London: Hutchinson, 1978.
LIEBERSTEIN, STANLEY H. *Who Owns What Is In Your Head?* New York: A. Howard Wyndham Company, 1979.
LINDSEY, ROBERT. *The Falcon and the Snowman.* New York: Simon and Schuster, 1979.
LIPSET, SEYMOUR MARTIN, and SCHNEIDER, WILLIAM. *The Confidence Gap.* New York: Free Press, 1983.
LOWI, THEODORE J. *The Politics of Disorder.* New York: W. W. Norton, 1971.
MADDEN, CARL H. *Clash of Culture: Management in an Age of Changing Values.* Washington, D.C.: National Planning Association, 1972.
MAY, STACY, and PLAZA, G. *The United Fruit Company in Latin America.* Washington, D.C.: National Planning Association, 1958.
MAYER, CARL. "On the Intellectual Origin of National Socialism." *Social Research,* IX:2. May, 1942.
McCANN, THOMAS P. *An American Company: The Tragedy of United Fruit.* New York: Crown Press, 1976.
McGOVERN, WILLIAM M. *Strategic Intelligence and the Shape of Tomorrow.* New York: Henry Regnery, 1961; Folkestone, U.K.: Bailey and Swinfen, 1961.
McLACHLAN, DONALD. *Room 39: A Study in Naval Intelligence.* New York: Atheneum, 1968.
MEADOWS, DENNIS, et al. *The Limits to Growth.* New York: Universe Books, 1972.
MELZER, MORTON E. *The Information Center: Management's Hidden Asset.* New York: American Management Association, 1967.
MILLER, ROBERT W., and JOHNSON, JIMMY D., *Corporate Ambassadors to Washington.* Washington, D.C.: American University Center for the Study of Private Enterprise, 1970.
MILLSTEIN, IRA M., and KATSH, SALEM M. *The Limits of Corporate Power.* New York: Macmillan, 1981.
MORGAN, RICHARD E. *Domestic Intelligence: Monitoring Dissent in America.* Austin, Texas: University of Texas Press, 1980.
MYAGKOV, ALEKSEI. *Inside the KGB.* New York: Ballantine Books, 1976.

NASH, L. L. "Ethics without the Sermon." *Harvard Business Review,* November–December 1981.

NEIER, ARYEH. *Dossier.* New York: Stein and Day, 1975.

NISBET, ROBERT. *History of the Idea of Progress.* New York: Basic Books, 1980.

NOVAK, MICHAEL. *The American Vision: An Essay on the Future of Democratic Capitalism.* Washington, D.C.: American Enterprise Institute, 1978.

NOVAK, MICHAEL, and COOPER, JOHN W., editors. *The Corporation: A Theological Inquiry.* Washington, D.C.: American Enterprise Institute, 1981.

PAGE, BRUCE; LEITCH, DAVID; and KNIGHTLEY, PHILLIP. *The Philby Conspiracy.* Garden City, New York: Doubleday, 1968.

PASH, BORIS T. *The Alsos Mission.* New York: Award House, 1969.

PATTERSON, ANDREW, JR. "Confidential: The Beginning of Defense-Information Marking." Unpublished manuscript, Copyright by Andrew Patterson, Jr., 1980.

PETRUSENKO, VITALY. *A Dangerous Game: The CIA and the Mass Media.* Prague: Interpress, no date.

PETTE, GEORGE S. *The Future of American Secret Intelligence.* Washington, D.C.: Infantry Journal Press, 1946.

PLATT, JOHN. "How Men Can Shape Their Future." *International Future Research Conference Proceedings.* Kyoto, Japan: April, 1970.

PLATT, WASHINGTON. *National Character in Action: Intelligence Factors in Foreign Relations.* New Brunswick, New Jersey: Rutgers University Press, 1961.

POOL, ITHIEL DE SOLA. *Technologies of Freedom.* Cambridge, Mass.: The Belknap Press of Harvard University Press, 1983.

POOLEY, JAMES. *Trade Secrets: How To Protect Your Ideas and Assets.* Berkeley, California: Osborne/McGraw-Hill, 1982.

PORTER, MICHAEL E. *Competitive Strategy: Techniques for Analyzing Industries and Competitors.* New York: Macmillan, 1980.

POUND, ROSCOE. *Privacy in a Free Society.* Cambridge: American Trial Lawyers Foundation, 1974.

POWERS, FRANCIS GARY. *Operation Overflight.* New York: Holt, Rinehart & Winston, 1970.

POWERS, THOMAS. *The Man Who Kept the Secrets: Richard Helms and the CIA.* New York: Alfred A. Knopf, 1979.

RALIS, MAX. "Workers' Social Perceptions," in *The Soviet Worker,* edited by Leonard Schapiro and Joseph Godson. London: Macmillan, 1982.

RANSOM, HARRY W. *The Intelligence Establishment.* Cambridge, Mass.: Harvard University Press, 1970.

Restatement of Torts, The.

REVEL, JEAN FRANÇOIS. *The Totalitarian Temptation.* Garden City, New York: Doubleday, 1977.

ROPER, CARL. *Agent's Handbook of Black Bag Operations.* Cornville, Arizona: Desert Publications, 1978.

ROSITZKE, HARRY. *The CIA's Secret Operations: Espionage, Counterespionage, and Covert Action.* New York: Reader's Digest Press, 1977.

———. *The KGB: The Eyes of Russia.* Garden City, New York: Doubleday, 1981.

RUML, BEARDSLEY. *Tomorrow's Business.* New York: Farrar and Rinehart, 1945.

Select Bibliography

SAMPSON, ANTHONY. *The Sovereign State: The Secret History of ITT.* London: Hodder Fawcett, 1973.

SCHRAMM, WILBUR. *Mass Media and National Development: The Role of Information in Developing Countries.* Stanford, California: Stanford University Press, 1964.

SIGMUND, PAUL E. *Natural Law in Political Thought.* Cambridge, Mass.: Winthrop Publishers, 1971.

SINGER, KURT. *Three Thousand Years of Espionage.* New York: Prentice-Hall, 1948.

SLOAN, ALFRED P., JR. *My Years with General Motors.* Garden City, New York: Doubleday, 1964.

SMITH, CONSTANCE BABINGTON. *Evidence in Camera: The Story of Photographic Intelligence in World War Two.* London: Chatto and Windus, 1958.

SMITH, RICHARD HARRIS. *OSS: The Secret History of America's First Central Intelligence Agency.* Berkeley: University of California Press, 1972.

Soviet Spies in the Scientific and Technical Fields. Wavre, Belgium: Ligue de la Liberté, 1968.

Stanford Research Institute International. *Business Intelligence Program.* Menlo Park, California (ongoing service).

STEINER, GEORGE A. *The New CEO.* New York: Macmillan, 1983.

———. *Strategic Planning: What Every Manager Must Know.* New York: Macmillan, 1979.

STERLING, CLAIRE. *The Terror Network: The Secret War of International Terrorism.* New York: Berkley Books, 1982.

STERN, FRITZ. *The Politics of Cultural Despair.* Garden City, New York: Doubleday, 1961.

STOESSING, JOHN G.; LEBOW, RICHARD; and HENDERSON, GREGORY, editors. *Divided Nations in a Divided World.* New York: David McKay, 1974.

STOESSINGER, JOHN G. *Why Nations Go to War.* New York: St. Martin's Press, 1978.

STRAIGHT, MICHAEL. *After Long Silence.* New York: W. W. Norton, 1983.

STRONG, KENNETH. *Intelligence at the Top: The Recollections of an Intelligence Officer.* New York: Doubleday, 1969.

SULLIVAN, DAVID S. "Evaluating U.S. Intelligence Estimates," in *Intelligence Requirements for the 1980's: Analysis and Estimates,* edited by Roy Godson. Washington, D.C.: National Strategy Information Center, 1980.

SUN TZU. *The Art of War,* edited and with a Foreword by James Clavell. New York: Delacorte Press, 1983.

SUVOROV, VICTOR. *Inside the Soviet Army.* New York: Macmillan, 1983.

SWEENEY, WALTER C. *Military Intelligence: A New Weapon in War.* New York: Frederick A. Stokes, 1924.

Telex Corp. v. IBM, 367 F. Supp. 258 (1973); and Telex Corp. v. IBM, 510 F. (2d) 894 (1975), cert. denied 423 U.S. 802 (1975).

THEOHARIS, ATHAN G. *Spying on Americans: Political Surveillance from Hoover to the Huston Plan.* Philadelphia: Temple University Press, 1978.

TOLAND, JOHN. *Infamy: Pearl Harbor and Its Aftermath.* New York: Doubleday, 1982.

TOWNSEND, ELIAS CARTER. *Risks: The Key to Combat Intelligence.* Harrisburg, Pennsylvania: Military Service Publishing Company, 1955.

TULLY, ANDREW. *The CIA: The Inside Story.* New York: Morrow, 1962.

Uniform Trade Secrets Act.

U.S. Department of State. "Soviet Active Measures: Focus on Forgeries." Washington, D.C., April 1983.

WALTON, CLARENCE. *The Ethics of Corporate Conduct.* Englewood Cliffs, New Jersey: Prentice-Hall, 1977.

WASSON, R. GORDON; HOFFMAN, ALBERT; and RUCK, CARL A. P. *The Road to Eleusis: Unveiling the Secret of the Mysteries.* New York: Harcourt Brace Jovanovich, 1978.

WEST, NIGEL. *The Circus: MI-5 Operations 1945–1972.* Briarcliff Manor, New York: Stein & Day, 1982.

WESTIN, ALAN F. *Databanks in a Free Society.* New York: Quadrangle Books, 1972.

———. *Privacy and Freedom.* New York: Atheneum, 1967.

WESTON, J. FRED, editor. *Large Corporations in a Changing Society.* New York: New York University Press, 1975.

WHITEHOUSE, ARCH. *Espionage and Counterespionage.* New York: Doubleday, 1964.

WHITESIDE, THOMAS. *Computer Capers: Tales of Embezzlement and Fraud.* New York: Thomas Y. Crowell Co., 1978.

WILCOX, LAIRD M. *Bibliography on Espionage and Intelligence Operations.* Kansas City: Editorial Research Service, 1980.

WILENSKY, HAROLD L. *Organizational Intelligence: Knowledge and Policy in Government and Industry.* New York and London: Basic Books, 1967.

WILLIAMS, OLIVER F., and HOUCK, JOHN W. *Full Value: Cases in Christian Business Ethics.* New York: Harper & Row, 1978.

WILSON, IAN H. *The Business Environment of the Seventies.* New York: McGraw-Hill, 1971.

———. *Corporate Environments of the Future: Planning for Major Change.* (Special Study, No. 61). New York: Presidents Association, 1976.

WISE, DAVID, and ROSS, THOMAS B. *The Invisible Government.* New York: Random House, 1964.

YARDLEY, HERBERT O. *The American Black Chamber.* New York: Ballantine Books, 1981.

YAVITZ, BORIS, and NEWMAN, WILLIAM H. *Strategy in Action: The Execution, Politics, and Payoff in Business Planning.* New York: Macmillan, 1982.

Index

Index

Index

256

Index

Index

Index

Index

Index

Index

Index

Index

United States
  diminishing power and prestige of, 91–95
  as an open society, 170, 171–172, 179–180
  "underground" economy in, 19
United States government
  concern of, for IBM's security, 216–217
  levels of classification of defense information, 50–51
  and technology transfers, 53–54
United States Senate, report of, on technology transfers, 15
University of California at San Diego, 181
U.S. Army, 16
  Foreign Materiel Branch of, 55
  late in creating an intelligence branch, 41
U.S. Customs Service, 175–176
U.S. export control restrictions, circumvention of, 174–176
U.S. Intelligence Board, 47
U.S. Leasing International Inc., 137
U.S. Navy, hesitant in creating an intelligence branch, 41–42
USSR, *see* Soviet Union
U.S. Steel Company, 88

Values
  corporate, 6
  as help in resolving ethical issues, 197–198
  implications of changing, 209–210
  legitimatize action, 198–200
  manifestations of, 194, 195
Value strategy(ies), 200 ff.
  and anti-growth philosophy, 207–208
  corporate, 185 ff.
  and defense of capitalism, 207
  organizational, 196
Value system(s)
  of contituencies of corporations, 194–195
  as guide and confidence-giver to decision-maker, 199–200
  of institutions, 209

Value system(s)—*Continued*
  of an organization, 196
  structure of corporate, 198
Verification, of application of dual-use materials, 14–15
Vietnam War, criticisms of U.S. intelligence during, 47
Violence, 19–20
  growth of, 7–8

Wallach, Judge Richard W. (New York State Supreme Court), quoted on *Laurie vs. Chesebrough,* 113–114
Wall Street Journal, 127, 129
Walsingham, Sir Francis, created first modern espionage system, 29
Wang Anshih, 27
Weapons technology, and restrictions on information, 35–39
Webster, William (Director, FBI), 172, 176, 182
  cited on Soviet and satellite diplomats in U.S., 149
Weinberger, Caspar
  quoted on Soviet espionage, 172–173
  quoted on trade with USSR, 176
Weizenbaum, Joseph (computer scientist) quoted, 62
Wendin, Daniel G., 125
West Germany, 156
  intelligence community in, 48
Whiteside, Thomas, quoted, 135
Wiesner, Jerome B., quoted on possibility of nuclear war, 218
Wohlgemuth, Donald, sued by B. F. Goodrich, 124
Work ethic, 192–194
Wu, Theodore Wai (Assistant U.S. Attorney), exposed Maluta's operations, 173–175

Xerox, 66
Xerxes, 26

Yardley, Major Herbert O., 43

Zacharski, Marian (Polish intelligence officer), relationship of, with William Bell, 151–153
Zeiss, Carl, 12

About the Authors

RICHARD EELLS is Special Adviser to the President of Columbia University, Counselor to the Dean, Director of the Program for Studies of the Modern Corporation, and Professor of Business (adjunct) at the Graduate School of Business. He has been at Columbia since 1961. Earlier, he was Manager of Public Policy Research at the corporate headquarters of the General Electric Company in New York City. Prior to that, he was Chief of the Division of Aeronautics at the Library of Congress, holding the Guggenheim Chair of Aeronautics. Professor Eells has been a consultant and/or adviser to many corporations and institutions and is a trustee of several foundations. He was educated at Whitman College and Princeton University and holds an honorary LL.D. He has received awards from both the Alfred P. Sloan Foundation and the Rockefeller Foundation. The first edition of *Conceptual Foundations of Business,* by Professor Eells and Professor Clarence Walton, received the McKinsey Foundation Academy of Management Award. Professor Eells has represented Columbia University at numerous international conferences and, in the summer of 1979, was the court-appointed observer for the United States Court for Berlin. He is the author, co-author, or editor of fifteen books and is the series editor of thirty-four volumes of the Program for Studies of the Modern Corporation.

PETER NEHEMKIS, a member of the faculty of the UCLA Graduate School of Management, has had a career that included government service, the practice of law, and business management. A graduate of Swarthmore College and the Yale Law School, he was an early staff member of the Securities and Exchange Commission. In 1960 he was a member of a study group that prepared for President-elect John F. Kennedy a report entitled "Alliance for Progress." A founding trustee of the Pan American Development Foundation, he is the author of *Latin America: Myth and Reality* and, with Neil Jacoby and Richard Eells, an author of *Bribery and Extortion in World Business.* Also author of numerous legal and business articles, he has lectured at the Foreign Service Institute and George Washington and American Universities, and has been a consultant to the Departments of State and Commerce, several foreign governments, and a number of U.S. companies.

PROGRAM FOR STUDIES OF
THE MODERN CORPORATION
Graduate School of Business, Columbia University

PUBLICATIONS

FRANCIS JOSEPH AGUILAR
  Scanning the Business Environment

MELVIN ANSHEN
  Corporate Strategies for Social Performance

MELVIN ANSHEN, *editor*
  Managing the Socially Responsible Corporation

HERMAN W. BEVIS
  Corporate Financial Reporting in a Competitive Economy

COURTNEY C. BROWN
  Beyond the Bottom Line

COURTNEY C. BROWN
  Putting the Corporate Board to Work

COURTNEY C. BROWN, *editor*
  World Business: Promise and Problems

YALE BROZEN
  Concentration, Mergers, and Public Policy

NEIL W. CHAMBERLAIN
  Social Strategy and Corporate Structure

CHARLES DE HOGHTON, *editor*
  The Company: Law, Structure, and Reform

RICHARD EELLS
  The Corporation and the Arts

RICHARD EELLS
  The Political Crisis of the Enterprise System

RICHARD EELLS and PETER NEHEMKIS
  Corporate Intelligence and Espionage: A Blueprint for Executive Decision Making

RICHARD EELLS, *editor*
  International Business Philanthropy

The colophon for this book as for the other books of the Program for Studies of the Modern Corporation was created by Theodore Roszak